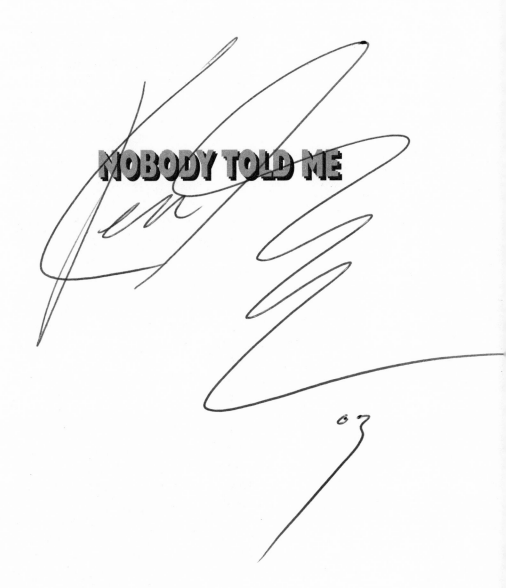

NOBODY TOLD ME

NOBODY TOLD ME

From Basement Band to Jack and the John Lennon Sessions

Ken Geringer

A Hipway Book published by
Hipway Press, New York

Grateful acknowledgment is made to the following for permission
to reprint the following photographs:
Bob Gruen: photo of John Lennon
Fantail Productions: photo by Bob Gruen, photo of George Mazzola,
Lauren Smolkin, Jack Douglas and Christine Desautel,
and photo of Jack Douglas and Christine Desautel
Fantail Productions for the following photos: photos of Tony Schittina,
Lauren Smolkin, Ken Geringer, George Mazzola—Ken, Pearl, Ezra—
Lauren Smolkin—Gypsy Queen—Pearl Livingston-Marley—
Jack Douglas, Rod O'Brien—Lee DeCarlo—Paul Ill, Alissa Geringer—
Neil Levine—Pam Mattioli, Randy Jackson, Paula Mattioli,
Jack Douglas and Ken Geringer—Inner Circle—Cheap Trick backstage.
Special thanks and acknowledgment is made to the following:
Kathleen Tallarico for Steven and Cyrinda photo
Jon Swift for Skunk Hollow Halloween photo, photo by Jon Swift

Publisher's Cataloging-in-Publication
(Provided by Quality Books, Inc.)

Geringer, Ken.

Nobody told me / Ken Geringer.—1st ed.
p. cm.

1.   Geringer, Ken. 2. Rock music—United States—
Biography. 3. Popular culture—United States.
4. Radicalism—United States. 5. Sound recording
executives and producers—United States—Biography.
6. Lennon, John, 1940-1980. I. Title.

ML429.G47N63 2001   781.66'092
                           QBI00-901986

Library of Congress Control Number: 00-136555

ISBN 0-9707126-0-X

Hipway Press
PO Box 764
Rock Hill, New York 12775

For information contact:
hipway@in4web.com

Visit our web site at:
www.hipway.com

This book is dedicated to:

George Haber,
age 19, who was killed while standing outside the Nassau Coliseum
during a Led Zeppelin concert

Phil Desemini,
age 21, shot in the head during a drug deal

Mike Colorado,
age 17, crushed under his car when the jack broke

Crystal Smith,
age 20, whom I loved, and who died in a fire

Rob Lewin,
age 17, died of leukemia and was buried with his guitar

Sheila Lasini,
age 7, hit by a car while walking to Hillcrest

Ellen Lewis,
age 15, run down while crossing Rt. 306

Mrs. Ralph Breeden,
age 19, died in a car accident on New Year's Eve

Kevin Folley,
age 18, who took his own

And to all the other young casualties of the '60s, '70s and '80s
who never made it into the '90s

Contents

PREFACE

"FUCK NAVARRO! FUCK! FUCK! NAVARRO!" the crowd roared as Luther and his 2 Live Crew rapped their raunchy lyrics to the beat of pulsating laser beams dancing crazily through the smoky club. In the streets several hundred more fans seethed around Luther's black stretch limousine while armies of police officers, reporters and cameramen squared off, anticipating the band's emergence from the front door. Scenes of chaos from inside and out were being broadcast live into millions of living rooms worldwide, and I was huddled backstage, anxious to put my escape plan into action.

The date was Saturday, June 9, 1990. Months previous, I had booked this concert with the hunch it would be the hottest ticket in town, and at the time I had no idea how right I was. The weeks preceding the concert showed brisk ticket sales and I felt smug and successful, until, like so many times in the past, and as always due to circumstances completely beyond my control, my foolproof plan was blown to bits.

Only two days before the band was scheduled to perform at my Broward County nightclub, a federal judge ruled the 2 Live Crew's songs obscene, and later that day I tuned in with the rest of South Florida to watch Sheriff Nick Navarro and his deputy execute a live news conference. They stepped up to the microphones and announced that effective immediately, 2 Live Crew songs were to be banned from Broward County.

"Are you aware the band is scheduled to perform at Club Futura the day after tomorrow?" shouted reporters.

"What will you do if they sing the illegal lyrics?"

The sheriff's deputy glared straight in the cameras and declared, "I will arrest anyone who sings those disgusting words at Club Futura Saturday night!"

Instantly my office phones were ringing off the hook. One reporter after another—from the state, from across the country, and even a few from foreign lands—asked if I was going to cancel the show or plead with Luther Campbell to tone down his lyrics.

"Absolutely not," I replied to each and every caller. "I do not believe in censorship. The show will go on exactly as planned!" Even after all these years, I was still a rebel, and I always refused to back down when I believed my actions were correct.

The band took hurried bows and dashed backstage. I rushed them out the back door and into a beige sedan that had been idling in the dark and deserted alley. I regularly helped performers sneak out the back door to escape crazed fans, but that night my mission was to help the band escape arrest.

The plain car disappeared into the night, and, laughing to myself, I turned and headed back inside. As I stepped through the door two sheriffs grabbed my arms and dragged me through the delirious crowd. Loud cries of "Let him go!" and "He didn't do anything!" followed us all the way to my office where I was shoved through a crush of cops and reporters. Additional cameras were beaming, and curious fans and employees were trying to squeeze through the already jammed doorway.

"Where is Luther Campbell?" demanded to know both cops and reporters, at which point all eyes, ears and cameras turned to me. Except for the soft shuffle of the cameramen the room was silent, and the bedlam in the next room seemed a distant echo.

I said nothing.

An angry-faced officer strode forward. "You are under arrest!" As the cold steely handcuffs tightened around my wrists I wondered, after all I'd been through (I'd left home at fourteen, quit public school at fifteen and entered the adult world at seventeen) was this to become my fifteen minutes of fame? As the millions of people in their living rooms watched me, I knew this moment didn't define who I truly was. My thoughts were of all that had happened: from basement band to Jack and the John Lennon sessions, and then, from the 2.2 to the 2 Live Crew.

I always believed life existed for me to conquer, and if I didn't ever give up, the world would be mine. My story is one of deep loves and soaring successes, and of disasters and despair, and my wonderment of all the possibilities that once lay before me. I remember all and I will tell, and I will start at the beginning.

CHAPTER 1

Really Love That County— Ain't No Lie

j. scherman

It was back in good old 1970. One might call it those coming out days; with the '50s in a swing and the '60s in a roar, the early '70s kind of put it all together.

The movement was happening! Put down your guns and throw away your shields. Let us be brothers—peace, love and non-violence. It almost looked real, but they say good things never last.

Anyway, I'm thirteen again, just recently bar mitzvah'd and living in Rockland County, New York. The suburbs! Like most families on our street, mine had worked their way out of those changing Bronx neighborhoods. Before we moved here, we called it *the country*. Real backyards, and if you were lucky the developers left a tree or two on your quarter-acre plot.

Up until now, coming from a conventional background, I'd been sheltered, seeing only bits and pieces of what was going on in the world around me. The earlier years showed me a happy family life where Dad was out working, keeping it all together, while Mom stayed at home always looking good and Grandma shopped for toys for me and my younger sister, keeping us spoiled and happy.

With an upbringing like that, one might assume school would have been an important part of life for a person my age. If not to give the family the privilege of raving about A grades on a report card, then maybe being the star of the school football or basketball team would have put a twinkle in Dad's eye. Well, to put it bluntly, I never brought home an A or a B, and the closest I ever made it to the football or basketball team was the second-string soccer team in the eighth grade. I never could understand how other kids were able to participate in class with ease when in order to just pass I had to spend hours studying things I would forget the next day. For all my efforts, if lucky, I'd wind up with a C-minus and be put in a separate class with misbehaved kids, mostly rough-looking greasers. This made me an easy mark, especially since I was dressed nice like all the other kids in my development (who also took pleasure in picking on me for being in those classes). At this point you might think of me as being quite stupid. I know I did.

I saw no way out—didn't even know there was a way out—until I attended the very straight and conservative Kakiat Junior High School. For example, soon after I started eighth grade, the principal had just begun to allow girls to wear slacks to school, but only after students staged a protest march down the halls. Poor Kakiat had never witnessed such a thing. I had never witnessed such a thing! Did students actually have the right to say *no*? After all, we weren't allowed to vote until we were twenty-one, and before we reached that age of enlightenment they'd make us go fight in the war in Vietnam, which was escalating.

I experienced a new sensation walking home from school that day. Discovering power and freedom is a feeling one never forgets, but I was soon to find out there was no one I could share my joy with.

"You mean you walked out of class? I can't believe you would do that!" The neighborhood kids were making fun of the protestors, and they were shocked when I announced I had joined the march. Their mentality was choking me; I knew I didn't belong here, and I was confused. I had to cut loose. There wasn't much else available, but my eyes and ears were open and I was ready.

Then, it happened . . .

Hair!

Not just on old bums in the city, but on Dean and Michael and other guys who the year before looked as goofy as I still looked in my tight bell-bottom slacks, turtleneck sweater, shiny brown loafers and Beatle haircut complete with bangs. Not knowing or caring what it was all about, I had to become a part of it. I was aware, but didn't care, couldn't care, what I'd have to put at stake. It was beautiful—they were one in a crowd, a mystery to all. It was the most intriguing part of my existence.

By the end of 1970 my hair had grown past my shoulders. I wore dungarees with velvet patches on the knees, a faded flannel shirt and an old leather jacket found at a thrift store. I had an earring and wore Frye boots that carried me inches above the ground. Man, was I ever high on being alive for the first time in years! Unfortunately, the people around me, including the neighborhood kids and their parents, were unable to share in my happiness. I think my family would have abandoned me as well, but being a minor they were obligated to keep me.

And so began my revolt against all that had been taught me thus far. Things I had never considered before began to matter. My parents came from hard times and left the Bronx with the intention of giving us opportunities they never had. It took constant work, and as rewards for their labor, like most, they would buy things. It was the era of keeping up with the Joneses and for a while my family was the leader on our block. Material things just didn't hold much meaning for me. You either had it, or you had nothing, and I was more concerned with the have-nothings. What was supposed to matter, didn't matter. I was changing and no one understood, not even me. Junior high became tougher now that I had to defend my new look to those around me, but there were others and we'd pass in the halls or hang out at lunch, and that made it all right.

I was bursting with energy to see, to do and to experience the world around me—I wanted it all, and I wasn't going to let school interfere. I was too young to drop out, so I started cutting classes, then entire days of school. It was at this time that I learned of Skunk Hollow High School.

Let me explain. Situated just north of New York City, Rockland County lay between the banks of the Hudson River and the base of the Catskill Mountains. Beautiful as it was, it attracted quite a few artists, actors and a variety of freethinking, progressive individuals who either wanted to live in these serene wooded areas (before all the developers invaded) or wished to be close enough to the city to have both lives. Skunk Hollow was an unaccredited high school launched for four students who came from those progressive families.

Many years prior, not agreeing with the rules and disciplinary methods employed by the public school system, their parents had created their own elementary school. They named it The Project School, and their philosophy was that children learn more readily when the pressure to do so is removed. After all, we learn from the day we are born. Was there ever a case of a baby who was ready and able, not trying to walk? Learning

3

starts out as a natural procedure for all of us. Nobody can demand a baby to walk—it just happens. Students at The Project School learned, at their own pace, about any- and-everything that interested them. For example, if a kid (who in public school would have been in sixth grade) was learning to write short stories, any other kids, regardless of their ages, could participate in that lesson. Because the school didn't believe in competition between students, there were no tests or report cards—nor were the students separated into classes, grades or levels. They were free to roam about the cozy home-like schoolhouse that was situated on a mountainside within sight of beautiful Rockland Lake.

When the original four students graduated Project School and were faced with returning to public school, Skunk Hollow High School was born.

My first visit to Skunk Hollow was made in the dead of winter midway through ninth grade. I was sitting in social studies with a girlfriend named Roberta, and, not feeling like finishing school that day, we decided to find something better to do. As soon as the bell rang we ran out a side door, up the hill beyond the football field and into the woods. What an adrenaline rush! It was like participating in an episode of *Mission Impossible*. Well, once this was accomplished, Roberta told me she had been hanging out at a really cool place, and always being ready to check out something new, I said, "Let's go!"

We hitchhiked to the town of Blauvelt, a long journey of fifteen miles. Hitchhiking was probably one of my favorite pastimes. It was always an adventure wondering which car would stop next, not knowing what experience lay ahead, and there were usually plenty. Our last ride took us to within a mile of our destination. After walking down winding roads that cut through mountains with snow all around, we got to this castle-like stone church with a graveyard in front. It looked like something out of an old movie, and, as we walked toward the building, I saw the most interesting, beautiful faces I'd ever seen in one place. Before anyone noticed us, a funny feeling came over me. It was as if the mists of my confusion were at last clearing away. All that mattered was that this place was here, and so was I.

The day turned out to be one of the most memorable I'd ever spent. I stayed outside throwing a football with Matthew and Wally, while Roberta went inside to look for Tilly, a teacher she knew. Matthew, a few years younger than I, didn't seem to like outsiders much. He had this toughness about him, and the nicest, thickest head of straight hair I'd ever seen. He'd lean forward and let it fall to the floor, then swing his head up, and I'd watch all that hair fly over his head and cascade down his back like a waterfall. Wally asked me where I went to school, and he made me feel right at home. Wally, with his great big beard and long hair, was a teacher at Skunk, as well as a professor at Long Island University.

The huge building had an upstairs and a lower level, and, as I explored the premises, all these great looking people would appear. What I noticed most was that everyone had his or her own look. At Skunk Hollow, there were no rules governing what clothes the students could or could not wear. Each person possessed total individuality. They were proud of themselves and of their school. Everyone was talking and laughing, happy with the moment and eager for the next—quite the opposite of Kakiat, where I spent lifetimes imprisoned behind my desk hoping the bell would hurry up and ring.

In the kitchen, a student named Maude was gathering everyone for lunch. When she saw me, she unquestioningly loaded up a plate and handed it to me. She had cooked a big pot of spaghetti with an unbeliev-able sauce, a salad, and apple cider As she handed out plates, people gave her change—I guess to pay for the food. Students came in slowly at dif-ferent times, maybe from a class on Greek mythology, or algebra or from taking a walk in the woods. They were in control and this was their school. It almost felt too good to be real. I thought maybe I had taken a wrong turn or ride and we were in some other world, or maybe I was dreaming and would soon wake up to find out it was time to get ready for Kakiat.

That night, sitting in my room, thinking about Skunk Hollow and Kakiat Junior High, it became clear what I had to do. I realized most peo-ple spend their entire lives looking for their rightful place in this world, and many never find it. That day I had stumbled upon mine, and there I would remain. Thus began the final stage of my revolt against the pub-lic school system.

CHAPTER 2

Haze Daze Indeed

Soon after my discovery of Skunk Hollow and due to my lack of class attendance, I brought home failing grades, so now, more then ever, I had to prove that public school was not for me. Sure, I'd failed subjects before, but never several at once, and this meant the worst to my parents who now refused to reward me in any way. After weeks of trying unsuccessfully to get them to at least take a look at Skunk, I decided to run away from home.

Tommy and I packed our bags and met at midnight. We were on our way to Florida, a place that always held a special attraction for me. I had never been there, but had always heard great stories from kids with divorced parents who always wound up in Florida during vacations.

It was cold out, very cold. We made it to the parkway and then had to wait about two hours to get picked up. Our first ride was with an older guy headed into Manhattan—a quick ride, just enough to warm up. He went a few miles out of his way to let us out at the on-ramp of the New Jersey Turnpike.

I-95 south! We stuck out our thumbs and within minutes a dilapidated van chugged off the highway in front of us. We hopped in to meet a young couple with whom we immediately identified, then Tommy and I fell asleep in the back of the van. They woke us a couple of hours later to ask if we wanted to spend the day with them, and if so, they would drive us back to the highway the following morning. We looked at each other, said "Why not?" and fell back asleep.

We were somewhere in Virginia on what seemed to be a farm, with chickens and even a goat. I'd never seen that before! Our new friends were Jesus freaks home from a get-together in upstate New York. They didn't talk much about Jesus, but instead wanted to know about us and where we were headed. It was fun being on a farm, and that night we had a big dinner followed by a sound night's sleep. The next morning our new friends discovered we only had seven dollars between us, so they gave us another ten before dropping us off at the highway ramp. We were rich and ready to continue.

After a few minutes a car pulled over and we dashed to catch the ride. As we ran closer, hair flying, a man's head came out of the passenger window to get a better look at us.

"Shit! They're guys!" he yelled. The driver rammed on the gas and screeched into the path of an oncoming truck. The truck skidded, just missing them and almost causing a major accident, all because we were, in fact, guys.

After a few more rides we arrived at South of the Border, a giant Mexican-themed pit stop that lies on the border of North and South Carolina. Our driver was going a few miles into South Carolina, but after laughing at all those stupid "Pedro Sez" billboards for the past one hundred miles, Tommy and I wanted to check the place out for ourselves. We took a quick tour before heading back to the highway and our next ride, which dropped us near a small town in South Carolina. The highway was closed for repairs so we had no choice but to hitch on the alternate route that ran right through town, and sure enough, we ended up in jail. It was okay. We were halfway to Florida, further south than I'd ever been, and we were on our own. It was hard to take our situation seriously.

The two officers that picked us up were right out of a TV sitcom. One was short and fat and the other tall and skinny. The short, fat guy's pants, topped by a gun belt, hung so low we couldn't help noticing his boxer shorts. We knew better than to laugh out loud. The jailhouse was a two-room building with one cell that became our bedroom. That night, the short officer kept trying to scare us by saying he was going to send us to a chain gang, while the tall officer kept telling him to knock it off.

Tommy and I didn't care—we sat back thinking we were James Cagney and Humphrey Bogart. We checked out every crack in the wall and the bars on the window in preparation for our death-defying escape. We were the tough ones, and our captors were Bud Abbott and Lou Costello.

7

Daylight found us back in the patrol car, and an hour later we were on a plane headed for Kennedy Airport. We entered the plane in handcuffs, making it obvious to everyone on the Eastern flight that we were dangerous criminals. Bud and Lou put us in the possession of a great looking southern stewardess, who, I think, if given the chance would have loved to free and run away with us both.

At Kennedy Airport all four of our parents were waiting, mothers weeping. I think my father was more upset with me for getting caught and him having to pay my bond and plane fare than for my running away in the first place. All the way home my mother was in tears and my father kept saying, "Look what you're doing to your mother!" Whenever I did something wrong, my mother would blame herself and wonder where she went wrong. It made me fear that I was in fact an awful kid. I loved my parents and wanted to tell them I really wasn't bad and it was all right, but they would never have understood. My younger sister was their reward for having to put up with me, and I think if not for her being the good one, they would have felt like complete failures.

The next step was family therapy at Summit Park Hospital Complex where we sat around with about six other families, with the therapist trying to pit everyone against each other. I detested it, and so did my father who would do anything not to air family laundry in public, but my mother insisted we go. It seemed someone with a college degree recommended it to her. My parents never made it to college so anyone with a degree had to know what they were talking about. After a few weeks my father copped out and refused to attend any more sessions. When my mother and I showed up without him, the therapist suggested I go to the Community Center.

The Community Center became my new haven away from home. In front was the administration office, and behind it a huge room with mix-and-match couches where we sat around smoking cigs. There was a ping-pong table and a stereo that played Zeppelin, Hendrix and the Grateful Dead throughout the day. Although we did have to go to group therapy sessions and it almost seemed like the therapists understood us, the best part about the center was the other kids. Most were around my age, and had been sent to the center for causing trouble in school or smoking pot, and some were really tough kids but we all got along.

The therapy sessions were held in the back room. We sat in the multi-colored vinyl beanbag chairs scattered around the floor, but only after we prepared by taking a stroll through the run-down town of Spring Valley to smoke a joint or two.

In my neighborhood there was a kid named Scott, who drove a motorcycle. I had a mini bike. He had long hair and a moustache and listened to rock n' roll. I could hear it from his window. One day he talked to me, invited me in. He put on a record he said was just released called "Purple Haze," then he opened a drawer, took out some foil, rolled it into a pipe and cut out a little round piece of his window screen for a filter.

"Look at me," he commanded. "Do what I do."

He put a piece of *hashish* into the pipe, lit it with a match, took a puff, blew out and then started breathing heavily, hyperventilating. At that point he slowly fell to the floor with his eyes closed.

"Oh no," I thought. "He's dead!"

Then he opened his eyes and exclaimed, "What a rush!"

This was it! There was no turning back. I sucked on the pipe, coughed out the smoke, breathed heavily, closed my eyes and fell on the floor.

Looking up at Scott, I said, "What a rush!"

I had just passed my eleventh birthday.

I hung out with all the center regulars. Glenn, a few years younger, had a brother in high school, and sometimes Glenn would sing in his brother's band. Crystal was a year older and was like a cuddly puppy dog. Everyone loved her except her mom. Poor Crystal, it was a few years later I heard she was pregnant and living with a drug dealer on The Hill, the worst place to live in Spring Valley. She died when someone set her apartment on fire. Angela Paone, at fifteen, was the sexiest Italian girl you'd ever want to meet. Vinnie Palozolo was street-wise and could con anyone out of anything. His girlfriend, Joy Breeden, was a few years older than I. The first time I walked into the center, Joy was sitting in the front room sewing patches on Vinnie's jeans, and I immediately developed a crush on her. Vinnie lived on the streets and Joy took care of him. Tina and Nancy Garrison were two beautiful sisters who were the first to turn me onto the Grateful Dead record *American Beauty*. Bimbo was an amateur boxer, black, and always in trouble with the police, and for a while he lived at my parents' house. There were others, and during the day we'd meet at the center and at night hang out at Hillcrest, a shopping center near my house.

On those gritty summer days when the sun's rays sizzled Spring Valley's cracked sidewalks and the thermometer punched ninety degrees by nine in the morning, we'd hitchhike to a mountain named Bailey's, then hike to a waterhole deep in the cool woods. Everyone would shed their clothes, go swimming and hang out naked on the rocks in the sun. Sometimes we'd take a two-hour hike to Pine Meadow, a clear, untouched lake on top of the mountain. We knew and relied on each other and there were rarely any outsiders. The summer was filled with hope. I had found friends that felt as I did, and we mattered. The girls were beautiful with flowing hair, long dresses, peace symbols and marijuana. It hardly seemed that two years before I was thirteen and at summer camp in upstate New York. It was a ranch camp where each camper had his own horse and they let us take horseback rides on the camp's many acres. During one of these rides we saw outsiders constructing what looked like homesteads on the camp's property. "Long haired hippies!" the camp director called them; they were camping by the streams on his property. Naked people running in and out of the water was not a spectacle he wished his innocent campers to see.

It was the summer of Woodstock and the homesteads were being set up by some of the overflow. I really liked what I saw and almost had the guts to take my horse and go for it, but I would have been on my own as none of my peers had any feelings except to laugh at what they viewed as a carnival or freak show.

Now, two years older with one lifetime behind me and another ahead of me, my parents started to cool out. They knew I wasn't going to change, they didn't want to deal with me running away and they certainly didn't want to attend any more therapy sessions. What else to do they figured, but pretend it was a phase that I was going through, and I'd grow out of it?

Summer was drawing to a close and I was facing my first year of high school. I met Peter and Carl at the center on the last day of summer vacation. Peter was twelve, but looked older, and sort of like a pirate. He had a long face, brown hair that grew in ringlets, a red velvet shirt with two pockets, and he carried a pack of Marlboro's in each one. I later learned that his nickname was Captain K.

Peter's parents were both artists. His mom was a painter and his dad was head of the art department at the local community college. Peter told me about the time when his older brother Lawrence had attended Kakiat and the principal called their father in for a meeting. It seemed that

Lawrence's hair had grown over his collar, and long hair on boys was strictly forbidden. When their dad got to the meeting, the principal was speechless seeing his hair down to the middle of his back! When I met Peter's parents, it was my first experience with meeting adults who were cool—it was all right to speak, think and let them know what was going on, and I'd always wonder why my parents never took the time to understand what I was really about instead of having these hallucinations of what I was supposed to be like.

Carl was fifteen. He had big round glasses, straggly hair, and wore clothes that hadn't been changed in a week. His background seemed similar to mine, except he had an older brother who helped pave his way. Carl would sit for hours playing licks on the guitar, listening to Grateful Dead music and making up outrageous stories, usually about himself. Carl had a reputation for being a liar and a petty thief. He would steal your change to buy a pack of Marlboros or a Kraft macaroni and cheese dinner. He already attended Skunk Hollow, and Peter was enrolled to start that year. He was coming out of seventh grade and going directly into Skunk. I envied Peter and Carl, and was in dread of the following morning when I'd have to walk up the hill behind my house to attend my first day of school at Ramapo Senior High.

That evening, after the center closed, I invited Peter and Carl to spend the night at my house. The house had two levels; upstairs held the kitchen, living room, my sister's and parents' rooms, and down below was my room. I had removed the screen from my window to make it silent and easy for me to come and go, or for friends to come see me after hours. My possessions amounted to a cheap stereo with a turntable, records, psychedelic posters on the walls, a pile of clothes thrown on the floor in my closet and a Rupp Roadster mini bike in the garage.

After a brief encounter with my parents we went down to my room and it was cool. Carl said he had a couple of hits of blotter acid, a mild form of LSD and asked if we'd like to trip. I admitted I had never tripped before, but Carl looked at Peter and said, "I know you have!"

Up until then I had only heard stories about acid, as half of the center kids did it regularly. I also thought about what I was taught in school about LSD—how it would erode my body and my mind, I'd have flashbacks for the rest of my life and if I ever had kids they would come out deformed—but worst of all, it would lead me to shooting heroin in some ghetto alley somewhere.

I looked at Carl and said, "Yeah, I'll do it!"

The acid was on paper. We put it on our tongues and swallowed. "Easy enough," I thought, and I wondered how a little ripped piece of paper could have any effect on my mind. We sat around talking, mostly me asking questions about Skunk Hollow.

Carl kept saying, "I think I'm getting off!" It wasn't like smoking pot, where you'd feel it right away. No, this feeling crept up on us slowly.

We were laughing. Something was going on and it was good. I noticed that my room was quite colorful with pink carpeting and paneled walls swimming with bright posters and colored lights. Suddenly Carl said, "I gotta split!" We asked him what was wrong but he only said, "Don't worry, I'll be back," and he crawled out the window.

That left Peter and me. Our conversation went from hating public school to music. Then Peter started checking out my records. He put on Jimi Hendrix's *Smash Hits* and said, "Listen to that, did you hear that?" It was the first time in my life I was not only able to hear the music, but I saw it, felt it and it became a part of me. I heard everything as the music took over. Peter was in charge. He played Hendrix, the Stones, the Grateful Dead, and more Hendrix. I sat on the floor deep in thought, totally entranced by the music.

As the sunlight crept through my window we started talking about how the patterns on the paneling looked intense, and as I moved my hand in front of my eyes it left trails. All of this was too cool to handle. I went to use the bathroom and the toilet looked like a giant hole. When I flushed, I stood there in amazement watching the water circle round and round. When I looked in the mirror my face looked like a cartoon and my hair looked like straw. I could only laugh.

I realized I was about to begin my first day of high school at Ramapo Senior High. Peter assured me it would be all right. "I'll go with you," he said, and that made me feel better.

Suddenly there was movement outside. A garbage truck was stopping in front of the house. Each noise was amplified and we laughed at the strange sounds. A car passed by. Then, footsteps. The movement upstairs grew as my father and sister got ready for work and school. A door slammed, a plate rattled. Muffled voices. A drawer slid open, silverware hit the table. I was a producer and the house was filled with an orchestra of sounds, and it was all in my mind.

It was hard to believe that my father took no notice of all the swirling sounds and flashing lights when he came downstairs to make sure I was up and about. I had to reassure myself again by asking Peter if everything was all right, and he, being the experienced tripper that he was, assured me all was fine.

It was a beautiful morning. The sun was shining, the sky was bright blue and the grass emerald green. The only drawback was being stuck in the middle of this housing development. At the time, Rockland County was still in its early stage of growth. Years before, there was no Palisades Interstate Parkway. To get to Rockland from Manhattan you had to drive bumpy and winding country roads, but in the late 1950s the parkway was built. A smooth, idyllic half-hour's drive took you from the George Washington Bridge all the way up to Harriman State Park, and this brought a rush of land developers who came to Rockland County to make their fortunes. I was six years old when my family moved there, and our house was one of the first on the street. It was fun to watch the work crews cut down trees, and we played in the houses as they were being built. When I was eight years old my father bought me a toolbox. We rode our bikes around collecting scrap lumber, and occasionally a few two-by-fours and some nails to create what we called furniture.

As Peter and I cut across a neighbor's lawn and walked up the hill, Ramapo Senior High School came into view and looked like a huge cement iceberg floating in a black parking lot ocean. We walked in the front door, went straight through the building and out the back door. Peter led me across the football field and through the woods to an abandoned graveyard. Already there was a gathering, and the sweet and sharp odors of marijuana and cigarette smoke mingled in the cool morning air. Surprisingly, a lot of people knew Peter; though he was only twelve, throughout the elite Rockland music and art scene, he and his parents were well-known.

The bell rang and we hurried to find my homeroom class. I sat in the back of the room feeling quite alone since Peter had gone back to the graveyard, but he told me he'd hang around and meet me in the cafeteria during lunch. Suddenly, a loud voice came over the P.A. "WEELLLL-COOOMMEEE-TTTTTOOO-RRRAAMMAPOOOO-SSSSSEEEEENNIORRR-HHHIGGGHH-SCHOOOOOLL . . . " It went on forever.

That is all I remember about that class, except I did say "*here!*" when my name was called. I was back in school and I didn't want to be there. After the bell rang, I located Peter and we cut out. I had just attended my first, and last, class at Ramapo Senior High School.

It's funny how one school experience can have such a powerful influence over one's life. I remember well my first experience in a classroom. It happened when I was five years old and my family was living on Commonwealth Avenue in the Bronx. My father was a traveling salesman selling a line of socks, and every morning Mom walked me to kindergarten.

On my way to school we passed by the Yeshiva, a school for religious Jewish boys. The school was set back on a hill with a chain link fence around it, and it had a playground that came up to the fence. We walked by the school every day where kids with yarmulkes and paises were running around. It was a sight I always looked forward to.

One night I heard my parents arguing about enrolling me in the Yeshiva. I didn't know why Mom wanted me to go. We weren't religious, I had no paises, and I was doing fine in kindergarten, but Mom won out and took me in to register the next morning.

The school had no kindergarten; it started at the first grade. These kids were already learning their ABCs, but at PS 143, we were still playing with blocks. Maybe my mom wanted to show everyone how smart I was by moving me up from kindergarten to the first grade, or perhaps she had an urge to give me a shot of religion, but either way I was not happy to be changing schools, especially since I looked nothing like the Yeshiva kids and I'd be the different one on the other side of the fence.

The next day I was up early and ready to go to school, except for one minor problem. I owned just one pair of shoes and that morning I could find only one of the pair. After a massive search throughout the apartment my mother had me dressed in the shoe and one brown vinyl bedroom-slipper decorated with little cartoon characters. We were late, and Mom walked me into the first structured classroom I had ever seen. I marveled at the neat rows of desks and kids identical in uniforms and yarmulkes, and everyone turned to stare at me. With a sick stomach I motioned good-bye to my mother as she threw me a kiss. I managed not to shed a tear, and I was determined to fit in and do my work as well, if not better than my new classmates.

The teacher, a very serious, big man had me sit in the front row. I was given a pencil and paper, and the lesson began. While giving the instructions, the teacher directed his talk to me and looked into my eyes. He said, "Copy onto your paper exactly what I do on the blackboard!" First he drew a big chalk square on the blackboard to represent the piece of paper we had in front of us. I drew a big black square on my paper and glanced around at the other boys' work.

Their papers were still blank. I was the only one following directions, I was on my way to being grown-up, and I felt proud! Then, words started appearing in two columns. I could do that too. When we were done it was time for recess and I could hardly wait to be one of them now inside the fence, kicking the ball while the traffic of passersby looked on. It was fun and I was a playground prince.

After recess, rather than taking me back to class, the playground teacher took me to an office where Mom and my teacher were engaged in a heated argument. Mom had found my missing shoe and when she happily came back with it, the teacher informed her that I wasn't ready for the first grade and I didn't fit in at the school. The playground teacher said I did great out in the yard, and he thought I should be given a trial period, but when my paper with the big black square was compared to the other kids' papers, it was decided I really didn't belong in Yeshiva school after all.

"I was following the directions!" I said, but no one listened to me. This was my first classroom experience and already I was being labeled stupid.

I spent my first week at Ramapo in the graveyard smoking cigs with some of the center gang and meeting new faces. Sometimes, I'd hang out in the cafeteria or just wander the halls looking for something to do. I had no idea what my schedule was, or what classes I was supposed to be in. No one questioned me—they must have assumed I belonged since I was there every day.

My dad was selling draperies and interior design and he just recently had bought out his partner. He was the new owner of Rockland Decorators and business was good, but it engulfed all his time. One day, I walked into the house and my mother was on the phone, crying to a neighbor. It seemed Ramapo High School had telephoned, wondering why I hadn't been to class for the past few weeks.

Sitting in Dr. Sugarman's office—the superintendent for the whole school district—I feared the worst. I was alone in the waiting room while he and my parents were deciding my fate. Then the secretary said, "Ken, you can go in now."

I sat at the round table: on my right, Mom, on my left, Dad, and across, Dr. Sugarman.

"Ken, it seems as though we have a problem. What do we do with you?"

I had the perfect answer, but why waste it on them? Obviously I was headed for reform school, and there was nothing I could do about it.

He continued. "There is a place I've recommended to your parents. It is new, and sort of experimental."

An experimental reform school didn't sound as bad as the regular type.

"Since your case is exceptional, and you feel there is no way you could fit in here in our school system, I am referring you to a private school . . ."

Not another Yeshiva!

" . . . called Skunk Hollow High School."

What?

Who would have thought a school superintendent, with a Ph.D., would wind me up in Skunk Hollow?

Skunk had moved into a Unitarian Church building just off Exit 11 of the Palisades Interstate Parkway and was quite close to my house. The school was in two low buildings set back in the woods and if not for the church sign, you'd hardly notice the buildings were there. My adrenaline was pumping as my parents and I pulled into the driveway. I could only dream that I'd ever make it there as a legitimate student and, as of yet, my parents still hadn't made up their minds.

We walked through the building, really just a giant room, and passed a ping-pong table, a drum set, and some guitar amplifiers, but no people. We left the room, which I later learned was called the R.E. room, exited the building through sliding glass doors and headed to the main building. We walked through another set of sliding glass doors and down an empty corridor. Where was everyone?

"Hi, I'm Tilly!" In her forties, with a long, thick, gray ponytail, Tilly had a wholesome look, the type of person it was safe to leave your parents with. She directed us into a room where we sat at a conference table, and she began to explain to my parents about the school. The only problem was, there was another person at the table, Janie German, and she was neither wholesome nor safe. As I remember, she resembled Janis Joplin as she appeared on the album cover *Pearl*. I never got to know Janie because she rarely spoke to anyone; instead she would just sit there and make funny sinus-related noises, snorting and grunting to herself. While Tilly was talking, I kept looking around wondering where everyone was, while my father kept sneaking glances at Janie.

It was getting scary. I didn't think we were going to make it to the signing of the papers, but we did—and I was in!

On the way back to the car my father asked, "What am I sending you to, a school for retards?"

CHAPTER 3

Freeway

I loved school for the first time in my life. It was Skunk's second year in existence and here I was at fifteen, part of one of the few real alternative schools in the country. Our philosophy: Do whatever you want, as long as you don't interfere with what someone else is doing (a rather Libertarian philosophy). There were weekly meetings to discuss what we wanted to do and how much money we had to do it with. As students we made the decisions to form a new class, go on an outing to see a psychedelic art exhibit in Manhattan or attend a twelve-hour Grateful Dead marathon show at the Grand Ballroom. Sometimes we'd vote on letting in a stray public-schooler who had been hanging around, as I once had.

Money was scarce at Skunk and it was hard to pay teachers. They were there because, like us, they wanted to be. I never trusted or respected any of my public school teachers, but at Skunk that changed. There was Bob and Nan, and you would rarely hear one name without the other. Nan had a petite, childish look about her and was a former public school teacher in New York City. She hated the public school system and was one of the founders, along with four students, of Skunk Hollow. You always felt safe with Nan around; no matter what you did, she was usually right there doing it with you.

Her husband, Bob, was a giant of a man in all respects. Standing over six feet tall with long black hair worn in a ponytail, he was the most logical, intelligent person I'd ever come across. He was a math professor at

Long Island University, but spent all his free time teaching at Skunk. Bob was our wisdom and we trusted him.

Nan conducted writing class, my favorite subject. We sat in the room and picked an object, phrase, or place and wrote about it. When the writing was done, each person read his or her story out loud. Grammar, spelling and penmanship were unimportant; it was only the content of your story that mattered. We sat in awe, listening, as each of us read our tale. We had the freedom to write and create with unlimited boundaries. In public school, my illegible handwriting and complete inability to spell made every writing assignment an exercise in failure, but at Skunk I never missed writing class. I was free to learn without the fear of condemnation and I became interested in everything. Life at home was improving, too. Skunk had no tests, no grades and no report cards, so how could I do badly?

Each morning the school bus picked me up in front of my house at around eight o'clock, then went on to Carl Cooperstein's house. Pauline got on next with Sam, her little black dog that always wore a red bandana to school. After about two more stops, we arrived at Skunk at nine.

Behind the school were woods that adjoined a progressive cooperative community called Skyview Acres. In Skyview, land was divided into two and three-acre plots, and each family was allowed to build one house on their acreage. Hardly any trees were cleared to build these houses, unlike the bare housing development I lived in. They also made a clearing for a baseball field and created a small lake called the Skyview Pool. There were no sidewalks or streetlights, and some nights it was so dark you couldn't see your hand in front of your face. Most Skyview parents were cool, and many sent their kids to Skunk. I loved being in the woods behind Skunk, so Skyview became one of my favorite places. Most Skunks took regular walks in the woods. If a student had something particular they wished to discuss, teachers could always be counted on for a walk in the woods. Some of my best memories are of just walking in the woods talking to Nan. It was the best therapy yet.

Joe Quesada rented a big dilapidated house next door to the church, played drums and was Skunk's music director. He was about twenty-two years old and looked more like a student than a teacher. From my first day at the school I was fascinated by the music jams. The R.E. building contained the music equipment and it was always on, usually at full volume, and there were big old chairs where I spent a good part of my day

19

lying back and listening. It was known that Skunk was happening, and musicians from all over the county came to play, usually Hendrix-type jams that went on for hours. Eventually, Joe taught me a drumbeat and from that day on you'd find me on the drums at every opportunity. If someone else wanted to play, they'd first have to drag me off the drum set.

I hung out a lot with Peter and he spent half the week over at my house. We were popular with the Spring Valley girls and often walked to Hillcrest at night to pick up chicks, and many afternoons we hitchhiked to Ramapo High School to see some of our girlfriends. Kids that had to go to school at Ramapo and Kakiat envied us and we knew it, and we had a lot of friends in the public schools.

Once while visiting Ramapo, I was enjoying a leisurely cigarette outside the school door when a teacher grabbed me by the collar and escorted me to the principal's office. Not wanting to admit I was from Skunk Hollow (information that would result in me being barred permanently from school grounds—and my girlfriends!) I told the principal my name and phone number only. When he disappeared into the inner office, presumably to call my parents, I took off. Later that day, when I arrived home, my mother said she had gotten a phone call from someone claiming to be the principal of Ramapo. He told her I was suspended for a week.

This time she didn't cry. She hung up on him.

Among my friends, a person's age, color or religion was unimportant. We were a group of individuals, not only at Skunk but also throughout the county. A core group of about two hundred attended parties held in various homes nearly every weekend. The crowd included both Skunk and Project School students and teachers, Skyview-ers, public schoolers, older artists and musicians (who were the originators of the scene) and always new faces. All were welcomed and no one was ever turned away.

By this time, the Vietnam War was going full blast and we were against it, so when a protest was planned in Washington, D.C., many of us decided to go. I hitchhiked down with Crystal, one of my center girlfriends, and we joined the thousands of people who came from all over the country. Some of the speakers were veterans who had just returned from Vietnam, and I particularly remember the sad, horrible stories they told, but the people around me were beautiful and I was proud to be one of them. Psychedelics, peace signs, and banners, and people chanting, "Hell no, we won't go!" Then it got ugly. Suddenly, tear gas was everywhere, people were running in all directions and policemen in space masks were hitting us with clubs. In the confusion I lost Crystal, but later found a group from Rockland County who gave me a ride home in their old Volkswagen bus.

I hadn't found any one girl interesting enough for me to restrict myself to seeing her only. I had many girlfriends and devoted myself to adding to my collection, until the day of a picnic at the Skyview pool. Johnny Hill, Danny Toan and David Snider—all three great guitar players—were jamming. Danny had spent a year locked in his room with his guitar, and could imitate Hendrix note for note. Johnny played bass and David played drums. It took two guitar players to back Danny, one on drums and one on bass, and they were Rockland's version of the Jimi Hendrix Experience. I was hanging out with a friend of mine from Kakiat named Dean who was there on his horse and looked like a cowboy with his fringed poncho and suede hat.

A beautiful young girl with hair that fell below the pockets of her Levi's was sitting by herself at the edge of the pool. I kept sneaking looks at her and wanted to go over and talk to her. Dean told me she was Mr. Gurowsky's daughter.

Mr. Gurowsky was a teacher at Kakiat, and he was no ordinary teacher. He was the science department chairman and was known as the strictest teacher of all. Once in my Kakiat days, I was walking through the halls when Mr. Gurowsky took me to the office after I refused to tuck in my shirt. Dean had him for a teacher and they hated each other, mainly because Dean refused to do any work. Dean had a genius IQ and went from ninth grade directly to college, but because he would sit in class and daydream, Mr. Gurowsky thought he was stupid.

I wondered how this little girl with the velvet patched jeans, sitting there like the Goddess of the Lake, could belong to him? It made me want to talk to her even more. Slowly, I walked up behind her and tapped her on the shoulder, and when she turned, I looked into her brown eyes (God, I wanted to kiss her) and asked, "Are you Mr. Gurowsky's daughter?"

She said, "Yeah," and turned back around.

Nervously, I walked away thinking, "Boy, did you ever blow that one!"

The Gurowskys had bought land in Skyview and built their own house, but Murry Gurowsky never really got along with any of his neighbors. He had another daughter, Sue, and a son, David, and while the other Skyview kids were growing up in permissive families, Sue and

David were taught not to question authority and had a very strict and studious upbringing. But I knew this daughter was different and she intrigued me, and I knew it was only a matter of time before our paths crossed again.

Most other people seemed capable of following rules easily, but not me. Being too young to obtain a learner's permit, I taught myself to drive by stealing my parents' car when they weren't home. They often went out at night, leaving the Buick Electra in the garage, and Peter and I would take turns driving it around the development.

In addition to making my own rules, I continually craved excitement, and when it could not be found in Rockland County, New York City was just around the corner. One day Peter and I were hanging out at Hillcrest when we ran into Butch and Guy. Butch was a bad ass from Spring Valley who looked like he could have been my older brother, but when it came to his friends he had a heart of gold. Guy was a criminal, did a lot of drugs and had been in and out of reform school. At eighteen he was best known for ripping off houses. Butch and Guy may not have had many social graces, but they were an easy outlet for excitement.

The Rolling Stones were playing at Madison Square Garden that night, as their album *Sticky Fingers* had just come out. Even though they did not have tickets, Butch and Guy were on their way to the concert, and Peter and I decided to tag along. We used up all our money on the bus tickets to Manhattan, and when we followed Butch and Guy into the subway, Guy jumped the railing. The three of us followed suit, and when a transit cop called for us to stop, Guy yelled, "Fuck off!" and we darted onto the train just as the doors slid shut behind us.

When we arrived at the Garden, there were people everywhere—scalpers selling tickets, policemen on horseback and crowds hurrying up the steps to get to their seats before the concert began. Guy said he was going to steal a ticket, and he took off. As the night progressed, the crowds swelled, streets were roped off and armies of police on horseback moved us from side to side like human ping-pong balls.

Eventually the concert let out and the crowd thinned. Guy never made it into the show, but he did get beat up by a street gang in the process of trying. Again, the four of us snuck into the subway tunnel and hopped a train headed toward the George Washington Bridge. Upon disembarking, we found ourselves in the middle of Spanish Harlem and, hoping to wrest additional fun from the still young evening, we decided to explore.

We happened upon a street-vendor selling egg rolls. I was keeping pace with Guy, walking ahead of Peter and Butch, when Guy stopped at the man's pushcart, looked at me and asked, "You hungry?"

"Yeah!" I was half starved, and assumed that Guy held a secret money stash.

We were each handed an egg roll, and as the vendor said, "That will be—" Guy yelled, "Run!" and he took off down the street, leaving me standing there about to take my first bite. I threw my egg roll in the air and tore after him. Guy had ducked into a narrow alley between two buildings, and I found him crouched down munching his late night snack. He looked at me and asked, "Where's your egg roll?"

I had to smoke a cigarette to calm my nerves, and then we resumed walking the streets looking for Peter and Butch. Suddenly we heard a loud shout from behind, "There they are!" We turned to see a group of street thugs barreling toward us. Right away we were off and running again, Guy in the lead. He flew into an old building and up the creaky stairs, with me close behind. At the top of the stairway we went through an open hole onto the roof. Guy walked around commenting on how cool the view looked, while I sat and wondered how cool it would feel having my throat cut.

Guy peered over the edge of the roof. "There's Butch and Peter," he said, pointing down. "Yo! Up here!"

I peeked over in time to see the street thugs surround Peter and Butch, then the gang raced into the building.

I heard Peter warn, "Get out of there! They have knives!" I was so scared I thought I would pass out before anyone had the chance to kill me. Meanwhile, Guy calmly stood at the edge studying the roof of the next building. Without warning, he stepped back, ran, lifted off and dropped safely on the neighboring roof. In a flash he disappeared down the stair hole.

I heard voices behind me. The building next to me was not that far away—a rather easy jump—but from this height it appeared impossible. The voices were getting louder, so I stepped back, ran like hell and pushed off. I sailed over the alley like a cat and almost landed in the stair hole! I slammed the door shut behind me, clattered down the stairs and into the deserted alley.

Guy was nowhere in sight. I slipped down back alleys, circled tall buildings and scrambled over brick walls in an effort to shake the gang that was undoubtedly still hunting for me. Even with all the excitement, I still could not believe people actually lived in these decrepit buildings, but they did. Televisions and radios were blaring, and one woman spotted me as she hung out by her window. She threw something in my direction while yelling at me in Spanish.

Finally, I found my way out of the apartment maze and onto the busy city streets, and as I hurried toward the George Washington Bridge, I thanked God to be alive and headed for home. It was a windy night and I felt scared walking alone across the bridge that gently swayed back and forth high over the Hudson River. At the entrance ramp to the Palisades Interstate Parkway, I stuck out my thumb, and within no time at all I was home, safe and sound, and asleep in my bed.

An experience such as this would probably discourage the faint at heart, but not Peter and me. A week later we were back in New York City, and again, we unexpectedly took another of life's lessons on the realities that lurked beyond our safe haven called Rockland County. We whiled away the day and most of the night hanging around Washington Square Park checking out the street musicians and comedians. When we returned to Port Authority at two in the morning to catch the bus back to Rockland, we were told that the last bus had left an hour earlier. Rather than ending it by hitchhiking home, we headed back to the streets and hung around Times Square rapping with the prostitutes and eating pizza. There was nothing more appetizing than New York pizza, and these prostitutes weren't bad either. Two girls, not much older than us, said they had run away from somewhere in the mid west, and they offered us blowjobs for twenty-five dollars, which we declined. Eventually, we headed back to Port Authority to crash in the lobby of the enormous bus terminal with the rest of the New York City street people.

Peter was half asleep when a man moved next to where we were sitting. The man and I got to talking, and he invited us to crash at his apartment. I elbowed Peter, who said, "Cool," and off we went. This guy had to be okay, after all these were not dangerous times, and we rarely thought twice in a situation like this.

He told us we could crash on the bed. Assuming we had the room to ourselves, we stripped down to our underwear. Peter was out like a light while I was thinking how fortunate we were to have met this guy. I was just about dead to the world when I felt a hand crawling up my leg.

Thinking Peter was having a bad dream, I rolled away and yelled, "What the fuck are you doing?" The next thing I knew, our host was naked on top of me, trying to kiss me and grab my balls. I jumped out of bed, snatched my pants and boots and ran into the living room. The guy immediately tried the same moves with Peter, who joined me in throwing clothes on as quickly as possible. The man kept saying how sorry he was and promised to leave us alone if we stayed the night, but we said "No thanks!" and headed back to the bus station.

I didn't mind someone being gay, as long as they kept their hands off my balls—even though some of my friends and I were naïve and a bit sheltered, we had respect for others. One thing about our upbringing, we weren't prejudiced. It was okay to be different, and we tried to be open minded. Those were the days of race riots; the country was in turmoil but attitudes in Rockland were changing for the better. Maybe it was the place, or just the time, but I didn't realize until years later how deep prejudice ran in so many parts of this country.

CHAPTER 4

"Call My Mother!"

Neil Levine was a year younger than I and, at fourteen, he already had a moustache and a beard. He played the sax and we often jammed together at Skunk.

Nineteen seventy-two was a cold, hard winter. I was sick of shoveling snow, so one especially freezing day, Neil and I decided to hitchhike down to Florida where it was warm, and where his older sister lived. I went home and packed a knapsack, determined this time to make it all the way to Miami. I figured I didn't need much in the way of belongings; I was only going on vacation, not running away! I told my sister I was leaving, said goodbye to everyone at Skunk and we were off. We had fifty dollars between us and, being the day of twenty-five cent pizza slices, we thought it was plenty of money to see us to our destination.

When I called home the first night out, my parents weren't pleased with my decision to take off. My mom said that I shouldn't expect her to pay for me to come home like last time, and my dad said I shouldn't expect him to pay my tuition at Skunk Hollow anymore, but I had a big adventure ahead so there was no time to worry.

When Neil and I arrived at the spot where Tommy and I had been arrested, we tiptoed through town hiding our hair under ski hats. We weren't taking any chances this time! We traveled all that day and through the next day and night, and we were only two hours from the Florida state line with a ride that was headed into Jacksonville. I was asleep in the backseat, happy with the thought that as soon as I stepped out of the car, I would be in Florida. Neil woke me up just as we were passing the "Welcome to Florida" sign, and in a few minutes we were at our driver's exit. He let us out and took off.

We threw our bags in the air and shouted, "We're in Florida! We made it!"

Just as we picked up our bags, a police car with its lights flashing and sirens wailing pulled off the roadway and aimed right for us. Suddenly the car started talking. "Put down those bags and put your hands to your sides!" The trooper eased out of the car, and he was a giant. He was wearing boots, a perfectly pressed uniform, a large gun, cowboy hat and dark sunglasses. He glared down at us and drawled, "What type of drugs are in those bags, boys?" When we tried to answer, he snapped, "Shut up and show me some ID!" What was ID? We knew who we were. Then he asked to see how much money we had, and we handed over a few bills and some change. He counted out nine dollars.

"You are under arrest. You have the right to remain silent. Anything you say . . ."

We were handcuffed and stuffed into the back of his cruiser. He unloaded us at the police station where they took our fingerprints; we smiled for a picture, and then they put us in a big cell with a lot of other prisoners.

This was the cell where they put people they weren't quite sure what to do with. A guard said if we were seventeen or older we'd remain in jail, but if we were sixteen or younger they'd ship us out to Juvenile. Looking at Neil, they were relatively sure he was seventeen, but they had their doubts about me. Soon Neil was taken to another cell, and I was left alone for an hour until a cop came and yanked me out. "You're goin' to Juvie."

"I'm seventeen!" I swore repeatedly as we drove. "Can't you call my house and ask my parents?"

This guy didn't like me; I was a pain in his ass. "I hope you like to work!" was all he said.

Again I was locked in a cell. This one had a bench, a sink, a toilet, and a door made of bars. Looking through the bars, I caught glimpses of the other inmates. They were all kids, and they all looked identical in baggy, gray uniforms and—crew cuts!

Now I knew I had to get the hell out of this place, and besides, there was no one to talk to and I was hungry. Suddenly I heard a cart rolling down the corridor. Yes, lunchtime! I looked and sure enough a cart pushed by a rather big guard, was coming my way. The cell door opened and he shoved the cart inside. It held an enamel pot of water, a folded towel, two scissors, and an electric razor. One look at the razor, and I panicked.

The guard had a stupid grin on his face, complete with a hole where a tooth was missing. He grabbed his scissors and said, "Ya know what I'm here for?"

I backed into the corner yelling, "I don't belong here! I'm seventeen—take me back to the jail!" As he approached, scissors waving, my fists began to fly and I tossed my head from side to side in an effort to keep my hair from between the sparkling blades. The guard flung the scissors back on the cart, grabbed the front of my shirt and threw me down on the bench. Then he produced a great big billy club, held it to my face and snarled, "We can do this two ways. One, with you awake, or two, with you out, and it don't matter to me either way." As this was transpiring, one of the administrators came into the cell. This guy wore a suit and actually talked to me, trying to calm me down.

"Son, we have no proof you are of age, which means you're our responsibility. These are our rules, and unless you can show me proof of your correct age, we are stuck with each other."

While he was talking, the guard held me down and grinned like a monkey. I looked at the suit guy and whispered my last desperate plea. "Please, can't you call my mother?"

"We already called and your sister told us you were fifteen."

"She doesn't know anything, she's only a baby!"

The guy paused to think, then he said, "All right, we'll try one more time, and if we reach your parents, and they confirm that you are seventeen, we'll transfer you back to the jail." I think he wanted to send me back to the Jacksonville Police Department as badly as I wanted to go.

As we walked to the office, I realized it was late afternoon. I thought about calling Skunk Hollow, but if that failed I'd have a new hair-do. We got to the administrator's office and lucky enough he handed the phone to me. I dialed my number and once more my sister answered the phone.

"Are you in jail, again?" she asked in her little girl voice.

"Get Mom!"

My mother was furious with me, but I asked her—pleaded with her—to tell them I was seventeen so they would take me back to the jail where Neil was.

"If you don't tell them I'm seventeen, they're going to give me a *crew cut!*" I was desperate.

My mother responded, "Why should *I* tell him anything, *you* ran away, remember?"

It was just then that the guy in the suit took the phone, politely intro-duced himself and asked, "How old is your son? Okay, thank you ma'am," and hung up. I was trying to see my reflection in the window, hoping to get one last glimpse of my hair. The man looked at me and said, "Back to the cell," and sure enough, Egor the Barber-ian was still there.

The administrator said to him, "You can go, Dave. We'll have to move him back." For the first and last time in my life, I was thrilled about going to jail. All right, Mom!

A new officer drove me back to the jailhouse. "What have we here, a vagrant? Oh, that should guarantee you at least thirty days on the labor farm, kid." With my hands handcuffed behind my back, I tried to enjoy the ride, all the while hoping he was just trying to scare me. Upon return-ing to the jailhouse I was escorted upstairs where one of the officers who recognized me from before said, "I don't envy you. You should have stayed where you were!"

They took off my cuffs and tossed me into a cell with four other guys. There was a phone on the wall and I waited my turn. I couldn't make a collect call to Skunk because all the school had was a pay phone, so I gave the operator a made-up credit card number and my call went through.

Wally answered the phone, and when word got out I was in Florida, and in jail, everyone wanted to talk to me, like I was some kind of hero. Then, an operator cut in to inform me my card was unauthorized, and the phone went dead. When the other prisoners in the cell heard I killed the phone, they wanted to kill me. These were not the kind of guys you mess around with, so I sat with my back to the wall and hoped the phone would be restored, and restored quick.

From a cell down the hall someone was yelling, "Help, help!" He kept screaming without pause. I thought Neil might be somewhere down the hall, so I called for him. Sure enough he answered, and I felt better.

I hollered to Neil that there was a phone in my cell, and he replied, "Call my mother and tell her to send bond money!" This triggered the crazy guy who had been screaming "Help, help!" to begin screaming, "Call my mother! Call my mother!"

As I waited for the phone to come back on, a big fat guy came over and demanded, "Give me a blowjob!" and he insisted I do until a guard removed me to a holding cell. There were ten or eleven inmates there, including a few old bums, two young guys who were caught trying to rape a girl in the middle of town, two of the bad asses who were in my original cell and a tough guy who escaped from prison in Atlanta. Neil was there, too.

Neil had already established himself with this crew, but I was fresh meat. As soon as I walked into the cell, one of the bad asses said, "The fuckin' mountain climber's back!" while pointing to my suede knee-high boots with fringes. When his buddy mumbled, "Yeah, that's the asshole who fucked up our phone," I knew I was off to an unhealthy start. Neil tried not to laugh and acted like he didn't know me. Just in the nick of time a guard opened the cell door and handed me the half-pack of Marlboros that had been taken away from me earlier. All of a sudden everybody was my best friend, the cigarettes were passed around, and jail became fun.

Neil and I were the youngest prisoners in this Jacksonville jail, and we were taking it all in. The guy who escaped from prison was a heroin addict impatiently waiting for his methadone. If he wasn't pushing someone up against the wall, he was yelling for the guards to find out where his meth was. The crazy guy down the corridor was still yelling, "Call my mother!" and at one point we heard what sounded like a bunch of officers beating the shit out of him. Dinner was rolled in—a boloney sandwich, beans and a plastic cup of orange juice that tasted like warm water. We sat on the floor against the wall, Neil on one side of me, an old bum on my other side, and next to him, nibbling on his food, the escaped addict. When I saw something crawling in my beans I threw my plate aside, and within seconds the bum was finishing them off.

Just then a guard opened the cell. He held up a Dixie cup containing a small amount of orange fluid. The addict leaped forward, took the cup and dropped down between me and the old man. He gazed lovingly into his cup and breathed a long, racking breath of relief. Then he tapped the old man, held the cup out to him and said, "Fill this with water."

The old guy, barely aware of what was going on but satisfied after finishing both his dinner and mine, took the cup and shuffled away. Neil and I watched as, in one quick motion, he turned the Dixie cup upside down and dumped the methadone down the sink. Then he filled the cup with water, turned and headed back toward us.

Neil and I looked at each other, our eyes wide open and jaws dropped, speechless.

Mr. Escapee grabbed the cup from the old man and gulped down the contents, but the water came spewing out of his mouth when he realized his methadone wasn't in it. He threw the cup across the room, grabbed the old man by the throat and banged his head against the wall, screaming, "*WHAT*(bang!) *THE*(bang!) *FUCK*(bang!) *DID*(bang!) *YOU*(bang!) *DO?*(bang!)"

As he slammed the old guy's head into the wall, the two would-be rapists picked up the cup and, with their fingers, tried to scoop out any leftover methadone-flavored water. The old man was crying as a few of us tried to pull the attacker off him. After a long five minutes a guard came, then two more, and they removed the old man from the cell, leaving us with the madman.

As the cell filled up with new prisoners, others were being taken out. Neil and I wondered why people who arrived after us were leaving before us. After several more hours of waiting, a cop told us that Neil's sister, Nancy, was coming up from Miami to bail us out. By the time they took Neil out, there were mostly new faces in the cell.

"What about me? Hey, Neil, make sure I get out!"

"Don't worry," he called over his shoulder.

The minutes were now like hours and, as I paced back and forth wondering how I was going to handle this by myself, panic again flashed through me. To add to my desperate situation, one of the cops told me that Nancy brought only enough money to pay Neil's bond. I was crushed. Was there any way we could mail you the money?

"In the morning ya'll be in front of the judge to find out how long ya work sentence'll be, kid." Another half hour passed, and I was convinced it would be a long time before I saw Miami Beach, or any other beach for that matter.

Just then the cell door opened and a cop took me downstairs where I was handed my knapsack. I was getting out! The reason they refused to let me out earlier was because I wasn't related to Neil's family, but after an argument with Neil's brother-in-law, Bill, who was an Air Force officer, they finally let me go. Our bond was fifty dollars each, the vagrancy fine for not having enough money.

Now we were really on our way to Miami Beach, and in style, too, sitting in the back of Bill's big air-conditioned Cadillac. Neil's sister was "very disappointed" in us, and she elaborated on this theme during most of the six-hour ride to her apartment.

We arrived in Miami Beach at nine o'clock in the morning, and man was it beautiful! The sun was shining, it was eighty degrees out, and to think that only a few days earlier, we were up to our knees in snow! We laughed at the thought of all our friends freezing in New York, and agreed that a stopover in jail was a small price to pay to get to this place, where everything, including the apartment complex, seemed unreal. We were in a wonderland of newly constructed buildings painted wild colors like pink, yellow and turquoise. Exotic flowers, palm trees and swimming pools were everywhere we looked.

Nancy was very straight. She treated us like babies, but the minute she left for work, Air Force Bill pulled out a bag of pot and rolled a fat joint to smoke with us. Nancy didn't know that Bill smoked pot, and God forbid if she ever found out that he was turning us on! After we left Bill's smoke-in, we made it to the beach at last. Not having slept in almost two days, Neil and I crashed out on lounge chairs alongside the pool at the Aztec Hotel, and that night we hung out at the Castaway's Wreck Bar. Wayne Cochran was playing, and his bass player, a guy named Jack, snuck us in.

The next day Neil and I decided to hitch to Key West. We promised Nancy we'd be back in a week, at which time she had arranged a ride for us to New York with one of Bill's military buddies. On the way through the Keys we stopped to check out a campground on Sugarloaf Key, which was about twenty miles from Key West.

Bow Channel Campground looked like a tropical Woodstock. There were hippies camping in tents, trailers, old school buses, or like Neil and me, sleeping on the ground under the stars. We learned to make a hut out of palm fronds and to weave hats out of reeds. I had never felt so free, and I vowed that someday I would come back to Bow Channel. Before returning to Nancy's, we made it to Key West in time to watch the sun slide through orange and purple clouds into the Gulf of Mexico.

We were headed back to New York with Bill's friend T.J. in his Volkswagen Bug. As we passed Daytona Beach, T.J. decided he was too tired to drive. He pulled over and asked which one of us wanted to take the wheel. Neil and I both jumped at the opportunity, but Neil had never driven a car, and because I had experience driving Dad's Electra, I got the job. The fact that I was underage, had no driver's license and had just been released from jail didn't seem to bother T.J. in the least. All he wanted to do was crawl in the backseat and fall asleep.

The problem was, I had never before driven a car with a stick shift.

After almost being blown off the road by a semi, I finally got the car into the proper gear and we were on our way. T.J. was out cold, the 8-track tape was blasting, Neil was grooving to the music and I was King of the Road. As we passed the first Jacksonville exit signs, Neil and I laughed at our recent Jacksonville experience, making fun of the prisoners and performing imitations of the cops. This time, we were in the fast lane doing sixty-five, listening to the music and glad about how soon this town would be a thing of the past. Suddenly, the road divided, and before we knew it, we were off the highway and on the streets of the city of Jacksonville.

While Neil screamed that I should have gone the other way, I tried to shift into a lower gear. We must have been a sight, a Bug lurching down the street of what seemed to be one of Jacksonville's nastiest neighborhoods. Neil attempted to wake up T. J. as I imagined what it would be like back in the Jacksonville jailhouse. Finally, T.J. rose from the dead, and to make matters worse, he let us in on a little secret—there was a kilo of marijuana in the trunk, on its way to being delivered to his connection in D.C.! Strangely, my thoughts were on Nancy. Either she was real naïve or maybe she didn't care what everyone around her was up to. I came to the conclusion that she was just slow on the uptake.

Miraculously, we made it back to the highway, and by the time we got to D.C., I had mastered the art of driving a stick shift.

I loved my freedom—it was the most important part of my life. I did not want anyone telling me what I must think or believe or what I must say or not say, and I didn't want to take anything from anyone, not even my parents. To become fully independent, I'd need to earn my own money, so I decided to get a job.

Some of the Spring Valley guys hung out at Mickey's Mobil on Route 59. There was this kid named Ira who worked nights at the station. He was kind of dim-witted and tough looking, with acne and scars all over his face, and I figured if they hired him, it would be a cinch for me to get a job. I had never pumped gas before, am hardly what you might call mechanically inclined, and, I had to lie about my age—but in a few days I received the call telling me I was hired.

I was assigned to work the graveyard shift from midnight to seven in the morning. In those days, there was no such thing as self-serve, and we washed windshields. On my first night, Ira, my supervisor, had been instructed to train me, but instead he took off. As soon as he was gone, some guy pulled up with a Porsche, lifted up the hood and told me to "Fill 'er up!" The only problem was, I couldn't find the gas cap. There were several caps under the hood, so, using some logic, I opened the biggest one and filled 'er up. It only took about twenty cents of gasoline. The driver who had gone to the men's room came back, started the car and told me the gas gauge still read empty. He couldn't understand it because his car was brand new. We decided there must have been something wrong with the gauge, and he drove away. When Ira returned, I told him about the Porsche and he told me I had filled the oil tank with gasoline, and the poor guy was probably stuck up the road somewhere with a fucked-up car. Ira thought it was hysterical, but I felt really bad about it.

We had the place to ourselves, and Mickey's Mobil was known as one of the hot places to hang out. I was host of the party and getting paid to do it. I was always on time, did what I was told and made sure nothing was ever taken, but Ira was stealing money any way he could. I hated it, but didn't want to rat on him. We all had our honor, and you never told what you knew. Even if you didn't agree with what someone was doing, we would never narc on him or her. We knew people who had turned in friends to keep themselves out of trouble, and we considered them lowlifes. One night, a customer left her credit card and Ira got hold of it. He started ringing some of his cash sales on it and putting the cash in his pocket.

Another night, Peter was hanging out with me. When Ira heard us talking about wanting to pick up a girlfriend, he told us we could take a customer's car that was in for a service. He assured us that nothing was wrong with the car, it was just there for a check-up.

We had to drive down South Mountain Road, a narrow country lane that clung to the side of a steep mountain, and just as I was negotiating a hairpin turn, smoke started pouring into the car. Soon, the whole car was filled with smoke, and even after we opened all the windows I still couldn't see where I was driving. We wondered if the car might blow up and kill us, and we almost went over a cliff because I was trying to work the pedals and turn the steering wheel, with my head sticking out of the window.

We pulled into Mickey's Mobil in a cloud of smoke. As we scrambled from the car, Ira strolled over and calmly remarked, "Oh yeah. That's the one with the broken heater hose." When we informed him that we almost got killed on South Mountain Road, he gave us one of his great insights. "Life is what it is, and if it was meant to be, you'd be dead." Thanks a lot, Ira!

I was falling into a routine of working nights and sleeping days—one that would haunt me through much of my life—and it suited me just fine. I couldn't function in a nine-to-five schedule, and I loved to sleep while the rest of the world was awake. The graveyard shift foretold of the vampire years that followed.

At about five a.m., the diner across the street from Mickey's opened and we'd be the first ones in, anxious for that first cup of coffee. At six, it was time to find the darkest sunglasses in the place. I don't know why, but the world looks brighter in the morning when you've been up all night than when you're first getting up.

At seven o'clock, I'd either hitchhike or Ira would give me a ride to Skunk, where I fell asleep in the R.E. building until around noon when the music started. At home, after dinner, I'd usually get a few more hours of sleep before going back to work.

One afternoon when I got home from Skunk, there was an FBI agent waiting to question me. It seemed someone at Mickey's Mobil was running up bills on a missing credit card, and most of it was during my shift. I never did rat on Ira, but after being harassed by the Feds, the local authorities and even Mickey, I quit. Eventually Mickey figured out that Ira was stealing, and Ira was fired. No one ever apologized to me, but I thought I did the right thing by not turning in Ira. I learned that it didn't matter what other people thought. What mattered was what I knew to be true. We all have to live with our actions, and I didn't bother to explain my side to anyone.

CHAPTER 5

Jack and the John Lennon Sessions: The Meeting

In the late '70s, Jack Douglas and his fiancé, Christine Desautels, lived one block from Central Park West in a brownstone apartment on West 76th Street, a pleasant neighborhood with quaint shops. Their apartment was in the same neighborhood as the Dakota, the famous building where John Lennon and Yoko Ono lived. John was known to occasionally stroll the neighborhood streets. The merchants all knew him, and many had put an autographed picture of John wearing his NYC t-shirt in their shop windows. John loved the streets of New York, and they loved him (or so he imagined).

Jack and John had become friends years earlier when Jack worked as an engineer at Record Plant Studios. John sometimes accompanied Beatles producer George Martin on his trips to the United States to finish albums at Record Plant, and Jack was usually the assistant George called upon.

After not seeing John for years, Jack was on his way home from the gym when again, their paths crossed. When John saw Jack he became as excited as a child. He said he was writing songs again, and might want to go back into the studio. He asked Jack if he would consider taking him into the studio; Jack was speechless. It had been over five years since John had done anything musically. The world had all but forgotten John Lennon the artist, composer, and musician. He had reportedly taken up the new profession of raising his son, while the world waited patiently for a Beatles reunion.

Upon returning to his apartment, Jack didn't know what to think. He wondered if John was daydreaming about making a comeback or if he was serious, but he had said he would call, and Jack had a funny feeling that he would.

CHAPTER 6

She Stayed Long Enough to Rescue Me

I was sixteen that November, when Ramapo held its yearly music concert. The Skunk Hollow Band was scheduled to play, and I was appointed official roadie. After setting up the drums and doing a sound check, I spotted Angela Paone. Angela liked older guys, which I wasn't, but she liked me sort of as a younger brother. It worked for me because with sexy Angela hanging all over me the other girls would take notice, and that made it easy for me to meet them later.

They were just starting to let people into the auditorium when Angela grabbed me off the stage and we found seats a few rows from the front. Sitting in front of me were two girls. One was sort of a bookworm type, but it was her friend I couldn't help noticing. Her hair was cascading over the back of the seat in front of me, and I could almost smell it. Then it hit me! It was the same girl sitting beside the Skyview pool—Mr. Gurowsky's daughter! This time, not feeling at all awkward, I was determined to get to know her. I climbed over the row and sat in the empty seat next to her. Again, the same line came out of my mouth. "You're Mr. Gurowsky's daughter, right?"

This time she smiled. "Yeah, and you go to Skunk Hollow, right?"

That was it! The ice was broken, and it was all right to be there. When the show started, we couldn't let go of each other's hand, and it seemed she liked me as much as I liked her. After the concert, and a few kisses in the hallway, I walked her outside to meet her mother, who was waiting to pick her up in the family's 1964 Studebaker.

One can always feel the tension when a parent looks you over, and meeting Alissa's mother caused me plenty. Elsa, the school nurse at a local junior high, was cold but cordial, and before she drove off, Alissa and I arranged to see each other the following day.

In the morning I picked her up in my mother's red Cutlass to take her to Harriman State Park. As soon as she got into the car, Alissa said, "I had a hard time convincing my parents to let me go out with you. My mother even asked me, 'Does Kenny smoke pot?'"

"What did you say?"

"I told her, 'If he does, it doesn't matter, because I don't!'"

I thought that was the wrong thing to say, and it gave me a bad feeling, but I soon forgot the whole incident as we drove the winding roads, walked to waterfalls and found a secret place in the woods where we smoked a joint supplied by Alissa. We even stopped at the Bear Mountain Inn to attend an arts and crafts fair. It was our first "date," and I wanted more.

The next day was Monday. Unable to wait until the afternoon to see me again, Alissa cut school and came to Skunk. That morning, she got on the bus in front of her house as usual, then got off at the next stop and walked through the woods to visit me. She had never been to Skunk before, and didn't know where the front door was. Tilly spotted her as she walked past one of the sliding glass doors. Never having seen Alissa before, Tilly opened the door and said to her, "I don't know who you are, but you're welcome to come in and join us!"

I was sitting on the floor of that class. Nervously, Alissa walked in and all eyes were fastened on her as she crossed the room and sat down next to me. Mr. Gurowsky's daughter was the last person they ever expected to see at Skunk Hollow . . . least of all with me!

This wasn't the first time Alissa had cut school, but it was the first time her mother had forgotten to leave the house key under the doormat. You can imagine the shock Elsa received when she called Ramapo to tell Alissa the key would not be there, only to be told her daughter was absent that day!

Unlike her sister and brother, who were doing great in college, Alissa had lost interest in school. We agreed public school was intolerable; it was like being locked in a prison, unable to experience the whole wide world that lay beyond. Alissa, especially, felt trapped. She always wondered why her family stayed to themselves and why the other Skyview kids rarely had anything to do with her or her brother and sister. Now she was fifteen, she knew me, she was hanging out at Skunk, and for the first time, the other Skyview kids were taking notice of her. All she ever wanted was to feel she belonged, and finally she did.

It was after six-thirty that night before we could let go of each other. It wasn't unusual for Alissa to come home at this hour, as she would often visit after school with her friend, Sue. When I kissed her good-bye, I knew no one else could ever make me feel this way, and I wanted to tell her everything, but she already knew.

Alissa walked into her house and headed to the phone to call Sue to make sure everything was okay, but when Sue answered the phone, she was crying hysterically. "Your mom called me, and I couldn't lie. She knew you cut school and there was nothing I could . . ." Just then, Elsa took the phone out of Alissa's hand and hung it up. With the new strength that arose from the special feeling we had shared only a few moments before, Alissa decided for the first time in her life to stand up to her parents.

"Where were you? Who were you with? Was it that boy? Were you at that school . . . Skunk Hollow?"

"Yes, I was with him, I was at Skunk Hollow!"

Then her father yelled, "I suppose you smoke pot, too?"

Alissa had a friend, Stevie Mednick, a loner from Skyview, who had turned her on to pot several months earlier. They frequently cut school and hung out in the woods getting high. Or, to be more accurate, Stevie would sell Alissa pot and then stick around to help her smoke it all up.

"Yes!" she answered.

That was more than Murry could handle, and he was determined to get even with that Skunk Hollow trash he was sure had corrupted his youngest daughter and disrupted his perfect family and perfectly planned life.

Murry Gurowsky hated the outside world. His mother died during a flu epidemic when he was an infant, and Murry was left with his father and three older sisters. His sisters had the responsibility of raising him, and they resented it. Murry was alone, and remembered when times were so tough they did not always have food. His father owned a wholesale nut and dried fruit company with his cousin, who was a thief and eventually destroyed the business. Murry's father was left without a company or a job. When Murry was old enough he joined the Navy and worked in the shipyards and became mechanically skilled. Around that time he met Elsa, his future wife. Murry then became a schoolteacher, and Elsa was a registered nurse.

Murry learned of a cooperative community that was forming in Rockland County, and he bought his two and a half acres of what was soon to become Skyview Acres. As the years passed, houses were built and the community grew. Skyview evolved into a close-knit family of friends that had moved out of New York City, seeking to live cooperatively in a natural environment.

Eventually a meeting was held to find out why Murry had not built his house. All the available land had been sold and built upon, and many residents had a friend or relative who had changed their minds and now wished they could live in Skyview. Murry was the only one with land but no house, so it was decided they would try to take back his land. The lady across the street told Murry that she had overheard some talk coming from his driveway, and she had listened as they discussed the possible ways they would divide his land up for themselves once they got it back.

With two small kids, a pregnant wife and a full-time job, Murry was forced to break ground and build his house years before he had planned to. His fight with Skyview was never to be forgotten, nor was the pain of his childhood. There were very few people Murry got along with, and he made his family aware of how he felt and kept them sheltered from the outside world. Now he had a new problem. His youngest daughter had been corrupted and demoralized, and like all other fights, this was one that Murry was determined to win.

Alissa was permanently grounded. She was not allowed to receive phone calls or see friends, and she was never to see that boy again!

What he didn't count on was the bond between Alissa and me. We sensed this was IT—we had found the course of the remainder of our lives. We were meant for each other, and our love was stronger than Murry's resolve, so we devised ways to see each other. There was an hour between the time Alissa got home from school and her mother got home from work, and I usually spent that time with her at her house. A week after Alissa was grounded, I had my next encounter with Elsa. I had just left their house and was walking up the hill when Elsa came driving around the bend. and she spotted me. She was furious and warned me to keep away from her daughter.

Alissa and I were in love and would do anything to see each other. It took a lot of planning, but we succeeded, and with each encounter fell more in love.

CHAPTER 7

By the Time We Got to-
Watkins Glen

We students, along with teachers at Skunk Hollow, built an eight-track recording studio in the R.E. building, and I was introduced to the multi-track recording process. Recording music fascinated me, and I wanted to learn all facets of the music business, but attending concerts was still my number one priority. Woodstock had passed into the history books, but this was the summer of Watkins Glen, another three-day rock n' roll festival being held in upstate New York. The Grateful Dead, the Allman Brothers and the Band were scheduled to play, and there were rumors that Bob Dylan would also appear.

We met at the Skyview pool, Neil with his saxophone and me with my drumsticks. Alissa came to tell us good-bye. We had dreamed of us both going, but at the last minute she decided not to go. I wish we had kidnapped her.

I was driving my first car, an old gray American Motors Gremlin hatchback. It felt great to zip down the highway behind the wheel of my own car with a load with supplies and a wad of cash, and even greater not to be hitchhiking with a backpack, a candy bar and a five dollar bill. When Neil and I arrived in Watkins Glen, the concert was still a week away. With only a few campsites scattered around, the fields were almost empty. We helped unload lumber that was used to build the stage and hung out with the Grateful Dead roadies.

The festival attracted people from all corners, and at night we sat around campfires listening to interesting stories. Colorful buses and trailers trickled in along with hikers, bikers and VW Bugs. It seemed any-one who was at Woodstock would be here—The Farm, the Rainbow People, and the Hell's Angels—and those who had missed Woodstock certainly would not miss this one.

There was a stream, and we went skinny dipping in the water holes. We slid in the mudslides when it rained and spent the nights around bon-fires, meeting brothers and sisters from all over the country. Lots of sis-ters—there were wild women everywhere and they were determined to have as much fun as we were. Concert time drew near and the crowd swelled.

Then one night it happened. As the sun was going down, the "setting of the sun" jams were starting up. There were a few guitars, lots of drums which included pots, pans, sticks or anything that could create a sound and, of course, Neil on his big old tenor sax. The chanting had begun. "Whoa, whoa, whoa, whoa"— Cat Stevens meets Santana meets Miles Davis. I was hanging around the fire listening to the music and, as usual, sipping on the bottles of wine and toking on the joints that were being passed around. Suddenly I started to feel weird. I imagined it was the pot, but the feeling began to get intense. Neil stopped playing, turned to me and said, "I think I'm tripping!"

Doing acid was something we always planned ahead of time, sometimes weeks in advance. We would plan a trip like one plans a vaca-tion. For example, we might decide on Friday to hike up to Pine Meadow and drop acid, or if someone's parents were going out of town, we'd do it at their house. We would take care of every detail right down to the records we were going to play. The worst thing that could happen was to be dosed out without your knowledge.

Neil seemed content to play his sax while I hung out next to a couple of guys that had ridden their Harleys down from Vermont. It was dark by the time I decided to go back to our pup tent. I took about twenty steps, figured it was a bad idea, and thought I should return to the fire. When I got back to it, all these different people were there. I tried to get a grasp as to what was going on but everyone seemed twice as fucked up as I was. There were fires everywhere, so I tried listening for Neil's horn, but I heard it coming from more than one direction. I don't remember much, except I think I walked for hours following the directions people gave me when I asked them if they had seen a guy with long hair play-ing a saxophone.

When dawn finally broke, I found myself in a strange tent cuddled in the arms of a strange girl, and I had no recollection of how I got there. Without waking her up I put on my dungarees and crawled outside, leaving my shirt and shoes in the tent.

Green, blue, red and yellow tents covered the hills, rising and falling in every direction as far as the eye could see. I stood in amazement staring at what looked like thousands, perhaps millions of tents! People everywhere were walking around and partying, the smoke from thousands of campfires hung low in the early morning mist and the soft rhythmic thump of conga drums carried far into the cool, still air. I watched for a long moment then turned to go back and meet the girl I had just left, but had no idea which tent I'd come out of. That's how many tents there were.

It was like nothing I had ever experienced. I gave up hunting for my clothes after looking in four or five tents. I couldn't imagine where my car or tent was, or where Neil might be. The concert was to start that day, and suddenly I came to the realization that I had no shirt, shoes, car, tent or friend. I was surrounded by a million strangers, and I was not going to eat or drink anything that was unwrapped or open! But I wasn't alone for long though, because it was easy to fit into whatever was going on.

I remember even less about the performances, except I wound up close to the stage for most of the concert, it rained, and there was a big jam with members of all three bands. As the concert ended and the people thinned out, I ran into Neil. We watched the people melt from the fields, leaving their muddy tents and campsites behind, plus tons of garbage that was scattered for miles. We stayed an extra few days and joined in picking up and burning the garbage. Finding food was easy because the locals came around with sandwiches and drinks, and things (including our minds) slowly returned to their preconcert condition.

I'll always cherish the memories of being a part of Watkins Glen. There were over 300,000 of us, and we all shared the common belief that it was better to love than to fight. For a few days we created a city within a small area, and it worked. One guy died when he jumped out of an airplane holding sparklers that set his parachute on fire, but a woman gave birth to a baby boy. We believed in what we stood for, and we were united in this massive celebration. As we went our separate ways, it was like we knew it was okay to return to society because we were all here together, and we'd all take a little of this back with us.

I believed this feeling would last a lifetime. It was not just a stage I was going through; this is how I was, and how I always would be. Believing everyone around me felt the same way was a powerful feeling and I was sorry Alissa couldn't have been there to share it with me.

Neil and I packed up my car, and headed to Canada. Neither of us had ever been across the border, and Montreal was only a few hours away. We picked up a hitchhiker and with him and his stuff, the car was full. None of us were prepared for what happened next.

It was nighttime. I was driving through pouring rain and could hardly see the road in front of me. Neil was sitting next to me and the hitchhiker was in the backseat. A semi pulling a double trailer passed us, and it started to turn into my lane a bit early. I slammed on my brakes and jerked the wheel to the right. Immediately my car spun off the road, rolled over twice and landed in a ditch. No one moved or said a word. The only sound in the car was Jimi Hendrix singing, "If I don't see you in this world, I'll meet you in the next, and don't be late . . . " I thought I was dead. Then I realized Neil and the hitchhiker weren't making a sound, and I thought they were dead.

I yelled "Neil!" and I heard him say he was all right. We helped each other out of the car, and then we panicked. What about the hitchhiker? He was silent, but after we helped him out of the car he said he was okay; just a little nervous was all.

Then I saw my Gremlin. It had taken months of working at Mickey's Mobil to save the money to buy it, and now it was destroyed! As I mourned the loss of my car, Neil turned to the hitchhiker, who had a tiny trickle of blood running down his forehead, and told him that his head was bleeding.

The hitcher started freaking out. "Oh no, is my brain all right?"

Neil was furious. "How can you worry about your brain, when this guy just lost his car?"

Eventually, a trucker picked us up and took us to a hospital in a nearby town. The hitcher was still panicked and crying about his brain. He had a tiny cut and even less blood, and his treatment consisted of a drop of iodine and a Band-Aid. To make matters worse, his father was a lawyer who eventually sued me for emotional stress. The case was dropped as soon as he found out I was underage and under insured.

As soon as Neil and I returned home, I immediately started working towards a new car. I got a job stocking shelves at the Waldbaums Supermarket, and also a part-time job at the Grand Union Supermarket. Both jobs were, of course, graveyard shifts. I would get home from work at dawn and sleep until Alissa woke me up.

CHAPTER 8

Your Daughters are Beyond Your Control

Every morning, as usual, Alissa took the bus to Ramapo High School. Upon arrival she got off the bus, walked in the front door, traveled straight through the school and out the back door, and then walked down the hill to my house. Once there, she climbed through the window and crawled into bed with me. Murry suspected we were seeing each other and although he couldn't prove it, he threatened to gun me down on sight. There were also threats leveled at Skunk Hollow. Little did he know that I was sleeping with his daughter, and with her school in my backyard, and my school in her backyard, it was easy to see each other.

A few weeks after Watkins Glen, Neil moved out of his parents' house, and into a tiny bungalow about two miles from both our houses. I thought the whole idea cool, and moved in with him, and thus began my bungalow days.

When you entered the tiny wooden structure, you were in a kind of narrow hallway. The kitchen was part of that hallway. There was a small bathroom on one side and a mini bedroom on the other. The strangest thing about this bungalow was that the heat came out of the floor through two big steel heating vents. It was hard not to step on these grills, and even harder to put shoes on all the time, so many mornings we departed with checkerboards on the bottoms of our feet. The place fit five people comfortably, but there were many nights when we had no less than twenty-five, and it quickly became a popular place to hang out. One morning I came home from work and as I approached the door something came flying out the kitchen window in an explosion of shattered glass. It was getting too crazy, so we stopped the parties and tried to discourage people from visiting us.

Once a week, Neil's mother picked him up for his therapy appointment. I tried to convince Neil there was nothing wrong with him (which there wasn't) but he would always say, "No, I'm messed up! My therapist says so." It pissed me off that they were tinkering with his mind, trying to get him to behave how they wanted, and I vowed that no matter what, I would never make my kids think there was something wrong with them. People are just different, that's all.

One day Neil and I decided, for health reasons, to quit smoking cigarettes. We went out and bought a couple of ounces of pot, which cost fifteen dollars an ounce. We rolled joints and filled empty Marlboro boxes with them, the philosophy being, whenever we felt like a cigarette, we'd smoke a joint instead. It worked until we ran out of pot, and besides, cigarettes were much cheaper, about fifty-five cents a pack, and there was a cigarette machine on the sidewalk in front of every store in town.

We all wanted to be gardeners and there were many gifted green thumbs among us. Not to be outdone, Neil and I decided to give it a shot. We sprouted the seeds in our bathtub under a fluorescent light bulb. It was amazing to watch the seeds open, and soon our bathtub was filled with thirty or forty cute little pot plants, each in its own little pot. Now it was time to find a garden. We picked a spot about ten miles upstate, near Bear Mountain in Harriman State Park. Hidden in the woods we found a secret place, and we put in our plants. We dug up the earth and mixed it with horse and cow shit, and left our babies there feeling they were quite safe in the hands of Mother Nature. Within a few weeks, they were on their way up. Periodically, we'd go to Harriman and top them (pinch off the top leaves) to make them grow thicker and bushier.

I once hitched up to the garden with a friend, Jeff, and we took two plants that looked like Christmas trees back with us. As we were hitchhiking with the plants in a Hefty trash bag, a sheriff pulled off the road in front of us.

I thought we were headed for jail, but the sheriff just looked at the two big marijuana plants sticking out of the bag and admonished, "Don't you boys realize what you are doing is illegal? This is a state park! I don't ever want to see you two pulling up our plants again!" After giving his little lecture he pulled away, leaving us holding the bag. When we returned to the bungalow we hung the plants upside down in the bathroom to dry. There was a real feeling of accomplishment that went along with smoking the plants we grew from a tiny seed into a tree.

After I moved out of my parents' house it was harder to see Alissa, but we managed, and after another fight with her parents, Alissa decided she was fed up and couldn't stand it anymore. She ran away to the bungalow and declared she wasn't ever going back home, which was fine with me. We started making plans to leave Rockland County, get jobs and support ourselves in some other town. No one would know where we were, and we were not afraid.

Later that night, my father, who by now had totally cooled out about me being the way I was, drove into the driveway. He told us Alissa's father had called him and threatened to call the police unless she came home immediately. My father convinced us it would be best if he took us to her house, and he'd be there to back us up. That made us think that maybe there was a chance Alissa's parents would realize there was less harm in letting Alissa and I see each other, than in us sneaking around behind their backs. We wanted them to see how much we loved each other.

Up until this point, Alissa's father hadn't seen me since Kakiat. Alissa had told him I once attended Kakiat, but I wasn't sure if he'd remember my face, or our shirt-not-tucked-in incident. As my dad pulled up to Alissa's house, I realized I was wearing an outfit most guys wouldn't deliberately select to meet his girlfriend's parents in. My dungarees had ripped open from knee to ankle but I had mended the gash with a ladder of safety pins. I had on an old pilot-type leather jacket with a zipper that wouldn't zip. A long earring dangled from my left ear, and my hair was especially wild that day. This is how I normally looked, and Alissa didn't want me to hide it. When I attempted to tie my hair back, she grabbed my hand and said, "No."

Elsa opened the door, and tried to be polite. "Won't you come in?" she said. Alissa and I held hands and stayed close together as we tiptoed through the living room and sat down on the couch next to my father.

The tension in the room was thick. The Gurowskys seldom had any company, and they tried to remain to themselves as much as possible. It was their daughter's doings that were now bringing outsiders into their lives, and they resented it. Murry detested things like big, flashy cars, and my father had just parked one in his driveway. Murry also despised cigarettes, and I don't think anyone had ever smoked anything in his house. My father, who was unaware of the house rules, pulled out a huge cigar and lit it just as Murry entered the room, making a dramatic entrance, and we all became very still. He saw me sitting next to Alissa and as I let go of her hand I saw his eyes grow bigger and rounder till they were bursting out of his head. He turned to his wife and said, "*That's* him?"

I guess he remembered me after all!

As our parents discussed the situation (in a steadily thickening cloud of smelly cigar smoke), things progressed from terrible to worse, and my father's presence did not help a bit. The Gurowskys loathed me, and didn't want me near their daughter.

Their voices grew louder, I guess because it was getting hard to see each other through the cloud. At one point, Alissa's mother stood in front of her, looked into her eyes and asked, "I suppose you've had sex with him?"

Alissa answered, "So what if I have?"

That was it. I was trapped, like a rat in a cage, and there wasn't much I could say. Everyone's voices were overpowering mine and, besides, no one was paying attention to what I had to say.

Then Elsa slapped Alissa across the face. That was more than I could take. I grabbed Alissa's hand and started towards the door. Alissa, recoiling, stood still and said, "No, you go."

I ran out the front door, like a prisoner escaping to freedom. I raced up the hill and through the woods to Jonathan Best's house, a Skyview neighbor who went to Skunk Hollow. I wanted more than anything to pull Alissa away from her parents, but I knew she was one prisoner who wouldn't escape for a long time.

I thought about not seeing her anymore. Maybe I was causing her more troubles than it was worth? If I wasn't around, if her parents knew I was gone, then maybe, slowly, they would let her out of the house again. I decided the only thing to do was to stop thinking about Alissa for now. I'd go back to Florida and not return until the day she turned eighteen. On that morning, I would walk right up to the front door and take her away for good, and there would be nothing Murry could do to stop me.

CHAPTER 9

Jack and the John Lennon Sessions: The Call

When the call finally came it was from Yoko. She insisted everything had to be done in secrecy. She instructed Jack to go to 34th Street where he was to board a seaplane that would take him to the Lennon mansion on Long Island.

Yoko met him at the mansion. Jack was told that if anything said to him were ever repeated, there would be no deal. Jack was given an envelope marked "FOR JACK'S EYES ONLY." In it he found a single cassette tape along with a letter from John. The letter read, "I think I want to go back, would you be interested in producing my album? Here's a bunch of my songs. I think it's the same old shit—tell me what you think."

John had recorded the songs in Bermuda so Jack called the cassette "The Bermuda Tape," and on it John played piano and acoustic guitar, and John's assistant Fred Seaman played pots and pans. The songs were as good, if not better, than anything John had done in the past. He had been busy during his time spent in seclusion, and it showed in his music.

The Bermuda tape consisted of about twelve finished songs. John had earmarked a song he had written and had planned to give as a gift to his good friend, Ringo Starr. The song was titled "Nobody Told Me." John introduced the song by saying, "This one is for Richard Starkey, former-ly, late, of the Beatles. This one's for Ringo, yeah, this one's got to be for Ringo." Then John launched into an acoustic version of the song.

In addition to John's Bermuda tape, Yoko sent Jack a box filled with tapes of her own compositions. Yoko told Jack that she was going to sing her songs on the album, too. For every one of John's songs, she would record one of her own. Yoko's tapes seemed to last for thousands of hours. Unlike John's Bermuda tape, these were unarranged bits of Yoko screaming and howling. It was a mess, but Jack was determined to listen to every minute in the hopes he would find something he could use.

Yoko made it clear to Jack that if John was going to make an album, she was going to have complete control, not only of John but the album as well. Jack had worked with Yoko in the past and was always patient with her while other producers found her relentless and difficult. She trusted Jack, and that was probably the reason why she had made the initial phone call to him. If John had any intentions of working with someone Yoko disapproved of, he wouldn't have been allowed. Yoko had no enthusiasm for her husband's music. Her sole interest lay in whether Jack had listened to her songs, and which ones they would record.

Since their chance meeting on the street, Jack hoped for the honor of working with John Lennon, and now that it was fast becoming a reality he was eager to begin the sessions.

CHAPTER 10

Highway Chile'

I was headed south again. I hitchhiked with Carl Cooperstein. Coop hadn't changed since the night he crawled out of my bedroom window while Peter and I were tripping. Actually, as time went on, he grew progressively worse and it was hard to trust him. It was like having a bad brother you had to put up with, but that aside he was the only one available on that particular day to go with me to Florida.

The hitch went smoothly enough, except for the first night. It was windy and very cold, and we tried desperately to get a car to stop before we froze to death. We stuffed a bag of clothes up the front of my jacket in an effort to make me look like a pregnant lady, and Carl put his arm around me.

It took us three days to make it to the Ft. Lauderdale strip. The strip was happening and there were young street people everywhere. Sleeping nights on the beach and hanging out on the strip during the day was the norm, and the police rarely bothered anyone. There were tourists everywhere; groups of college kids intermingled with the older retirees and everyone was having a groovy time. Carl and I met this gay black guy named Randy who was cool, letting us crash on the floor of his hotel room.

I wanted to offer proof to the Gurowskys that I had moved away, so I called Alissa's house and instructed the operator to say that the call was from "Kenny in Ft. Lauderdale." I figured Murry would be answering all calls that came to the house. After two rings I heard him pick up the phone and say, "Hello?"

When the operator said, "I have a collect call from Kenny in Ft. Lauderdale," Murry hung up. I didn't expect him to accept the call, but hoped it would buy Alissa her freedom once her parents knew I was far away in Florida.

When Randy checked out of the hotel, Coop and I met three guys from Ann Arbor, Michigan, who let us crash on their floor. We were looking for steady jobs, but in the meantime we worked for Labor Force. I (and occasionally Carl) got up at 5AM and waited outside the Labor Force office. If lucky, I got hired for the day and was paid cash at the end of the shift. The work usually involved carrying lumber on a construction site, unloading trucks or painting a building. It was hard work, but it felt good to get paid and to be able to walk across the street and afford dinner at the Royal Castle.

One day, I arrived home from work to find the three guys from Ann Arbor wanting to murder me. Someone had stolen one of their wallets with money in it, and some other things. Coop and I were the only ones who had access to their room, and I hadn't seen him since that morning, so the three guys took turns giving me a nasty beating. Coop just up and split for New York, leaving me to take the blame for what he had done.

It was definitely time to move, so I rented a room at the Broward Hotel, a place where old men living off their social security checks resided. The lobby was musty; it was a place for these men to gather, drink cheap wine and tell their worn-out tales to one another. The lobby was always filled and someone was usually creating a scene. It was amusing to me, and I enjoyed listening and watching. I became friends with several of the old men and sometimes went to the store to pick up food or cigarettes for them.

The owner of the Broward Hotel was renovating another hotel on the beach, and he gave me a job. I worked outside, across the street from the beach. It was a great place to meet girls and I started a new collection, but after Alissa these girls seemed less than fascinating. I preferred to hang out at the clubs on the strip and jam with the bands, and I loved getting up on stage whenever I had the opportunity.

Life was improving, but soon the work I was doing would be complete, the Broward Hotel was to be condemned, and it would be time for me to find a new job and a new place to live.

After job-hunting for a week, the only steady work I could find was as a dishwasher at a Ranch House Restaurant. The manager tried to encourage me by telling me that after a year of working for the company, I'd be eligible to go to school to become a Ranch House Manager, just like him! I couldn't imagine spending a year washing dishes, nor could I imagine spending the rest of my life managing a Ranch House Restaurant, but I needed this job and was determined to hold onto it.

As soon as I cashed my first paycheck I went to a rental agency to look for an apartment. The agent told me of a house near Broward Boulevard that would be available in one week, so I paid him one hundred fifty dollars for the first month's rent. That night, Neil called and told me he was flying down for a vacation. I proudly told him that I had just signed a lease on a house, and so he would have a place to stay.

Moving day finally arrived! I had spent my last week at the Broward Hotel daydreaming about how great it would be living in my own house. I envisioned the day I'd have enough money to buy furniture, TV, a stereo—the works! After work, I gathered my belongings, said farewell to the Broward Hotel, collected the key from the agent and called a cab.

We drove down some well-kept streets before the driver turned a corner and drove into a decrepit looking neighborhood. (Hey, I knew I couldn't afford the nicest part of town!) As we got closer, the houses started to look more like shacks. The cab parked in front of what seemed like the most run down shanty on the street.

Playing in the front yard were two of the cutest, blonde, curly-haired girls about five years old. As I got out of the cab and said, "Hello," a man's loud voice called from the house, and the girls hurried inside.

The agent didn't tell me the building was a duplex. When I finally figured this out, and found my front door, I thought about Neil flying down the next day to hang out at my 'house'. An hour before I was thinking about how I had my shit together and I couldn't wait for Neil to see the place, and as I turned the key I hoped that it wasn't as bad inside as it was outside.

It was worse. The smell was putrid. It was damp and moldy, and whoever just left did so in a hurry. There were McDonald's and candy bar wrappers on the floor, ripped up couches and a crooked bed. There were no light bulbs and it was starting to get dark. I wanted to find a store but was afraid to walk the streets.

This wasn't a house, it was a room, and it made the Broward Hotel look like The Ritz. Neil planned to meet me at the Ranch House after he landed, so I figured there would be time enough in the morning to clean up the place before he saw it.

As it got dark, weird things started to happen. The walls were thin and it was easy to hear people talking next door. I was having a hard time falling asleep, but eventually, it grew quiet. Suddenly, I heard faint scratching noises, then they got louder. Half asleep, I imagined they were coming from next door, and that it was a cat. Just as I was nearly asleep, I felt something smooth touch my hand, and I swatted it like a fly. Then I felt something crawling inside my sleeping bag. I jumped to the floor and heard the crunch of cockroaches under my feet. I had never seen a cockroach till I saw one in the kitchen at the Ranch House Restaurant, and it was like seeing a creature out of a monster movie. I had always hated bugs and was afraid of spiders, but this was a brand new bug and I didn't like it.

I stood in the middle of the floor in a strange, dark room surrounded by hoards of wild cockroaches. My worst nightmare had come true. I felt like screaming, "Help! I'm being attacked!" but who would hear me? I batted the bed and floor with a pillow, and it became quiet. I swept my hands over the sheets to make sure there were no roaches on the bed, but as I crouched on the corner of the mattress and listened intently, the scratching noises started up again. There was no way in the world I was going to fall asleep. I thought of what it would be like dozing off and letting the cockroaches attack my body, and I had visions of myself lying there with hundreds of different sized bugs crawling in and out of my mouth.

I asked myself, "What the hell am I trying to prove here in Florida? I could be at home in my room, at my parents' house!" I thought about the bungalow days, and how nice it would be if I could wake up from this nightmare and be there. Then I thought about the two little twin girls next door, and I felt like crying for them. This was only a bad dream for me, but it was their life. I couldn't stop thinking about those girls, and I felt guilty, yet thankful, for the childhood I'd had.

As it got light out the bugs began to disappear, but I was in for a second surprise. On the ceiling right over my head crawled the wealthiest, most obese cockroach known to mankind . . . it was shiny, black and disgusting. As I slowly moved off the bed, it flew right at me! If not for the door being close to me, I would have run right through the wall to get out of there.

57

I sat on the front step trying to figure out what to do next, and pretty soon the twin girls came out to play. They were beautiful, and I love kids. I asked them if they had bugs crawling in their house, and they said, "Oh yes! They're our pets . . . " and they started to tell me their names. They actually named their cockroaches! They also told me about their mom who had left with her boyfriend after their dad beat her up. I vowed that if I were ever lucky enough to have a wife and two children even half as beautiful as these girls, my wife would never leave me, and my kids would not have cockroaches for pets.

Soon the voice from the house bellowed out, and the girls disappeared inside. The two little girls left me there full of emotions—I felt happy and sad all at the same time.

That morning it was hard to find the bus stop and I was late for work. I was tired and hardly felt like washing dishes. Neil popped in around lunchtime, all bright-eyed and ready to party, and when my shift ended we headed back to the house.

I tried to warn Neil that it wasn't the greatest place, but he assured me not to worry. "How bad can it be? I'm here for the beach and the chicks, not the house!" We stopped at a 7-Eleven where I bought mega amounts of bug spray and light bulbs. When I opened the door of my castle, I saw the shock on Neil's face, and then he started to laugh! He just kept laughing and saying shit like, "I can't believe it! You live here? What a joke!" I tried to explain how the night before was the first time I'd ever seen the place, but he just kept on laughing. To make matters worse, he let me know Alissa had a new boyfriend. I no longer cared about the day Alissa would turn eighteen, and I knew Florida and I were through for good.

I was broke. The rental agency refused to refund my money, and when I told my boss I was leaving he refused to pay me for the days I had worked since my last paycheck. Neil had money, but not enough for a hotel, so he figured the next best thing to hanging out on the strip would be to go back to Bow Channel and spend the week camping there. I just wanted to go home to New York and see Alissa.

We took a bus to the Keys and found things at Bow Channel the same as before. I didn't want to ask Neil for money, but I was starving, and after a couple of days of having very little to eat and with everyone around us cooking up great meals as the sun went down, I did something I normally would never do. I went into the General Store and walked out with a can of pork and beans.

The owner of the campground caught me, and he was horrified. He asked me, "How could you rip me off?" We had to leave. I was embarrassed and felt like a traitor. I had just gotten thrown out of a place I loved, over a can of pork and beans.

Neil wondered why I hadn't gone for a steak.

On the way to the Ft. Lauderdale airport, Neil gave me what was left of his money. It turned out to be enough for a Greyhound bus ticket to Daytona Beach. On the bus, I kept thinking about Alissa. A few months had passed since I'd seen her, but I knew what we had could never die. I had met other girls, but that was different. Alissa and I had this special bond—it was as if we both knew we would be together forever. From the moment Neil told me about this new guy, I couldn't wait to head home, and now I was on my way. I thought about what had happened at the Keys, and wished I'd never gone to Bow Channel. I should have just hitchhiked home.

When the bus stopped in Daytona, I hid in the bathroom. No one seemed to care, and I knew the bus was going through to New York City. There was a long stop the next day in D.C. where we got a new bus driver, and this guy was checking tickets and bathrooms. As he walked toward the back of the bus I thought about getting off, but the lady next to me told me to duck down, and she put her coat and bags on top of me. She was from Georgia, on her way to Harlem to see her grandchildren, and she carried a lot of presents. It was the middle of the night by the time I made it to Rockland and crawled gratefully through my window.

To my surprise, Carl Cooperstein was asleep in my bed.

I could have strangled him! What the hell was he doing snug in my bed, while I was getting beat up on his behalf in Florida? Coop swore to me that he didn't take that guy's wallet, that he split Florida because he just couldn't take it anymore. I knew he was lying, but . . . he was my (fucked up) brother.

My parents had hearts of gold and were suckers for down-and-outers like Coop. Often I'd bring someone home for a night, and they'd end up staying. Someone like George Haber.

George cherished life. There was nothing that could ever bring him down. That is, nothing until the time George went to the Nassau Coliseum to a Led Zeppelin concert. He was tripping and somehow wandered outside the Coliseum. When he tried to get back in, an officer was called, and before George had a chance, he was shot dead. No one could understand why, as George was one of the kindest, gentlest people we knew.

The next morning I woke up early and walked up the hill to Ramapo. In the hall I spotted Shelly, an old friend, who, like Neil, couldn't wait to tell me about Alissa and Jon. He was new in town, she told me. His father was a judge, and Jon was tall, dark and handsome. It seemed I didn't have a chance. To top it off, Alissa's parents approved of him.

I finally got my first glimpse of Alissa after not seeing her for three months. She was walking into the cafeteria holding hands with the guy. I waited until the bell rang and stalked them down the hall. When they got to his class, she kissed him good-bye and I took her by surprise around the next corner. She turned around, and for a second we were speechless, checking each other out. I'd never seen Alissa look as sexy as she looked that day in her black mini-skirt and red velvet peasant blouse. But then, standing in front of her, I felt like I was staring at some other person, and I wondered if something had been lost between us. We were alone, next to a side exit door, and she was the first to speak.

"Thanks for calling from Florida! When my parents knew you were gone, they immediately let me out of the house again. That's when I met Jon."

Alissa never had a normal childhood, and little things other people took for granted meant a lot to her. She never thought much of herself, and never understood why other kids had lots of stuff. Her father didn't believe in buying things for any reason except out of necessity. It wasn't as if he couldn't afford to buy Alissa nice clothes, a pair of Frye boots or a new stylish coat. If it wasn't necessary, or was in the least bit frivolous, Murry's family wouldn't own it. When Alissa was younger and started going to friends' houses, she wondered why they didn't wear coats inside in the winter. Murry never turned the heat up since he didn't like supporting the oil and electric companies, and you never left a light on if you left the room, even for a second. Alissa was in shock when her friends left the refrigerator door wide open while pouring a drink or making a snack, or kept lights on when they left the room You didn't do that in her house, and she grew up thinking everyone was just like her family.

After staring at each other in a moment of silence, we cut out that side exit door, arm in arm, and headed down the hill to my parents' house.

CHAPTER 11

Two's a Crowd, Three's Not!

The weeks that followed were a true romantic time for Alissa and me. Her parents had no idea I was back in town. We were together again, and everyone in town knew but them. My parents loved Alissa, and they let me use their cars whenever I wanted, making it easy for me to pick her up and get her home. I was the first to buy Alissa a Big Mac and a Carvel ice cream cone. Even going to the movies was an adventure for her, and we spent a lot of time at my parents' house where the heat was always going full blast, and one rarely remembered to turn off a light. Life was simple, no one bothered us and we were determined not to ever let things go back to the way they were before.

I started installing drapes and making deliveries for my father's decorating company. We needed money, and continually made plans to leave town. We even talked about it with my parents, who recognized the taming effect Alissa had on me.

Alissa cut school and went with me to customers' houses as my helper. She had convinced her parents to let her attend a program called SWAS, "A School Within A School" held at Ramapo where sixty kids and two full-time teachers modeled their curriculum after the Skunk Hollow method. She would still earn her Regents degree, enabling her to enter a state college as her parents planned for her, but they weren't aware that her schoolwork could be done as independent study, and class attendance was voluntary. Alissa did have to show up at Ramapo once a week to turn in her work, but the rest of the time was hers to do as she wished, and her parents had no idea.

Alissa's mother suspected we were seeing each other, and she hated it. Elsa would do anything to hide this from her husband, but eventually he caught on. Upon learning I was back in the picture, Murry came up with his last ditch effort to try to scare us apart. Since he was supporting Alissa, and I was playing with her, then why not arrange things so that if I wanted to be with her, I would have to support her as well? He was quite sure if I was put to the test, I would run away, and in a week Alissa would be home begging to go to college.

I had a few hundred dollars, and with the two hundred dollars Alissa had saved from babysitting we had enough money to rent our own place. We found a one-bedroom apartment one mile from my parents' house. With furniture, dishes and stuff from my parents and the Salvation Army, we "decorated" the apartment and moved in. Halfway through the twelfth grade, Alissa was the only kid in her high school to have her own apartment, and she was ecstatic . . . and warm!

It was the first time in my life I had to be responsible for someone aside from myself, and when people told me I was crazy, it made me even more determined to succeed. Especially when word got out that Alissa was pregnant.

I remember sitting by the phone in agony, waiting for the results of the test. Two months previous we had driven down to Florida and camped at Bow Channel. I wanted Alissa to know and share every part of my life, and Bow Channel was one place that was about to take on additional special meaning. Alissa had been feeling sick, so we went to see the doctor. He suggested a pregnancy test, taking us both by surprise. Oh yeah— that night in the tent, we weren't so careful . . .!

We had never talked or even thought about having kids, but sitting here by the phone, we both knew how the other one felt. The phone rang. Alissa was pregnant.

I was stunned; I actually called the doctor back to make sure. Yes, I was going to be a father! It was hard to believe, and right then, there was nothing in the world we wanted more than that baby. We immediately started calling all our friends to spread the happy news, but we were confused and sad when even our best friends couldn't share our happiness. People actually got mad at us. They said we were just kids, we should not have the baby! Some even suggested we have an abortion. All their negative talk had the usual effect on me. Ever since I was a kid, I've always done exactly what others said I could, would or should not do.

My parents were as excited as we were about the baby, and they meant well when they told me I now had to get serious: cut my hair, put on a suit, and start being a drapery salesman like my father. Not only was my parents' attitude beginning to annoy me, people at Skunk were changing, too. We still hung out there, but as we made friends with the newer, younger students we saw the defiance, conviction and pride that always bonded us so tightly together erode to be replaced with acquiescence, doubt and immaturity. It was strange. With the dual adult responsibilities of supporting ourselves and expecting a child, we maintained our fuck-the-world philosophy, while many appeared to now question what we all had always been so sure of.

When my father's store burned down, he moved the business to our house at 99 South Gate Drive, and it occupied the entire downstairs, including my old room with the screen removed. Every morning, Alissa and I would show up at the house around ten and eat breakfast or lay around until my dad assigned us our route for the day. Then we'd load up the 1969 silver bakery truck, sporting the Rockland Decorators sign, with boxes of drapes, curtain rods, slipcovers, toolboxes and ladders and spend the day driving all over Rockland and the surrounding counties making slipcover and drapery installations. Most days we'd have time to stop at Skunk. We loved each other and our life. This was as serious as we wanted to get.

Alissa's mother, sister and brother were told about the baby, but no one had the guts to tell Murry. He had already cut all ties with Alissa, and if Elsa wanted to see her youngest daughter, she would have to sneak a visit. Alissa weighed less than one hundred pounds, so as the baby grew inside her, it was difficult for anyone not to notice. She had just turned eighteen, but could easily pass for thirteen or fourteen. Soon it was obvious there was a pregnant girl going to Ramapo High School, and before word got around the school district that she was Mr. Gurowsky's daughter, we knew we would have to tell him.

We went to his house, sat him down in the living room and Alissa said, "Dad, in November Kenny and I will present you with the first of many beautiful grandchildren."

Unlike our friends, Murry never suggested an abortion. But nothing else changed; he still hated me (now more than ever!) and would not speak to Alissa. I think he still entertained visions of Alissa running home, now with a little baby, full of apologies about how wrong she was and how right he was.

In between drapery installations one irresistible June day, Alissa and I stopped at the Skyview pool for a swim. While sunning on the dock, we met a fourteen-year-old girl named Robin Wolf. Robin was beautiful in a native sort of way. She hated the public school system, hung out at Skunk and wasn't getting along with her parents. A familiar scenario! She told us that her parents were assholes, she couldn't stand them any more, and she had recently run away from home.

Alissa and I had spent years trying to make our parents understand and accept us—we had to run away from home and endure many trials and tribulations, and in the end, we earned our freedom. Now, in front of us was a kid just stepping onto the path for the first time, and we felt compelled to help her. We talked it over and decided to take her in, and until we could sort things out and come up with a workable plan, we wouldn't tell anyone in the county where she was.

With Canada only eight hours away, what better way to throw people off her trail than to drive to Canada and mail a postcard to Robin's parents? We loaded up the Rockland Decorators van and took off. When we got to the border, we decided it might not be safe to cross with a runaway, so Robin mailed a postcard from the U.S. side, saying good-bye, and that she was about to cross into Canada. On our way home we picked up a hitchhiker dressed in his Navy outfit. We told him all three of us were married to each other, and Alissa was having our baby. "Two's a crowd, three's not!" was our motto. He was tempted to become a deserter and join in with us.

The postcard worked great, and when the talk around town was of Robin being in Canada, we devised The Master Plan. I had a two-week vacation coming up, so . . . we decided to drive to California to mail the next postcard. The three of us packed up my Chevy Vega (my dad needed the van) and headed for California. We drove west on Route 80, which unlike the undulating I-95 was quite scenic. Alissa's best friend, Mary Dee Reynolds, lived on a commune in Tecumseh, Missouri, and we made it our first stopover. It was the same commune we had sent Coop to a few months earlier in a final attempt to get him out of my parents' house. We even gave him money for a one-way bus ticket, but two months later, he was back again, this time with a new guitar and a knapsack.

East Wind was everything you would imagine a commune to be. About sixty residents did everything naturally, as a group, from building their own houses—they were cozy but looked more like dormitories—to growing their own food. All their clothes were kept in one big room, and when a person felt like getting dressed, they'd go to the room and put on anything they wanted. People took turns with the laundry, meal preparation and gardening. They were affiliated with another community in Virginia called Twin Oaks, and money was made at both by weaving hammocks and making sandals. No wonder Coop didn't last long. They probably required he work!

We arrived at the front gate, announced we were there to visit Mary Dee and were allowed to enter. As we puffed down the dirt lane we noticed the backs of three bare-chested, longhaired guys on a scaffold putting up a building. We parked and got out of the car, and when they turned around to look at us, I noticed one of them had tits. While I was checking her out, the guys were checking out Alissa and Robin.

We found Mary Dee in the kitchen preparing lunch, and she and Alissa had a tearful reunion. After lunch and a tour we went down to the stream where we spent the afternoon sitting naked in waist deep water. The amazing thing about this stream was that the bottom was a sheet of smooth slate. It was like sitting in a huge bathtub under a blue sky, with warm breezes and little fish all around.

Everyone kept coming over to feel Alissa's rounded belly. I tried to keep my eyes to myself and act normal around the young, pretty, naked girls sitting by us. At the same time I tried to keep my cool and not get jealous when the guys came around Alissa and Robin. Here I was with two beautiful women, but I couldn't stop wondering about the other girls around me. Since they shared everything, I was curious if that meant each other as well. When a beautiful blonde girl with breasts that pointed up to the sky sat sunning herself beside me, I couldn't help but picture her having sex with the fat, bearded guy on the other side of me who looked like he stepped out of a bad biker movie.

Many of the residents were musicians and they shared the guitars and other instruments. They had plans to build a recording studio and were in need of a drummer to do gigs in neighboring towns. When I mentioned I played drums and had some knowledge of recording, they asked us if we would like to join the commune. East Wind also planned to include children, and like their sister commune in Virginia, there would be separate housing for the kids. I couldn't imagine anyone wanting to share everything, even children! I had gone there with great expectations about commune life, but what I encountered was a bunch of rules. Alissa and I had talked about joining a commune, but driving down Route 80, I realized the only commune I'd want to be a part of was one I started myself, without all the rules. As I drove into the night I thought the three of us had real freedom. I started to laugh, thinking about when we heard mention of a missing guitar and knapsack. Coop, you fucker!

In the days that followed, the scenery constantly changed. The golden plains west of the mighty Mississippi shimmered under the endless sky; the jagged peaks of the Rocky Mountains defied my Chevy Vega and the desert sun broiled us through New Mexico and Nevada. The Grand Canyon was grand, but Monterey was magnificent. Alissa, Robin and I sat atop a mountain cliff and watched the huge orange sun sizzle into the cold blue Pacific Ocean. People were camping on the grasslands that stretched between the crashing waves and the base of the rocky cliff far below us, and we could hear an occasional laugh or tinkle of a guitar waft up from their direction. We had made it to California and this place was our reward. It looked like a mini Watkins Glen scene, but most of these people were surfers and used words like "hey dude."

At the campfire that night Robin paired up with one of the surfer dudes, and in the morning I got upset when Robin said she was thinking of staying in California with him. I told her, "No way!" I was responsible for her and knew she'd be safe as long as she stayed with us. Even though she was a runaway, she was our runaway.

Alissa began to dislike Robin. She felt we were being used and that Robin had put us in a position where we had to act as if we were her parents. To make matters worse, Alissa thought I was attracted to her, so she quickly went into action. Wherever we stopped to eat, Alissa ordered extra food and desserts and anything else Robin wanted. She kept an assortment of cookies and candies in the car, and Robin would eat it all. By the time we got back to New York, Robin had gained quite a few extra pounds.

As postcards from California arrived in Rockland, our friends began to suspect what we had done. When a posse from Skunk Hollow came to the apartment in search of Robin, she ran into the closet, but she was dying to tell everyone about her trip to California, so we agreed there was no reason to perpetuate our game. She popped out of the closet, and the posse was amazed at her appearance. They said they had pictured her as a starving runaway and had felt sorry for her, but not anymore, now that they saw how much weight she had put on. When people told Robin how fat she looked, Alissa sat back and grinned, pleased that her plan had worked best of all.

Robin's parents arranged a party, and Alissa and I were surprised when they invited us. We arrived expecting a hokey little deal with cake and balloons, but the party was a rock n' roll blowout. The Wolfs were nothing like the big, mean monsters Robin had described. They were young and hip, and lived in a huge modern house overlooking the Hudson River. I suddenly didn't understand what Robin was running away from. I thought about Alissa and me so close to having a child of our own. Would he or she want to run away from us?

The Wolfs had their party to show Robin how happy they were to have her home again, but just as the bash swung into high gear, Robin and her friends stole her dad's car and drove it across the Tappan Zee Bridge. Alissa and I were stunned by her ungratefulness. I found myself sympathizing with her parents, and that night I crossed a bridge of my own. For the first time in my life I was viewing a situation from a father's perspective—the father I was soon to become.

Back at our low-income apartment complex we were introduced to a new type of person. Nearly everyone I grew up with had both a mother and a father, and most moms stayed home while the dad went to work. But where Alissa and I lived, almost all the families consisted of single mothers. My heart went out to the little kids who played unsupervised in the ugly hallways and garbage-strewn parking lots while their mothers were away at work all day.

I was the only adult male figure many of these children knew. My favorite was Tommy Hill, a little boy who lived down the hall. We usually fed Tommy dinner, as his mom was always working and his older brothers and sisters were never around. Occasionally we took him to the drive-in movie theater. In the apartment below us lived eight-year-old Sheila Lasini. Poor Sheila was hit by a car and killed one day while walking to the store. She and her older brother were walking on the sidewalk, and he was holding her hand. The car killed her but missed him completely, leaving him standing on the sidewalk.

I found the neighborhood kids cute, but couldn't wait until the day my own child would be born. We attended Lamaze class, and planned to be together in the delivery room to watch the birth of our baby. Fathers had just recently been permitted in delivery rooms—in our parents' day, fathers were relegated to a waiting room to pace back and forth while his wife dozed through the blessed event.

Sonograms were not yet in use to determine the sex of the unborn baby. The only way to find out if we were the parents of a daughter or a son was to wait for the baby to come out and show us in person. We completed the Lamaze classes and went home to wait impatiently for Alissa to start her labor. It was unbelievable to think that soon there would be three of us.

CHAPTER 12

Jack and the John Lennon Sessions: The Sessions

Before John and Yoko could go into the studio, musicians had to be hired. Jack knew all the best studio players and proceeded to put a band together. Before Jack could hire any one musician he had to secretly obtain the birth date of the person so that Yoko, who was into numerology, could give final approval. Luckily, she approved all Jack's choices.

John had lost confidence in his musical abilities, and was not sure if the project would be a success. He swore Jack to secrecy, insisting that even the band members not be told they were going to play on a John Lennon album. Musicians were hired at a pay rate above scale, Jack called in friend and engineer Lee DeCarlo, and rehearsals at The Hit Factory got underway. Jack taught the songs to the band without them having any idea who the artist was. Even the owners and employees of the studio didn't know the artists' identity. All Jack could say was "It's a mystery artist." And he asked everyone to keep word of the sessions private.

When the song arrangements were made, Jack sang the vocals. Everyone thought the tunes were great, but as the days wore on and no artist appeared, they started to suspect that maybe Jack was the artist and the songs were his. The band apprehensively sat Jack down and told him, "Jack, these songs are great, but your vocals just don't cut it!"

One night soon after, John and Yoko appeared unannounced. The musicians rejoiced, not only because they had been chosen to play on John Lennon's comeback album, but also because they found out Jack Douglas really wasn't going to sing.

It took a lot of encouragement to get John to lay down his vocal tracks. He wouldn't record his vocals without using the effects that caused his voice to reverb and echo. Even when he sang dummy tracks, he only felt confident having his voice layered over with effects, masking the pure beauty of his voice. Not until the Bermuda tape or on early rehearsal tapes can a person hear John Lennon pure and unadulterated.

As the songs started to come together, John became satisfied with his music and grew eager to continue. He even began to make plans for a second album and talked about building a studio of his own. Jack was included in all of John's plans, which included co-writing songs— Lennon-Douglas compositions. After Double Fantasy was completed, John spoke of their co-producing a Ringo album. Jack was building his future around their relationship.

Initially, there wasn't a record label involved in the John and Yoko project. On August 12, 1980, it was announced to the world that John Lennon was back in the studio, and naturally all the record labels wanted in. One night, Atlantic Records president Ahmet Ertegun showed up at a session. Like all the other record company moguls, he had plans on making a deal with John. When Yoko saw Ahmet she told Jack to throw him out. Jack tried to tell Yoko that he couldn't kick out the president of Atlantic Records, but Yoko insisted, so Jack had to go into the other room and politely inform Ahmet that no one was interested in talking to him.

Though the Lennons could have named their price for an advance, David Geffen, president of the fledgling Geffen Records, was able to sign them to a contract that paid a three-million-dollar advance, a sum much lower than all the other offers. When David approached Yoko, he told her the reason he was so excited to have her and John come to Geffen was that he would not be signing one artist, but two, and that was what Yoko had been waiting to hear. Every other company was after John alone, but David cleverly considered Yoko's self-interest as well as John's talent. A recording contract was signed between Geffen Records and John and Yoko, as well as a production contract giving Jack a four-point royalty.

CHAPTER 13

Forever Young

The night before our baby was born, we had gone to the movies, and at one o'clock in the morning Alissa's water broke. I was the classic nervous father, and if not for Alissa being calm and collected, we never would have made it to the hospital in one piece. Alissa's labor progressed smoothly. I spent most of the night by her side, timing her contractions and coaching her on the breathing exercises taught to us in Lamaze class. At one point I went to the waiting room for a break, and one of the nurses remarked to me that I looked too young to be a father. I would hear a lot of that in the coming years.

By 9A.M., Alissa was in the final stage of labor, and in quite a bit of pain. She was wheeled into the delivery room while I donned surgical clothes, paper shoes and a mask. As she pushed, it still all seemed unreal, even as the top of the baby's head started to emerge. Just then, it all became very real. A tiny, perfect human ear unfolded in front of me. Within seconds, and with one last big push from Alissa, the rest of the baby slid out, and at 9:22 on November 21, our son Brian was born. He immediately started crying.

I would hear a lot of that in the coming years, too.

When Alissa's father came to the hospital he stood outside the nursery window next to my father. As they stood gazing at Brian, Murry said, "A Gurowsky!" My father responded by saying, "A Geringer!" and pointing to the sign on the crib, and they had a noisy argument over Brian's true last name.

One of the most memorable moments of my life occurred when we returned home to our apartment. I was sitting in an antique rocking chair holding Brian, by myself, for the first time. Moments like this come few in one's lifetime. There are things that are forgotten with the passing of time. Alissa must have known. She took a picture.

My life settled into a routine. Once again I felt things closing in on me. My parents and Alissa's mother had visions of me working for my dad and eventually taking over his business. Since I was the boss's son, the other employees assumed I was given special privileges. Yet, at the same time, no matter how hard I worked, my father felt that since I was his son and would someday be taking over the business, I had to work harder than everyone else. He always expected more from me. I didn't disagree, but my heart was not in it. I thought back to my dishwashing days at Ranch House Restaurant and had the same feelings of dissatisfaction. Did most people work their entire lives in safe, secure jobs, always wondering what they were really capable of? Was selling drapes and slipcovers all I was capable of? I was frustrated and scared—more scared about being stuck as a drapery salesman than of living a life with no guarantees. My father took risks to start Rockland Decorators and worked for years to build a great business, but it was his accomplishment, not mine. I envied his success, and from him I learned that with hard work, sacrifice and a desire to succeed, anything was possible. I knew that one day, as soon as I figured out what it was I wanted to do with my life, I would have to break the news to everyone that I was quitting dad's business. I was going to play the world like he had and see how far I could get.

Brian was almost four months old and everyone wondered if Alissa and I would ever get married. We never planned on it, until one particular day when I was on the volleyball court at Skunk Hollow. Just as my serve was coming up, someone inside yelled out to me that I had a phone call.

It was Alissa calling from her parents' house. "How would you like to go to Hawaii? My mother said she'd pay for us to go on a honeymoon to Hawaii if we got married!"

I hung up the phone and ran back to the courts yelling, "Hey, I'm going to Hawaii! All I have to do is marry Alissa!"

The school planned our wedding. A student donated his parents' house, a big old Victorian mansion with a wraparound porch and a beautiful view of the Catskill Mountains. Jonathan Best, or Jabe as everyone called him, was a minister from the New World Church, sort of a mail-in way to become a certified preacher. Our parents wanted a rabbi, and we wanted Jabe, so we all settled for a judge.

Everyone was told to bring a covered dish and we spent our own money renting tables and chairs. The Skunk band brought the music equipment and all of our friends came to play. We didn't bother sending out invitations. We just told everyone to come, and they did. The relatives included most of my aunts and uncles who came up from the Bronx expecting a typical, catered Jewish wedding. Alissa's mother, sister and brother were there, but Murry refused to attend until the last minute, and only because Alissa begged him. He ended up sitting one seat away from his ex-student archenemy, Dean, who was dressed in a big hat and cape and looked like Zorro. It was an interesting mix of hippies decked out in their most colorful finery and straight Jewish relatives in suits and gold jewelry.

One of my uncles still tells the following story: "I was seated at the table across from such a nicely dressed young man. He was wearing a new tuxedo jacket with tails, a starched white shirt and a silk top hat over his clean, long hair. But when he stood up, he had on old, ripped denim shorts, and was barefoot!"

Bob and Nan set up a piña colada table, and were busy all day running the blenders. There was plenty of food, from vegetarian tabouli to matzo ball soup. Everyone had a great time mingling, eating and dancing. Murry gave us no indication of his approval or support, and no one ever sent us to Hawaii, but because he did show up at the wedding, it was the beginning of the end of our cold war.

A few weeks after the wedding, I quit my job at Rockland Decorators. Alissa and I had three hundred dollars saved, and rent was due, so I had to think of a way to make money—fast. At the time, flea markets were the new rage, and I knew someone who had a booth at one of them and sold jewelry. I thought I could do something like that. The *New York Times* had a section called "Offerings to Buyers," and with the newspaper in one hand, and our savings in the other, I set out on a journey to buy something that I'd be able to sell at the Spring Valley Flea Market.

I spent the day in Brooklyn looking at t-shirts, the South Bronx looking at watches, and Manhattan looking at general merchandise. There wasn't much I could afford to buy, but there was one more place left to check out—Ross Cosmetics in Staten Island. Ross had a warehouse full of closeouts, mostly little make-up sets or colognes that the department stores would use as giveaways. He had hundreds of different items. I walked in, followed by a customer who was there to pick up a load of goods. I waited patiently while Ross put the man's order together, and when it was ready the handtrucks were wheeled out. I was given one and it took about forty-five minutes to load the guy's truck. When the truck drove away, Ross looked at me and said, "Why are you still here?" Ross thought I worked for his customer, and the customer had thought I worked for Ross.

I came home that night with a car full of cosmetics and perfumes. The next morning I rented a booth at the flea market. Alissa and I set it up with tables and shelves, and we were in (our own!) business.

After several more buying trips to Staten Island, Ross made an offer that gave me the opportunity for the success I had been dreaming of. He proposed giving me merchandise on consignment, and I agreed to pay for it as I sold it. Eventually, our apartment was filled with boxes of colognes, perfumes and make-up, and I held an open invoice to Ross owing thousands of dollars. I wanted to sell more than what was possible at the flea market, so I got the idea to sell to stores. When I wasn't at the flea market, I'd go to all of the drugstores, beauty parlors and clothing stores around Rockland County and sell to them wholesale. Business was good, and I was slowly building up my own wholesale company.

Alissa grew up in the woods and hated living in an apartment, especially one with creepy-crawlies, and we wanted to move out before Brian was old enough to start giving them names. As the business grew we needed more space, so in June we rented a big old house that was surrounded by acres of trees and had a huge yard full of wildflowers. Alissa adored it, and spent her days outside on the lawn with Brian. He was an active baby, constantly demanding attention, and by one year of age was not yet sleeping through the night. We could tell as soon as he was born that he was a smart baby. He was very alert, had an insatiable curiosity and was quick to react. Soon after we moved into the house he went straight from crawling to running (he took his first step at Skunk in the R.E. building), and run he did all over the place, with Alissa always right behind him.

To help pay the four hundred-dollar-a-month rent (double that of the apartment), we took in boarders. I bought a drum set and had jams in the basement. One night, two of our boarders, Mitchell Mednick and Claire Green, and a friend, Terry Miles, six feet tall and black, decided it would be entertaining to run up and down the street naked.

Twenty minutes later, a raft of police cars came screaming into our driveway. It seemed a passer-by reported that a black man was raping a white woman on our lawn, and the cops demanded to see "the girl" immediately. While I kept the cops busy in the front room, Terry and Mitchell slid through the back door and into their clothes.

"Officers, there are no naked people here!" I denied while trying to elicit a surprised expression. Just then, Terry and Mitchell strolled into the room, querying, "Why are the police here?"

The police insisted on us producing the girl, but Claire had run down to her room in the basement where I found her still naked and hyperventilating with fear. The cops wouldn't leave until she presented herself and declared that she was not being raped, so I tried to get her to breathe into a paper bag while Alissa attempted to shove her arms into her blouse. Claire wouldn't admit she had deliberately appeared naked in public because she was afraid of being arrested for indecent exposure, and she was panicking that Terry would end up in jail. We finally got her calmed down enough, and dressed to present herself upstairs and defend Terry's innocence. When the cops became convinced we were all safe from the Big Bad Black Man, they got in their cruiser and left, satisfied with Claire's appearance, if not a bit perplexed!

I expanded my business into New Jersey and upstate New York, and everyone wanted my closeouts. If a customer like a smaller beauty or nail salon was unsure, I opened their account on consignment and once a week they paid me for what they sold. Sometimes, after picking up my orders from Ross, I'd go into New York and buy a copy of *Screw* magazine. I went into the massage parlors and whorehouses and sold perfumes to the girls. I thought it was an original idea, until one day a guy came in selling watches. The girls often offered me a trade for my merchandise. Although tempted, I never did take the trade—wouldn't have—especially since my wife and baby were waiting downstairs in the car.

I worked out of the house so I was home a lot, which meant we were in control of our schedule. Nice day out? We'd take Brian on a picnic in Harriman and work the next day. Alissa could work anytime she wished, or not work at all. Elsa was happy to spend time with Brian whom she had developed a special relationship with. And when Brian was seventeen months old, Alissa informed me she was pregnant again. We were thrilled (if not surprised!) to be expecting our second baby.

Florida still held a special attraction for me, and I harbored the belief that if given the chance, it was a place where I could do better than dishwasher. As the months went by, Ross and I became closer, and I approached him with my desire to live and work in Florida; I had, in the short time I'd known him, sold over one hundred thousand dollars worth of his merchandise, and saved ten thousand of it. I was ready to take the next step.

All four of our parents pleaded with us not to move. My parents warned us it would be impossible to build a business in South Florida; if it were that easy, everyone would be doing it. Alissa's family simply didn't want her that far away. As usual, surrounded by all those negative opinions, I couldn't wait to get started.

Ross and I flew to Florida where we found a warehouse in Hallandale, and I rented an apartment in North Miami. Our plan was for Alissa, Brian and me to move to Florida where I would run my own company. Ross would send me shipments on consignment, and I would open accounts locally. Alissa and I named our new business East Coast Cosmetics. It was hard to believe I was returning to Florida, not as a disguised, pregnant, runaway hitchhiker in the snow, but as a businessman with a wife, a son and another baby on the way.

My father gave us the Rockland Decorators aluminum bakery truck as a going away present. On January 15, 1978 Coop, Alissa and I packed all our furniture and boxes into the truck and into my green Dodge station wagon, and when I stuffed the last item (a folding lawn chair) into the back of the overloaded car and triumphantly slammed down the hatchback, the rear window cracked into a million pieces and fell out all over the driveway—and I've not gone out without a bang since.

With the weather forecast calling for a blizzard, we left as soon as I was done taping up the window. I drove the truck, and Coop drove the station wagon. As the wind blew me from side to side and lane to lane, I wondered if Alissa would go into labor at her parents' house. She was probably cold, and I silently hoped her father would turn up the heat. The snow and hail were hitting like rocks, and from the holes in the floor, an icy wind flew up my pant legs. Lost in my thoughts, I didn't feel the cold of the unheated truck as I followed Coop down the empty highway. The weather report had warned us to wait, but I had only one desire—to get to Florida and send for my wife before our second child was born. The storm blew us all the way into Georgia before the weather warmed up. Coop pleaded for a hotel but I was determined not to stop, and we made it to North Miami in little over twenty-four hours.

Sail Cove Apartments were beautiful. The seven brand new buildings of the complex surrounded a seven-acre lake. They were painted pastel colors, and exotic plants and flowers draped the walls and walkways. Our ground-floor apartment had two bedrooms and two bathrooms, and everything in it was modern. Two big sliding glass doors opened onto a view of the grassy lawn and the lake, and little lights reflected off the water, making a rippling effect over the walls and ceiling. It was warm and tropical, and nothing like it existed in New York. I was worried that Alissa would miss having her own house, but thought she had to adore living in paradise.

I made arrangements for Alissa and Brian to fly down on the next available flight and was left with a day to unpack. When I picked them up at Miami Airport, I told Alissa I was thankful the baby hadn't been born in New York, and Alissa told me the phobic-flying lady in the seat next to her was thrilled the baby hadn't been born over the Atlantic. I arranged for a doctor and a hospital, we bought furniture for the apartment, and I hired an unemployed carpenter to build shelves in the warehouse to hold the expected delivery of boxes that, in addition to containing perfume and cologne, also contained our future.

The warehouse had two thousand square feet of space and looked huge. I tried to picture what it would look like filled with inventory. I had a sign made that said "Cosmetic Closeouts" and nailed it on the front of the building over the door. The warehouse complex ran along I-95, and the sign was easy to spot as you passed by on the highway. The apartment was ready for the new baby and the warehouse was ready for a new business. There was nothing left to do but sit back and wait to see what, or who, would arrive first.

CHAPTER 14

Isn't She Lovely?

The phone rang at 6:30 A.M. Alissa nudged me and I jumped out of bed prepared to dash to the hospital. I was dazed and anxious but Alissa calmed me down by telling me it was only the phone—Carolina Freight calling to inform me my merchandise was on the truck and ready to be delivered. As I was giving the driver directions to my warehouse, Alissa nudged me again and whispered in my ear, "That's not all that's being delivered today!"

At 9:59 on the morning of January 30, 1978, I witnessed the birth of our daughter, Rachel Nina Geringer. One hour later, I was unloading an eighteen-wheeler crammed with heavy boxes of perfumes. On the way out of the hospital, I squeezed in a phone call to Elsa. When she answered the phone, I said, "Elsa this is Kenny . . . Rachel's here!" Elsa and I had long since reached a truce, and by the time Rachel was born, she loved me.

Life was at its best. Rachel was a sweet, happy baby who would wake up, have her bottle and fall back asleep until time for her next feeding. With Brian (finally!) sleeping through the night, Alissa found caring for two babies easier than just caring for Brian by himself. I was working six days a week, sometimes putting in fourteen hours a day, and I was building up a great business. In the warehouse I set up a showroom and put one of each of the two hundred products I carried on display. I filled up a large carry case with samples and headed out to open accounts, usually in downtown Miami, a part of the city settled mainly by the Cuban immigrants who came to America when Castro took over. They hated

Castro and were pro-America all the way. I went from store to store showing my products and taking orders on my newly minted order forms. There was something for everyone, and the storeowners loved my close-outs. Anything cheap was easy to sell in downtown Miami. It was a Latin melting pot where tourists from all over South and Central America flocked to buy electronics, clothing and perfumes. Occasionally, a store-owner picked an item and wanted all I could get, and soon Ross was sending me shipments every other day.

Running a wholesale company seemed natural to me. There was no one telling me how to, or how not to, do things. I hired a bookkeeper and he set up a record-keeping system. All of my business and personal records were kept in one book. It was a shortcut to record keeping, but it worked. Things were moving fast and there was no time to stop and learn the conventional way to operate a wholesale company. There was only the "Ken" method, and I wasn't about to change, because I already had the confidence I needed to succeed.

Sail Cove Apartments were populated mostly by divorced women and their kids, and they reminded me of the women in our New York apartment building except they had a "Let's party!" attitude. They were seemingly shallow and carefree, and didn't have the sad, weather-beaten appearance of their northern counterparts. When our new neighbors got past the fact that Alissa and I were so young, they had to deal with the fact that we were actually raising our own children together, as a family. Something was missing. It was like they missed the '60s and were asleep in the '70s.

Our next-door neighbors were a newly married couple named Dale and Vikki, and they had a three-month-old baby. Dale appeared hip with his long hair, and Vikki was an attractive blonde who looked great in a bathing suit (which was all she ever wore). Kathy lived across the lake with her four-year-old son, Roy, and her brother, Robert. Kathy and Robert were from London. Kathy, a nurse in her early thirties, looked played-out, and Robert was in his late twenties.

Vikki and Kathy loved doing Quaaludes, and the two of them often stumbled around the lake all day. During the night while Dale was away at work, Vikki was in bed with Robert. The walls were thin, our bedrooms adjoined, and Vikki was a screamer. "Ohhh, Robert! Ohhh, faster! Faster! Faster! Oh, don't stop! AAAAAHHHHHH!" Alissa and I would sit, listen and laugh.

One night, Robert and Vikki apparently were so fucked-up they fell asleep, and continued to sleep soundly until Dale got home from work. You guessed it! There was crashing and smashing, a lot of yelling and Dale moved out. The next morning, Robert moved in. Alissa and I were amazed at how easily Dale had left his wife and child, and how quickly Vikki replaced him with a new guy. I tried to imagine Brian and Rachel with a new Daddy, but I couldn't.

CHAPTER 15

Hot Fun

I loved the lake and spent all my free time running in and out of it with Brian. He had long golden curls, which we let grow down his back. People thought he was a girl until we called his name or took his diaper off to let him run around naked. Brian and I were a big hit with the Sail Cove kids, and I felt safer with them than with their parents. Most of these kids were neglected. All their parents wanted to do was get high and be rid of them. Months would go by before I would notice one of their mothers outside, and only because she was looking to put the kid in for the night. Alissa and I loved being parents, and couldn't understand why they would rather ignore their kids than enjoy them. We felt sorry for these people—they had no idea what they were missing!

I gave Romeo Robert a job making deliveries for East Coast Cosmetics. He was responsible and dependable at work, but if you saw him ten minutes after quitting time, you'd have to hold him up. I was learning how hard it was to be the boss of people who you associated with in your private life. Robert may not have been a friend exactly, but his nephew Roy was, to both Brian and me, and that friendship kept Robert employed. I wrote a song entitled "Roy," one day when his mother was lurching around too stoned to take care of him. The first verse went like this:

> Roy, you're such a small boy
> Who's put that curse on your soul?

You've got to grow up and face life's realities
Mom's up and downed all over town
While Daddy's somewhere else
And who stole their minds?
And what did they expect to find?

The most awful culture shock hit me when I started to see the amount of prejudice that existed in Florida. I remembered how, in my junior high school years, the black kids kept to themselves. The black kids used to call me "fish lips" and knock my books down, but as we grew up, things changed, especially because kids were making the changes.

Gone were the days of the "We Generation," that to me meant all of us. Now I was in a place where prejudice was epidemic. Hatred was everywhere and nigger was a commonly used word. Anytime someone would use the word in front of us, we were horrified then we got mad and gave a lecture. If all else failed, I'd say, "Look. You can't talk that way in front of Alissa. Her mom's black (Elsa?) and she really loves her mom!"

At first people didn't understand us, but once in a while we would get through to someone and that would make everything all right. Since most people did like and respect us, occasionally there would be an opportunity to break on through, and break on through we did.

After we got past the black-white thing, there was the Jewish thing. Everywhere we went we heard stories about cheap Jews. I guess we didn't *look* Jewish—Brian and Rachel have green eyes and bleached blonde curls, and I have green eyes, dark reddish hair and a small turned-up nose. No one who met us thought twice when it came time to express their opinions about Jewish people, until we would tell them we were Jewish and then we'd get an apology. "Oh, we didn't mean you! You're not like that!"

The hatred we witnessed, unfortunately, was just the tip of the iceberg. The blacks hated the whites, the whites hated the Cubans, the Cubans hated the blacks, and everyone hated the gays. The '70s were coming to an end and I wondered what had happened to all the people who were going to stop this hatred? Did they ever exist? It was hard to understand what went wrong and we wondered if everywhere in America was like this. We realized how sheltered our childhoods had been, and how lucky we were to have grown up in Rockland County. We knew that we had something to teach the people in our new community, and we were determined to do that by being ourselves. We refused to change so we could fit in, or be better accepted.

In addition to carrying American closeouts, Ross started to stock loads of new French perfumes. He would buy items that had been diverted from the duty-free Caribbean Islands, enabling him to import them into this country at great prices. At the time, I didn't understand how Ross could obtain colognes such as Opium, Chloe and Chanel, but I did know he was dealing with Pete Scarpachi.

Pete Scarpachi was one of Ross's connections. Before I moved to Florida, Ross took me to Pete's office in the Bedford Stuyvesent section of Brooklyn. While energetically pumping my hand up and down, Pete said, "Kid, ya see my Cadillac over there? Well, they know it's mine. I could leave it out there for a week in this shitty neighborhood, and nobody, but nobody, would lay a finger on it!"

Pete and Ross then commenced counting stacks of hundred dollar bills out onto the floor. When Pete told Ross he had two thousand perfume pens for him Ross reluctantly tried to get out of buying them, but eventually I loaded them into the car. It was against the rules to say no to Pete.

Ross called me a few months after we had moved to Florida and told me Pete was en route to Miami. His teenage daughter had run away from his house to her mother's house in Miramar, Florida, and he was coming to retrieve her. He arrived with his eight-year-old son, Little Peetie, and as soon as we got to our apartment Pete had Alissa take the kids into the other room so he could lay out the plan. Women and children were not supposed to be around while the men talked business.

"When we go tomorow, my ex-mother-in-law might get in the way, so it'll be your job to break her arm." At first I thought he was joking, but he was dead serious. Alissa and I sat up in bed that night trying to figure out a way to tell him he had the wrong guy. The next morning Pete told me he had a new plan; he'd tell me about it when we got to my warehouse. In the car, I tried to tell him gently that I could not break an old lady's arm, or anyone else's arm for that matter.

"Pete, I . . . I don't think I could break anyone's arm," I said.

"Sure ya could, kid! But ya may not hafta. I have a friend, a retired Fed, and I'm gonna give him a call!"

Upon arriving at the warehouse, Pete started to inspect my merchandise and make expert comments, such as, "Ya only have a coupla hundred perfume pens. Remind me to send ya some more!"

Pete carried a wad of hundred dollar bills and he loved to flash them. Even if he were just buying a pack of cigarettes, he'd peel off a hundred and ask the girl if she could make change. Ross had mentioned I owned an old Triumph chopper, and Pete wanted me to take Little Peetie for a ride. When I told him the bike was in the shop and wouldn't be ready for a week, he insisted I drive him there where he personally demonstrated for me the necessary maneuvers that would persuade the owner to have it ready in one hour. Medford Joe deposited two hundred-dollar bills in his pocket and fixed the bike, while Pete was telling everyone how important he was.

Once back in the warehouse, Pete asked me if I had learned a lesson. "It's all who ya are! Just keep telling 'em who ya are!"

Later that day, Pete's friend showed up. He was in his sixties, and with gray hair and a potbelly he looked like the typical Florida retiree, but with an FBI badge. After Pete explained the situation, his friend said, "Look, I could get in a lot of trouble for this, and if it was anyone else, I wouldn't do it, but I understand. It's your daughter." I wondered what it was that Pete had on this guy to have him do what he was about to do.

When we got home from the warehouse that afternoon, Alissa took me aside and told me Little Peetie was crazy. He was bragging about a kid at school who had been picking on him, and his dad had the kid's house blown up. I was thankful Little Peetie liked Alissa and the kids, and I was extra careful when I took him for a ride on my motorcycle.

At midnight, the FBI guy showed up and Pete asked him where he kept his gun. He said it was in his car. We dropped Pete off at Mr. FBI's apartment to wait while Mr. FBI and I went to recapture the daughter. In the car I told Mr. FBI, "I don't think I could break anybody's arm." I was hoping he'd agree it was silly of Pete to want this.

But instead he said, "You don't need to break bones when you have a gun!"

I felt much better.

The house was shabby, not the kind you would expect the ex-Mrs. Scarpachi to be living in. When the front door opened, Mr. FBI asked the lady if she was Mrs. Pete Scarpachi. Behind her stood a little old lady and a teenage girl, who started screaming, "I'm not going back!" Mr. FBI explained that he had a court order to bring the girl back to New York.

Mrs. Scarpachi asked, "How do I know it is legitimate?"

Mr. FBI flashed his badge, then he looked at me and said, "Okay, kid give me a hand!" I wondered if this was where I was supposed to break the arm.

The mother started to cry. "It's no use. He always gets his way!" The girl reluctantly got into the car with us, pleading to be allowed to stay. Pete Scarpachi either had everyone living in fear or owing him a favor.

We drove back to Mr. FBI's house where Mrs. FBI, who looked like an aunt of mine, greeted us at the door. As we entered, I noticed the house was filled with official awards and plaques received for years of good work and honor. I thought of how corrupt this agent must have been for him to be paying back favors from Pete Scarpachi.

Pete came in from the kitchen, surprising his daughter, and she ran into his arms crying, "I'm sorry, Daddy, I'm sorry!" He told her it was all right, not to cry.

In the morning the happy family was packed and ready to fly back to New York. Before leaving, Pete gave me a hug and said, "Kid, if ya ever need me, just give me a call!" and he peeled two hundred dollar bills off of his wad. I tried not to accept, but he insisted. I felt good, knowing Pete owed me a favor! I never did hear from him again, except for the occasional perfume pen shipment.

I remember the day the Driggses moved into Sail Cove. One morning as I was getting ready to go to the warehouse, I glanced out the sliding glass doors and stopped to watch as Carl and his wife, Gail, strutted by. You couldn't help but stare—they looked like they had just stepped off the pages of a fashion magazine. Carl was a cross between Desi Arnaz and Freddie Mercury, the lead singer for the group Queen. His face looked carved from stone, he was six feet tall, perfectly built and tanned, and was wearing crisp, white shorts. Gail had a glamorous, yet rock n' roll look, with blonde wavy hair and a perfectly made-up face, even early in the morning. She was holding a pudgy baby who wore a designer bathing suit. This family definitely did not fit the stumbling Sail Cove image.

When we got to know Carl and Gail, we learned Carl was the lead singer of a Cuban-heritage disco band called Foxy. They were signed to a local record company called TK Records, who also had Bobby Caldwell and K.C. and the Sunshine Band on their roster. When you signed a contract with TK Records you signed your life away, or your share of the royalties if your record ever made it big. TK had its own studio, so if you signed a contract, you usually did make a record. This was enough to get any band to sign on the dotted line. Most of TK's successful artists wound up in litigation, but the most popular entertainment lawyer in South Florida was so closely hooked up with the record companies, it was hard to determine exactly whose side he was on.

Just as Foxy's first album was about to be released, Carl and his co-writer got into a fight and Carl quit the band. When the album was released, a song called "Get Off" became a big Top 40 hit. Carl formed a new band called Driggs and The News, and when Carl sang "Get Off" at crummy gigs on the Ft. Lauderdale strip, the small audiences went wild. I guessed that they thought Driggs and The News was a local band imitating the Foxy tune. Neither Foxy nor Carl Driggs made it out of obscurity, but "Get Off" is still played in clubs and D.J. mixes to this day. The frustration of becoming almost famous was too much for Gail. She wanted the glitter more than she wanted Carl, and their marriage broke up.

While accompanying Carl to his gigs I became infected with music business fever, and I knew someday I would become a part of the industry. Music was the one thing that was lacking in my life, and I promised myself to one day fulfill my dream. All I needed was the right opportunity.

Sail Cove was a transient place. Just as we got used to a neighbor, they would move out. We formed new groups of friends fairly easily and spent Sunday afternoons around the lake, usually barbecuing, always with music blaring from one of our apartments. Complaints started coming in from other tenants. They seemed to resent seeing a group of young people having a good time and complained about the music and the shouts of the kids who gravitated from all over the complex to join in the fun. I refused to think of children as being a nuisance, and no matter how low the music would be turned down, people still complained. So the music went back up, and the parties continued.

The rental office group hated Alissa and me the most; we were served with eviction notices on a regular basis. We discovered that an eviction takes several months to complete, and just as our eviction was about to become final, the apartment complex would be sold, new managers would trundle in, and the eviction became null and void. After that the parties, the music and the complaints would start all over again, then lo and behold, we would be served with . . . a brand new eviction notice!

Our best friends were Bobbi and Richard from upstairs. Richard, in his thirties, was about six-feet-two and almost completely bald. He looked like a typical businessman, yet was anything but. He had grown up in South Florida, but he hated the Florida mentality and wanted to escape. He had hopes of becoming a successful New York comedian, and he'd sit around all day smoking pot and dreaming about the big time. Bobbi and Richard were hippies from the sixties, and like us, they refused to change. They had two daughters: Merrick, a very savvy eight-year-old, and four-year-old Rachel, whom everyone called Big Rachel. Merrick, Big Rachel, Brian and I became a gang and specialized in terrorizing the other apartments. We planned on letting Little Rachel in as soon as she was able to walk.

When Richard had a fight with the landlord and got evicted, he pulled a better trick on the rental office than I could have. This is how it worked: One night while the rental office was closed, we helped Carl Driggs move out of his apartment (before his lease was up), and as the neighbors slept, Bobbi and Richard swiftly and quietly moved out of their apartment and into Carl's. Each month they gave Carl the rent money, and Carl would mail his check to the rental office as usual. The rental agent went crazy seeing Bobbi and Richard every day, but their apartment was empty!

Soon after, relations between the Geringer family and the latest edition of the rental people grew poor. If not for them being upset about Brian running around naked and pissing in the grass, then our picnics-turned-jams would really get them. One day, I took my drums out of the warehouse and set them up in the apartment. Alissa got out her Fender Mustang bass guitar and I announced a jam. Since she had the bass and I had the drums, all we needed was for someone to bring a guitar, and somehow word spread all the way to the Haulover Beach crowd.

The party was amazing. With longhaired musicians jamming and their girlfriends hanging out, it looked almost like our old Rockland County days, except most of our guests were still in high school and carried surfboards on top of their cars. At Sail Cove, Alissa and I were always known as the kids (even though we had kids) because everyone else was older. We had finally found a scene we liked, and now we were the older ones.

There were differences between our new friends and the ones back home, like the prejudice thing, but if anything it gave us an outlet to open these young people's eyes to the ways of the outside world that we knew.

These kids were young, hip, and beautiful looking, and being native Floridians they didn't experience the '60s like we did, but they were still defiant. To rebel against their parents, they would stay out late, listen to rock n' roll and experiment with drugs. The difference was, there was no unity or deeper reason for what they were doing. For us, it was the serious business of not accepting post WWII conformity and materialism, or the war in Vietnam. For them, it was just fun. These kids were the beginning of the Me Generation, not giving a shit about anyone except themselves. They looked a lot like us, but there was so much missing.

CHAPTER 16

Miami Meltdown

We were tired of living among incoherent drug people and playing eviction tag; we needed more space and wanted fewer rules. One day, after almost two years after our move to Florida, Alissa spotted a classified ad in the *Miami Herald* describing a house for rent a few miles from the apartments. What attracted us most was the part about the six bedrooms. When we went to take a look at the house we found it to be gigantic! It had a huge living room, a separate dining room as big as most living rooms, three bathrooms and six bedrooms going off in all directions. The rent was a whopping six hundred dollars a month: we took it on sight. We planned to rent four of the bedrooms and share the kitchen, and in no time at all the rooms were filled. A thirty-five-year-old hippie, an eighteen-year-old flower-child nymphomaniac, a bad guitar player, a surfer dude and his girlfriend and a motley crew of all their friends descended upon us before my signature on the lease had a chance to dry.

We charged from seventy-five to one hundred seventy-five dollars a month for each room. Not only did we live rent-free, some months we made money. I hung a bulletin board in the entrance hall for listing who was having a party in what room, free rides to the beach and concert tickets for sale. Initially we were known as "The Big House" and eventually "The Commune in North Miami." Word of our house must have spread as far as Rockland County, because one day there was a knock on the door, and when Alissa opened it, there stood Coop, guitar in hand. He moved onto the couch.

I was living in two worlds. In the morning I'd go to the warehouse and conduct business with storeowners, flea marketers and other wholesalers, and I was beginning to open accounts with chain stores like Fedco Drugs and J.C. Penney. It was as natural for me to function in this world of business as it was for me to venture back into our private commune at #436 NW 177 Street at the end of each day.

Everyone compared Brian and Rachel to the Woodstock babies, and at ages five and three, I think Brian and Rachel had more fun with our friends than we did. Just before Brian turned five he started kindergarten. One day, a few weeks after school began, Alissa got a note from his teacher requesting a meeting. Because Brian was smart and knew all of his numbers and letters, she was sure they were going to tell her that he really belonged in first grade, and all they needed was to ask her permission to move him up. She arrived at the school and sat down expectantly with the teacher.

Instead, the teacher told her Brian would not sit still and could not concentrate. She said Brian was disruptive and a slow-learner. As Alissa listened to her speak, her joy turned to dismay. She was sure they had the wrong kid! When we discussed the situation that night, we decided we weren't going to let anyone make us think there was something wrong with our kid, which there wasn't, of course—people are just different, that's all! That conference was the first of many we would endure over the years, and the first of many battles with the public school system that would last on and off for fourteen years.

Someone in the house was always playing an instrument, usually a guitar. Alissa and Coop once went into everyone's room, took out all the guitars and lined them up in front of the house for a picture. There were eleven guitars in the house that day, but the jams we were having kind of sucked until the night we met Tony. When he came into the house for the first time, he ran around like a crazy person, playing air-guitar, jumping on the furniture and making elephant noises. Coop threatened to throw him out, until Tony plugged in his guitar and played a few licks. After that our jams improved immensely.

Tony lived with his mother and grandmother. His grandmother, a Cherokee Indian in her late eighties, had a free spirit and a free tongue, expressing herself with more four-letter words than any one of us ever used, and Tony was just like her. He played a Gibson Byrdland guitar and was a friend of Ted Nugent, who also played a Byrdland. When Ted was in town, he often borrowed one of Tony's guitars. One day, Tony brought over a friend of his named George Mazzola. He told us George was a Jimi Hendrix fan and had recently been picked up by a local band (called The Kidds) after their lead guitarist got a gig with the Romantics. The twelfth guitar entered the house, along with someone who knew how to play it. Coop and I thought we had heard the best of them in New York, but none of them could even come close to George. He was Jimi re-born in a white boy from Miami. George was equally surprised at the Jimi-ness of Coop's bass playing and my drumming. He nicknamed me Mitch Baker, after two famous drummers, Mitch Mitchell and Ginger Baker. Any free time we had was spent jamming at the house. We started to tape the jams on my tape machine, and named ourselves "The Coop Experience." The music was as free as the life we were living, and it showed. We became the ultimate basement band.

As usual, during the holidays, I closed my business and flew the family to Rockland. We visited once a year, and each time we grew more homesick. On our return trip, we were booked into the last flight out of La Guardia Airport. While sitting in the empty lounge waiting to board the plane, a wild looking group of black guys wearing classy blue and silver jogging suits and hair resembling tubes of black Styrofoam came in and sat near us. We could hardly refrain from staring. It was obvious from their conversations that they were musicians. One of them came up to us and said, "That is a special baby." He was referring to three-year-old Rachel, who was smiling at him. Later, on the plane, sitting in front of me was the guy who had noticed her. He turned around and told me I reminded him of a drummer he played with in Jamaica. I had a Walkman with me, so I told him I was in fact a drummer, and asked him if he would like to hear some jams I had done with a friend of mine.

He listened, then rewound the tape and had the guy next to him have a listen. "Man, the man can play the guitar," commented the other guy, who mentioned he was also a guitarist (he didn't say anything about my drumming). The first guy gave me his phone number and invited me to come to his house in Miami to play soccer and meet his family. There was something special about this man—the way he spoke, his mannerisms and the way the others deferred to him. On the paper he had given me, next to his phone number, he had written "Robert Marley."

I lost his number and never had contact with him again, but as destiny would have it, I not only met and worked with his family after he died, but for a while I became a close part of their lives.

Most of my customers had stores in downtown Miami, and when the lease on my warehouse was about to expire we decided to move East Coast Cosmetics south to an area called Little Havana on SW Eighth Street. Three blocks east of me stood Tent City.

The United States had just opened the door to a new group of Cubans who were given permission by Castro to leave Cuba. There was a massive boat flotilla, and anyone who owned a boat capable of making the trip (and some that were not) was paid handsomely to retrieve the relatives of Cubans already living in South Florida. Some boat owners were paid up to ten thousand dollars per person, payable in advance. Boats came back full of passengers, but not always the ones they were paid to retrieve. It didn't matter. The boats were going back and forth and the dollars were flowing. The City of Miami panicked when confronted with the sudden influx of people and so it built a community of tents under a highway overpass to house them. Thousands of refugees were fenced into what looked like a prison yard, and the camp was dubbed Tent City. I passed it twice a day on my way to work and back. Some introduction, I thought, to The Land of Milk and Honey!

It was discovered that a large percent of the refugees were prisoners Castro wanted to rid Cuba of, and no one would be released from Tent City until everyone was sorted out. South Florida was in an uproar, and it became apparent that these refugees were not welcome. The prejudice between the Cuban and the non-Cuban communities became an open wound. I was the only non-Latin owned business on SW Eighth Street, but it never worried me, as I felt my neighbors were my friends, even after the cigar store three doors down was bombed.

I felt sorry for the way the non-Latin community viewed the Cubans who had made a prosperous life here. The Cubans built businesses and neighborhoods that stretched for miles to the south and west of downtown, and it was rare to hear a person speaking English. It never occurred to me that anyone would dislike a person speaking Spanish until we saw a bumper sticker that read, You're in Florida—Speak English! Alissa took a piece of paper and made up her own little sign. She wrote, You're in Florida—Speak Seminole! referring to the Seminole

Indians of Florida. She folded it up and slipped it under the car's windshield wiper.

The real sadness came from the way the Haitian refugees were treated. They crossed the ocean by rowboat and inner tube, just to be sent right back to Haiti to face jail, or worse. I saw the whole situation as unjust and prejudiced.

The pressure was building in the black community, too. First, a twelve-year-old black girl was raped by a white police officer. Then, cops with a search warrant broke into a black man's home and practically beat him to death, only to find out they were at the wrong address. Another time, the police followed a black man on a motorcycle to his home, then punched and kicked him till he was dead. The officers were tried and found innocent. The black community was enraged and riots ensued. In an attempt to tell the world about the unfair and unjust treatment the black people in Miami had to bear, they rioted and set fire to local neighborhoods. We could see the billowing clouds of smoke from our house in North Miami. My heart was with them and I felt their fury, but, never understood why they took it out on their neighbors and themselves. We thought it hopeless and we had grown very homesick. We put East Coast Cosmetics up for sale through Stebbins Commercial Brokers and talked about moving back to New York.

A Halston sales representative from Venezuela named Raphael Gutierrez was looking to buy a business in Florida. He liked my operation and offered me twenty thousand dollars for it, plus he would buy my inventory. We accepted his offer.

Once the deal was closed I flew to New York to find a house to rent. Sitting in the airport waiting for my flight, I felt overwhelming pride and joy. I had just sold my prosperous business, had and held a certified check for thirty-six grand in my pocket made out to Kenneth Geringer, along with a two-year note for another $20,000. I was so excited I couldn't sit still. I was now rich, returning to my hometown as a successful, upstanding member of society. I had gone to Florida, and conquered, and I wanted to shout it out to the world.

Eventually, two airport security officers approached me. They told me they had been informed by the ticket agent that I appeared anxious, and they wanted to know why. In one breath I blurted out, "I just sold my wholesale cosmetic business in downtown Miami, and I'm flying back to New York where I plan to move with my family," and I pulled the check out of my wallet to show it off.

It felt pretty good to have the opportunity to tell these two gentlemen my story and flaunt my success, and I was awaiting my reward—a pat on the back. Instead, I was handcuffed and taken to a back room at the Miami International Airport. They thought I was a cocaine dealer.

I had only tried coke once. It happened when I delivered an order to an old customer of Ross's. This guy had a ladies clothing store in a mall in Ft. Lauderdale. When he took me into his office to pay me, he had two Dobermans, one on either side of him, and when I reached into my pocket for the invoice, the dogs growled and crouched in attack-mode. After calling the dogs off and paying me, the guy pulled a big plastic baggie filled with cocaine out of his pocket and put huge lines of it on the desk. I thought he was nuts, but my adrenalin was pumping, and to be courteous I snorted a line of coke into each nostril. On the way home I had to pull the van off the road, and while puking my guts out all over the grass, I wondered what was so glamorous about cocaine.

After I was strip-searched and a meticulous search of my suitcases was made, I was allowed to leave the room. At that moment I vowed to myself: Never again would anyone abuse me and get away with what these guys did. I saw myself as a rebel who entered society and played by his own rules and prospered. While everyone else thought they had to go to college or business school to learn the accepted way to run a business, I went to a free high school, didn't have a diploma and was what society considered the least likely to succeed. Only I knew of the fire that burned inside me, and I was raging to show the world what I was capable of.

My plane had long since departed and the same ticket agent who had tipped off security reticketed me. This time I said to her, "I hope I don't still seem anxious to you!" After all, the steam had just been taken out of me.

CHAPTER 17

Onto the Past

I found a house to rent in Clarkstown, New York, and by November we were once again living in Rockland County. We were pleased to have Brian attend The Project School, but Rockland seemed stale in contrast to the busy and ever-changing life we had been leading in Florida. Each day in New York seemed duller than the previous. We figured we just needed some time to get back into the swing of things.

Ross wanted me to continue selling his products. He sent me on a trip to Texas to open up new accounts along the Texas-Mexico border. I had bags of samples and a list of the items Ross carried, and was astounded by the huge orders customers were placing. The stores wanted everything I had to offer, and my first day's gross was over twenty thousand dollars.

I wanted to venture into Mexico, so one of my new customers recommended I go across the border to a place called "Boys Town" in Matamoras. Boys Town turned out to be nothing more than rows of bars in decrepit shacks, with back rooms used for sex. The street was full of prostitutes, some as young as thirteen, and some as old as my grandmother. When you ordered a drink, a girl would sit in your lap and try to hustle you into a back room. It was wild. I was drinking tequila and feeling no pain when I decided to take a walk outside.

An ugly lady approached and propositioned me with rude gestures. When I motioned no, she started to scream at me in Spanish. Within seconds I was grabbed by a big, sweaty guy in a uniform and dragged into a dark room where there was another guy in a matching uniform.

They took my wallet out of my pocket and had me turn around. I tried to tell them that I was an American businessman, but they ignored me. They gave my wallet back to me, tossed me in the back of an old beat-up car and dropped me off at the border. When I looked in my wallet, my three hundred dollars was gone. I reported the robbery to the Mexican customs office, and they told me the men who just dropped me off were Matamoras police officers. I decided not to trust anyone on the Mexican side, so without making my complaint official, I hurried across the border back into Texas.

My customer was involved with the politicians of Matamoras, and he found out who the men were that robbed me. He said they were going to be hung up by their balls—not for robbing me, but because they didn't report the incident to their chief, who was furious about being cheated out of his share of the money. Reading about the incident the following day in the *Brownsville News,* I was satisfied knowing I had enough influence to make those guys pay a price for picking me to fuck with.

I soon realized how miserable Alissa was. While I was working with Ross, she was home alone all day in our quiet house. She missed our friends in Florida, but what she missed most was our independence. Our families were again lending their advice and opinions, and we resented it. After a few years of doing things our way, and doing just fine, we felt like life was moving backwards. Our old Rockland County friends had turned serious, and it seemed the common bond we once shared had disappeared. We attended a New Year's Eve party at a friend's house, and they actually had invitations and a guest list. Anyone who wasn't invited was thrown out. We hardly recognized anyone anymore. In Florida, we were living the life we thought we were missing in Rockland. We realized we had much to offer our friends in Florida, and in New York we had nothing to offer anyone.

When John Lennon was murdered that month, people viewed it as the irrevocable end of an era. The voice of our generation had been silenced, and though grieved, we were determined not to feel hopeless but to make a fresh start while retaining the old values. Even though Brian was happy in The Project School and I became a part-time teacher there, within a few months we packed up and headed home to Florida.

CHAPTER 18

Jack and the John Lennon Sessions: The Fall

Jack had escorted John and Yoko to their limo after a session at Record Plant. Jack usually rode home with John and Yoko, but that night he had a late gig at the studio with Patti Smith, so he gave them tapes of the session to take with them. Soon after the limo pulled away, Jack was called with the news that Lennon was shot. Jack and his fiancé Chris raced to the hospital, only to learn John was dead. Jack wandered the streets of New York all night, alone. He felt partially to blame for not being in the limo. Maybe if he had been there, somehow things would have been different and John would still be alive.

There would never be a greater musician on earth or in heaven than John Lennon. Jack could never produce music as great as he had been producing with Lennon. He was coming down the other side of the mountain—a mountain his future would show him was taller than he imagined.

Ken Geringer and Jack Douglas.

Skunk Hollow, first year (1970). Halloween party.

Cheap Trick, backstage.

Inner Circle, "Bad Boys, Bad Boys."

Cyrinda and Steven Tyler.

Ken Geringer.

Alissa Geringer.

CHAPTER 19

And Forever Futures

South Florida had become an open market, and merchandise from all over the world was flooding into the Port of Miami. I was back in town, with connections for buying, the money to buy with, and I knew who to sell to. I was back in business; we were having fun and life was great again. I set up a music studio in our rented house and decorated it with Hendrix posters. George was gigging with The Kidds, but spent his free time jamming and recording with Tony and me, and his playing was hotter than ever. Besides his guitar, George's only other passion was smoking pot, a ceremony he always performed before he picked up his 1962 Stratocaster guitar.

George's band The Kidds got a gig at the Rock Casino, a small club across the street from where the Seminole Indian Tribe now has huge gaming halls, in Davie, Florida. It was at the Rock Casino that George met Lauren. Lauren was nineteen and working on her acting career. She had just finished a bit part in the movie *Porky's* where she played a cheerleader. Lauren often went to the Rock Casino and sat at a table with her friends, acting unapproachable. She'd spend the night sipping a drink, looking very sexy and as if she was disinterested in every guy in the room. But George was in the band, he was in love and he had plans. After a long seductive battle, Lauren gave in and George had a girlfriend.

George and Lauren made an unlikely couple. They had little in common—Lauren had already been through her drug days, she was always dressed like she was going out on the town and she was a material girl with an attitude, while George was never without his pot and dressed like a starving musician. No one understood what these two opposites saw in each other, and no one believed their relationship would last, until the day George brought Lauren to our house.

Whenever they were together they fought constantly about one thing or another. Lauren hated everything George did, and George hated being nagged, but he had just discovered something new about Lauren. He had us set up an extra microphone in the jam room, then, before picking up his guitar, he proceeded with his usual pot ceremony. While he was smoking, Lauren paced nervously around the room, not talking to Tony or me but occasionally sniping at George, "George, haven't you had enough? When are you going to stop, George?"

The moment of truth finally arrived. George plugged in, did his usual loud licks to make sure his guitar was in tune, then had us start out with *Oh! Darling* by John Lennon. Lauren walked over to the mike, took a deep breath, and began to sing.

She started out softly, but slowly grew more intense. This sexy girl with the whining voice we heard constantly bitching at George possessed the most incredible singing voice I had ever heard. Tony and I couldn't believe what we were witnessing, and Alissa came running into the room. With our mouths wide open, we watched, played and listened as Lauren growled on with a raspy, nasty, unreal voice which grew so intense, that she was shaking by the end of the song. We had thought George's playing was hard to handle, but Lauren's singing was too much. It was the day Janis met Jimi, and it was happening in my house.

When she was finished, we told her how amazing her voice was. Lauren had had no idea she could sing until George heard her singing in the shower one day, and now, she wasn't only pretty, she could sing with the best of them. George started to bring Lauren to the house regularly, and we began to work out songs. The sessions ended with George, Tony and myself into one of our interminable Hendrix jams while Lauren and Alissa sat around talking and waiting for it to end.

Tony and I did everything we could to talk George into quitting The Kidds and starting a band with Lauren. The guys in George's band saw Lauren as a groupie/model who hung around the club scene, and they didn't take George seriously when he told them about her singing. George had some money and wanted to get Lauren on tape, so they started to write songs. George knew the guys in the Pat Travers Band, and when their bass player, Peter Cowling, or Mars, as he was called, heard Lauren sing, he found a studio drummer and the four of them went into the studio and recorded four of George and Lauren's songs. George was so busy gigging with The Kidds and recording Lauren that our jam time dwindled.

I was well established as a wholesaler, shipping merchandise throughout the country. I didn't need a warehouse. All I did was to call my suppliers, make a list of what they were selling, then get back on the phone and sell it. Then I picked up the merchandise at Point A and delivered it immediately to Point B. I was able to pick up orders and deliver them without ever bringing them home. Raphael from East Coast Cosmetics was one of my best suppliers, and I was even selling goods to Ross. As my bank account grew, I had the power to buy bigger and better deals. One fortunate day, I made five thousand dollars on a single phone call.

Once the goods were delivered, I had to wait several days to a week to get paid. All of my money was out. Unable to purchase or work until the money came back left me with plenty of free time.

I met Steve Shapiro through one of my accounts. In addition to buying perfumes, Steve was trying to break into the music business. He had just signed on as manager of a singer named Big Mama Blue. He knew Big Mama had cut a record that had gained some recognition, and he was convinced he had a star and it would be only a matter of time before he made millions. Big Mama kept Steve busy running errands, paying her bills and keeping her out of trouble. With a lot of gold jewelry and a hotshot attitude, he fit the manager stereotype. He knew nothing about the music business, and for this, Big Mama took big advantage of Steve.

Steve was looking for musicians for the band. I auditioned and became the drummer for the Big Mama Blues Band. The band's leader was a sax player from Brooklyn who had always been a backup player, not a bandleader, and at rehearsals there was no organization, but Steve thought we were great and lined up our first gig.

Big Mama was a three-hundred-pound white lady with stringy hair who wore cotton dresses and looked more like a farmer's wife than a blues singer. She was also a sloppy drunk with a bad cocaine habit. Poor Steve had to deal with all of her shit, and we in the band knew she wasn't going anywhere. To the band it was a paycheck, and Steve was paying us to rehearse.

Big Mama usually sang one or two songs with us, always insisting on "Stormy Monday," the song that needed the least work. She stood directly in front of my drums and gyrated her ass cheeks up and down with rhythmic precision, occasionally turning her head around to smile or wink at me. Then for one reason or another she would get up and leave, and Steve would have a fit and remind us about the upcoming gig. I sometimes closed my eyes and imagined it was Lauren in front of me—Lauren, who not only looked good, but with no experience could belt out the blues far better than this one-timer.

CHAPTER 20

This Is Reggaenomics

I met Leslie and Ezra a few days before the Big Mama gig while at Ace Music buying new drumheads. They were trying out guitars, strumming with this cool down-stroke that created a great sounding rhythm. I stood there mesmerized, and before I left, we exchanged phone numbers.

That night I called Leslie and invited him and Ezra over to the house to jam. Leslie and Ezra were from the Caribbean Islands and they were into reggae, a type of music I was only vaguely familiar with. Ezra was staying at Leslie's apartment, having just arrived from Houston where he had been in a band with his brother. They had made one record, and were well known in St. Lucia, but never gained recognition in the states.

When Leslie and Ezra plugged in and began to jam, we realized that I was ignorant as to how to play a reggae beat. This was new music, and I loved the groove, but my problem was that rock n' roll is played in four-four timing, and reggae turns that timing around, hitting the beat on three. It was confusing for me, but my teachers were perfectionists (who also needed a drummer and a place to rehearse).

The Big Mama Blues gig was two days away. I had played with Leslie and Ezra twice, and Steve had come over during the second rehearsal. He asked us if we would open the show for Big Mama, not seeming to know or care that this was only the second time we had ever played together, and I still hadn't figured out how to play in time. Ezra told Steve the music we were playing was called reggae. Steve had no idea what the music was supposed to sound like, but he was aware that there were people who liked it. Ezra had to talk Leslie into doing the gig because Leslie wanted nothing to do with it, but I was all in favor of it because I'd play anything, anytime, anywhere and with anyone.

At 7A.M. the morning of the gig, Leslie and Ezra showed up at my house to rehearse. I hadn't gone to sleep yet because the Big Mama rehearsal lasted until three, and when they walked in I was sitting at the drums in my underwear practicing a reggae groove. They were satisfied with my progress, and after I put my pants on we spent the day playing "Jammin" by Bob Marley.

We arrived at the gig in time to hear Mama giving hell to Steve. She had just found out there was to be an opening act, and this was her big comeback performance and she didn't want anyone cutting in on her show. Little did she know it was a three-piece reggae band with only three rehearsals to its name. Steve was smart enough not to tell her.

We opened with "Jammin," and for the first time I came in on time at the bridge of the song. We did three more Bob Marley tunes, and then said "Thank you!" The audience at this Pompano Beach club, which had recently changed its format from '50s music to whatever that night was supposed to be, applauded, and Steve asked us if we'd go on for an encore. We had never heard of an opening act doing an encore, but we said sure, not telling him that we only knew four songs, and we had just played them all. We went back up and played "Jammin" again, and this time I missed coming in at the bridge. No one but us seemed to know or care that I threw the timing off, and we were once again applauded.

Big Mama wasn't aware that I was in the opening act, and she was furious at me. She told me that no drummer of hers was allowed to be in another band, and she resented me for being in the opening act of her comeback show. Leslie and Ezra felt badly, having witnessed Big Mama's tantrum—half of the club was also aware of it—but we felt consoled when the rest of the Blues Band shook our hands and told us "Good show!"

After the gig, Steve related the news that the club owner wanted Big Mama and us back. The next morning he called and said he had to cancel the opening act because Big Mama wasn't going on if we showed up. That's when I quit the Big Mama Blues Band.

Ezra played bass and had stacks of original material. He was tall and skinny, girls loved him and he looked like a star. He grew up listening to

Calypso and Ska, but was dedicated to reggae. He had shoulder-length hair, but unlike many Rastafarians who wore dreadlocks, his hair was combed straight and stayed in one place.

I learned a lot about reggae. It was the new sound coming out of Jamaica after Calypso and Ska. It originated from centuries of oppression and used an ancient drumbeat. It was captivating and I understood why it was considered a spiritual form of music. I spent all my free time practicing with Leslie and Ezra, and after we learned many Bob Marley songs, we worked on originals. Tony and George joined in occasionally, but they had no real interest in playing reggae music. Leslie and Ezra loved it when George sat in, comparing him to Bob's guitar player, but the music bored George. Well, you either felt it . . . or you didn't.

We wanted to put a band together to do gigs. All we needed was a keyboard player and a lead guitar player, so I got in touch with Larry Dermer, who I knew from the Foxy days. He not only played with Foxy, he also was Miami's top studio session keyboard player. He liked the idea of playing reggae and hooked us up with a guitar player. Our sound and our band were growing.

The town of Coconut Grove, just southeast of Miami, was a trendy, pseudo-cool place to hang out, where yuppies, imitation hippies and neo-1980 trendoids gathered. Since reggae was the new hip sound, clubs in the grove were changing their formats to include reggae and calypso, and it was easy to line up gigs.

Our first gig was at a club called the Village Inn. We called ourselves the Reggae Rockers, a name we chose after days of suggestions and deliberations. Leslie and Ezra represented the Reggae, and I represented the Rock. Alissa suggested the name the Islanders but we felt it might get confused with the hockey team. Not only was I the drummer, my business experience made me a natural when it came to booking the band and arranging the rehearsals. Besides, I owned the PA system and a truck, two items a band needed to do gigs.

Most musicians I knew depended on the money they earned from these gigs to support themselves. Leslie, with a wife and daughter, had a job with United Parcel Service, but needed the extra money and took our band very seriously. Everyone supported themselves by gigging and doing the occasional studio session, except me. I was making plenty of money in my other business. My only reason for being in this band was my love of the music, but these guys depended on me, so I treated it like it was my only business and fought over pennies with the club owners.

We arrived at the Village Inn to find the club packed. We went on after the daytime band, a rock band called Gypsy Queen. The band had already left by the time we arrived, and their roadies were still loading out while we were loading in. We had no one but ourselves, and I realized that being in a band meant wearing many hats, including that of roadie.

In addition to the trendy yuppies in the audience, there were many Jamaican Rastafarians, and that meant we were facing a serious audience. It seemed people liked our name, but had no idea what to expect musically from the Reggae Rockers. Unlike the time we opened for Big Mama, we now had a big band and a big sound. The first set went off well. During the break, a woman asked us if she and her two cousins could get up and sing some Marley tunes with us. It was a smash. The woman who approached us was named Pearl, and she and her two cousins looked and sounded great on stage with us. Ezra felt like he was Bob Marley, with Rita Marley and the "I-Threes" backing him up, and it showed in his performance. To our great surprise, Pearl told us she was Bob Marley's sister! She extended an invitation for us to visit her at home the next day.

Bob had recently died of cancer, and his followers were still in mourning. When I had met Bob at LaGuardia airport, I didn't realize at the time the enormity of the encounter. I regretted never taking him up on the offer to visit and play soccer (second-string soccer player that I was) but now I had another chance to meet his family, and this time as a reggae musician myself.

Bob had bought a house in Miami for his mother, Cedella Booker. She had been living in Delaware, but decided to move to Miami in the late '70s after her husband Edward Booker passed away. Cedella Booker's house was a busy place the day Ezra and I visited. Pearl was just getting up, and Anthony, her (and Bob's) younger brother, was just getting home from school. Anthony, who looked nothing like Bob, and was sort of heavy with short hair, led us into the den to wait for Pearl. No one took notice of us, and it appeared we weren't the only strangers at the house that day. A salesman was in the kitchen with an aunt of Pearl's trying to sell a water filtration system, and out by the pool were a few Rastafarians going over some papers. A giant rug with a picture of Bob smoking a spliff was hanging on the wall. It was a replica of the cover of the album *Rastaman Vibration* and was given to Bob as a gift by a fan who had hooked it one strand at a time. There were signs of Bob everywhere, and although it was a mansion, the house had a warm, special feeling about it.

When Pearl finally came out, she took us on a tour that included the yard where sugar cane and banana trees grew. She introduced us to a woman by the pool who had blond dreadlocks down to her waist, a lawyer from Jamaica helping Cedella with Bob's affairs. We went into the living room where Pearl played some of her songs on an electric organ. Ezra had his eye on Pearl's cousin, and Pearl had her eye on Ezra.

Cedella was a commanding, yet gentle woman who wore African robes and shoulder-length dreadlocks. When she came down the staircase everyone was there to greet her. Her entrance was flawless, and one by one she greeted and chatted with everyone who had been waiting patiently for her. Her sister, who did the cooking and cleaning, informed Cedella about the cost of the water filtration system, and the kitchen was filled with people talking about how bad the water was in Miami, and how the chemicals would "kill ya after a while." Cedella was full of spiritual wisdom, and she often praised Jah in the middle of her sentences while trying to get her point across. She was everything you'd expect Bob Marley's mother to be.

I did wonder if, as a mother, she had been accepting of Bob before he became famous. I imagined how his turning into a Rastafarian may have been as unfamiliar and unacceptable to his mother as my turning into a hippie had been to my mother. It was not a religious thing for me, but this was the way I could compare the revolution that was happening in Jamaica to the one that happened in America. Each of the revolutions had begun with the kids, and each had a new music that tied everyone together. Now, here was Bob Marley's mother standing in front of me, speaking the very words that her son died preaching.

Pearl and her cousin joined the band, and for a while we continued our Sunday gig at the Village Inn. During this time Pearl spent many nights at our house, and Ezra and I visited the Marley estate on a regular basis, but what cemented the bonds of friendship was what happened the day Cedella called to tell me Pearl had been arrested.

Pearl had a friend visiting from Africa who was staying in a hotel on Miami's Biscayne Boulevard, a street that was also frequented by local prostitutes. Pearl was standing on the sidewalk in front of the hotel waiting for her friend when two Miami police officers pulled up in their cruiser and demanded to know what Pearl was doing, implying she was a prostitute. Pearl, who wasn't afraid of anyone, started protesting (loudly!) that they had no right or reason to bother her. Naturally, they threw her in the back of the cruiser, using fists and billy clubs to shut her up. Cedella's lawyers had returned to Jamaica, so when she ran into trouble trying to raise bond, she called me.

When I got to the Dade County Jail, I learned Pearl had been charged with probable prostitution, violently resisting arrest and assaulting a police officer. Because of a technicality in the way the deed to her house was written, Cedella could not post bond, so I put up the title to my car. Pearl was released and Cedella took her home.

Later that day, I took Alissa with me to the estate to see how Pearl was doing. When Cedella heard we had arrived, she walked down the stairs, knelt at our feet, kissed the floor and said that I was a messenger sent to her by Jah. We felt strange as we stood there with Bob Marley's mother kneeling in front of us; especially Alissa, who had never before met Cedella Booker.

Pearl's last name was Livingston, and she was also Bunny Wailer Livingston's half-sister. Bunny, along with Bob and Peter Tosh, started The Wailers, the group that eventually became Bob Marley and the Wailers. Like her brothers, Pearl had anger inside her and expressed it through her music. She was furious about the arrest and had already written a song about how Babylon had captured her and grabbed her by her dreadlocks. The song was great and I realized that, like the blues, reggae songs came from real life hardships and hard times. It was a struggle that fueled the creative fires, and I wondered how anyone could be creative when they were at peace.

Bob grew up in a poor section of Jamaica called Trenchtown, where he experienced poverty and oppression, and now his baby sister Pearl, who lived in the exclusive well-to-do world he left her in, could not escape cruelty and prejudice. She was arrested and beat up by Miami police officers because she was young, female, and black. For them, she was an easy target. The people who lived in the poor neighborhood she was arrested in had no means to fight back, and the police officers felt it was safe for them to harass anyone they chose. The lawyers did get the charges dropped, but that was of little consolation to Pearl and Cedella.

The incident happened during the era of President Ronald Reagan.

Ezra wrote a song entitled "Reggaenomics" and one of the verses went like this:

Show me a politician,
And I'll show you a bare-faced liar.
He'll show you a solution
Don't be fooled, he's just an actor.
And don't be the victim
Of his careful, conniving schemes.
You see I speak
Yet I'm silent.
You've got to protect the innocent!
This is Reggaenomics
This is Reggaenomics now.

Pearl had also written a song entitled "Sweet Mama." It was a beautiful song written for and sung to Cedella about Bob's death, and we wanted to go into the studio to record these two songs. I told Ezra and Pearl about an eight-track studio I knew of in Rockland County, and also about the New York musicians I grew up with. The decision to record in New York was easy for all of us. Pearl had never been there and loved the idea of going, Ezra wanted to see friends in Brooklyn, and I wanted to show everyone in New York what I was up to in Miami. The only problem was that Pearl was only eighteen years old, and Cedella was very protective of her. She had yet to allow Pearl to leave Miami. Pearl was afraid to ask permission and she wanted to surprise her mother with the song as a gift, so we waited for the week Cedella flew to Jamaica, and we flew to New York.

I booked time at a studio called Nyack Sound and started looking around Rockland for musicians. It was easy to find the best. A friend named Marc Davenport played keyboards, and David Snider, who was playing at the Skyview pool the first time I met Alissa, played guitar. Ezra played bass and I played drums. Marc, Ezra and Pearl were all singers so we had plenty of background vocals to work with. We rehearsed at Marc's studio in Stony Point. Marc lived in a cooperative called The Land, a beautiful property that adjoined Harriman State Park. The family who had built it owned each house, but all the members of the community owned the land cooperatively. They were very original and unusual houses placed artistically up the side of a mountain within earshot of a series of waterfalls. Marc and his brothers had built a rehearsal studio in an A-frame on the top of the mountain, high above his parents' house.

Pearl expected all of New York to be concrete and garbage, and could not believe the beauty of Rockland County. On breaks from rehearsing we took walks to the waterfalls, and after two rehearsals we were ready to go into the studio. We began by recording the bass and drum tracks to "Reggaenomics." Then, one by one, we added parts, like layering paint on a painting. The owner of the studio had to go to Manhattan to work on Devo's album so he left us with his engineer. Ezra and I acted as producers by telling him what we wanted as he mixed it down. The tracks were so full that to fit everything on eight tracks we had to put the background vocals and lead guitar on the same track, using every bit of available tape. We recorded "Sweet Mama" by having all the musicians play at once, and we were happy with the second take. The songs came out so good we talked about putting a band together and shopping the tape. I wished we had more time to work on vocals, but Ezra and Pearl were satisfied, and I was finally in the business end of the music business.

My parents were on vacation in Japan and left their house and Mercedes-Benz for us to use. Pearl and Ezra slept in my parents' room and I slept in my old room. The next day we drove to Brooklyn to check out Ezra's friends. While sitting in traffic on some shitty highway, a car plowed into the back of my dad's car. It was a nightmare. Pearl was not feeling well, it was cold outside, horns were honking everywhere and I was arguing with the man who had run into me. The car was dented, but drivable. We made it to Brooklyn, only to get lost. After we found Ezra's friend's apartment and stayed awhile, we drove into Manhattan, parked the car in a garage and ate dinner in a Chinese restaurant. After eating half of her rice, Pearl found out that she was eating pork fried rice, and pork is strictly forbidden by her religion. Then she really got sick and yelled at the waitress—who spoke very little English—things like, "Blood clat, me no eat them devil food, now I and I get sick, why tem no tell me tis pork in here?"

My sister, Amy, had a one-bedroom apartment in Manhattan that she shared with her roommate, Laurie. Amy had left me the key since she was on vacation with my parents. I slept on the pullout sofa in the living room, and Ezra and Pearl slept in Laurie's bed. I mistakenly thought

Laurie would also be away for the weekend. When she got home late that night she tiptoed past me into her bedroom, and sprawled across her bed were two naked black people with dreadlocks flying in all directions.

The next morning we went to visit Danny Sims, a businessman Bob had befriended early in his career, and from whom I learned how easily artists could lose control of the money their compositions earned. Bob had entered into a publishing deal with Danny, who also set up many other deals and projects, but mostly he made lots of money from Bob's works. Now Bob was dead, and there was a war going on between the lawyers, the record companies and the families. Cedella had told me that before Bob died, he let her know that his will gave her guardianship of all his belongings, including his house, his possessions and the rights to all his music, but after he died no such will turned up. Cedella believed it was those who pretended to be close to Bob, such as Danny, who were responsible for the will's disappearance. Jamaican law gave Rita Marley the rights to Bob's estate, and Cedella, who never got along well with Rita, had to accept small sums of money to meet house and car payments. She hated being dependent upon Rita, and the way Cedella felt about the situation was expressed by Pearl in "Sweet Mama":

"The war wasn't over,
We—his roots—are here to stay.
Mama,
Sweet Mama,
Don't you cry..yy..yy..."

The song also expressed the controversy surrounding Bob's illness and death. Cedella told me she believed that because he grew up in Jamaica, he was strong. She would say, "Them children of mine no have them diseases! My Bob a healthy man, he never do them things to bring cancer." She said that because Bob had many followers all over the world who not only listened to his music but believed in what he had to say about the struggle to overthrow oppression, and because the CIA had an open file on him, she was sure that during a show in New York the CIA had someone in the crowd inject Bob with a substance. Bob had told her of someone sticking him in the leg with a needle, and Cedella swore that that's how he contracted his disease.

117

Danny had us meet him at the studio where he was working on a Jimmy Cliff album. He invited us to his apartment where we were surprised to find Jimmy Cliff and his band. They were lounging about on mattresses and blankets. Four women were in the kitchen tending a giant simmering pot of soup. One of the women was Jimmy's wife, who was pregnant. She looked like she was due any minute, and Jimmy said he didn't want the baby born in New York and hoped to be finished with the album and back in Jamaica in a few days.

Pearl wanted to talk to Danny about all the music he had acquired of Bob's throughout the years. She demanded he tell her who was getting the money that was being made from these releases. Danny evaded Pearl's questions and said things like, "There is going to be plenty of money for all of us. I don't know why your mother won't talk to me. It is Rita who is the enemy!" Before we left, Danny gave us a copy of *Uprising*, the new Bob Marley album he was about to release. I left Danny's with an eerie feeling about what this music business was all about.

Ezra and Pearl flew back to Florida, and I stayed in New York to shop the tape. Most of the major labels had offices in Manhattan, and it was time for me to figure out how to get these bigwigs to listen to it. I found making the appointments easy, especially when I mentioned that Bob Marley's sister was the singer. The hard part was trying to figure out which department would listen to us. The labels had Artist and Repertoire (A&R) departments, and I was usually directed to their black music departments where they handled soul, blues and funk artists. It was as confusing to me as it was to them, as most of the young black A&R executives knew little about reggae, had no reggae artists on their rosters, and weren't sure if I even belonged in the black department. Reggae in the United States was listened to primarily by a white, yuppie audience. Eventually, someone would end up listening, and most everyone liked "Reggaenomics," but no one understood how Bob Marley's sister fit in. Everyone was polite, but I could see by the huge stacks of cassette tapes piled up all over their desks that there were many others trying to do exactly what I was doing.

A record deal seemed like a magical thing and there was an excitement that went with walking into big companies like Warner Brothers and CBS. I was sure we were to become big recording stars, and the feeling grew every time one of the A&R guys would like the tape enough to call the guy in from the next office to have a listen. No one turned me down on the spot and I was given assurance I would hear from them in a few days. Island Records, a company I was sure would sign us right away, said they weren't signing any new reggae artists, but they recommended I see a company in New Jersey called Shanachie Records.

Shanachie all but signed us right away. They were more like a distributor than a label, but offered us a cash advance to release the record, and even gave me a proposed release date for "Reggaenomics." They wanted to hold the song until Ronald Reagan was re-elected. Satisfied, I flew back to Florida to face Cedella.

Cedella was more than a little upset at us for taking Pearl to New York, but she was moved by Pearl's song. Like us, she thought it only a matter of time before the record companies would be calling, and she gave me all the rules and regulations regarding our coming and going with Pearl.

Responses did come in, but by mail, and consisted of a brief letter requesting additional material. I began to realize that record companies didn't want one-hit wonders, but expected multiple hit songs in return for their financial investment. Unfortunately, we couldn't send more material. Two songs were all we were ever going to have. We still had Shanachie Records, until they wrote us and explained that because they had just made a deal with Rita Marley to distribute her Tuff Gong Label, it would be a conflict of interest for them to work with Pearl.

Were it not for dreams, would life go on?

George and Lauren also had big dreams. George gave The Kidds notice and was teaching the tunes to his replacement. The night the new kid played his first gig with The Kidds, George, Tony and I went to check him out at our favorite local rock club, The Button South.

This guy was more than just a great rhythm guitarist. In addition to being able to play, he had amazing stage presence. He brought the band a new, younger image. He had a little James Dean in him, as well as a little teenage Elvis—handsome, tough, and sweet at the same time. While we were in awe watching him, Tony leaned over to me and whispered, "This kid's so pretty, I'd fuck him!"

The kid's name was Johnny Depp.

Ezra, Leslie and I continued to play gigs as the Reggae Rockers, and at one show a Jamaican producer named King Sportie approached us. He invited us to meet with him at Quadradial, a recording studio in North Miami where he was "doing something" with Bobby Caldwell. It seemed like what they were trying to do was determine who could inhale the biggest line of cocaine. Then, while Bobby pounded chords on the electric piano, King lectured us on the right way to sell a song, all the while reminding us what a serious man he was.

After Caldwell left, five kids that King claimed were his showed up to do a vocal session. The youngest kid was having a hard time singing in tune. King took him aside and started to pound on him. When this poor, shaken-up boy still couldn't get it right, King hit him again, pulled out a gun, aimed it at his son's head, and then waved the gun into the air and fired it, yelling, "I'll kill you, man!" (We were told the gun had blanks in it.) Later, King lit a fire on the ground just outside an exit door, preparing to cook a chicken dinner. Poor Bob Ingria, the owner of the studio, for having to have to put up with such shit! We declined dinner.

King insisted we come to his house where he, Leslie, Ezra and I sat around a massive conference table. King's seat was elevated and the chair he sat on was shaped like a throne. He announced proudly that he had played "Reggaenomics" for TK Records (remember Carl Driggs?), and he gave us one of their famous contracts to sign. We declined, but for fifty dollars a song we played back-up in the studio for some other acts that he was recording. I once saw one of the records on which we played. The credit for my drum parts went to an Imall Livingston.

In addition to having watched my first session in a 24-track recording studio with a real producer, I had cowritten and produced two songs, laid down studio drum tracks, and had been in contact with various major labels. I had taken my first steps into this wonderful business of music, and I was eager to see where the adventure would take me next.

CHAPTER 21

Cinderella from Porky's

Leslie had grown disenchanted with the Reggae Rockers lifestyle so he quit the band. Soon after, George and Lauren asked Ezra and me if we wanted to start a band and do local gigs. Their timing could not have been more perfect. We called the band Cinderella, and our first gig was at a game room in South Miami. We had to compete with the noise from hundreds of games, and our audience ages ranged from eight to twelve. When we complained about this to our agent, he assured us he had it all together, and the following week we were sent an hour north to Pompano Beach to do a private party. To our surprise, there wasn't a person under the age of sixty-five in the crowd. When we'd told the agent we didn't want to play for kids, this wasn't exactly what we had in mind!

After that, we were sent to audition at a club on the pier in Ft. Lauderdale. During the forty-five-minute audition, it started to rain. The roof had a leak and rainwater was pouring down directly on my head. No one in the band knew I was getting this shower, and I had to finish playing the set soaking wet.

Then, we were sent to a gig on the Ft. Lauderdale strip. The agency told the club owner that Lauren had played a cheerleader in the movie *Porky's*, and when we arrived we saw a giant billboard over the club which read, "Cinderella from Porky's!" Everyone thought it was hysterical. Everybody, except Lauren.

Next, we got a two-week gig at the Holiday Inn in West Palm Beach, and as part of the deal, I got my own room. Alissa and I packed up Brian and Rachel and we went on a family style rock n' roll vacation. Alissa loved the idea because she could come to the lounge every night after the kids fell asleep in the room. She had stopped coming to my gigs after attending the first few. It was great fun in the begining, but after a while, she grew tired of sitting in bars till sunrise while I played roadie. At the Holiday Inn, she figured she could go up to the room the minute it got boring, but that never happened.

The hotel manager had an artist create an advertising poster depicting a big picture of a horse and carriage, the carriage being a big orange pumpkin, and he cut Lauren's head out of her promo picture and stuck it inside the carriage. The poster was displayed prominently in the hotel lobby when we arrived. We found this even funnier than the billboard, especially because Lauren still wasn't amused.

By the second week of the gig, word got out that the Holiday Inn was rockin' and that the guitar player sounded like Hendrix. We packed the place, and at one in the morning, when the night desk manager got off work, the wild jams started. Each night local musicians would come to play with us. There was a guitar player named Keith who not only looked like Hendrix, he had the reputation of playing like him; he even played with his teeth. Keith was a computer genius and had built himself a computerized effects box he controlled with his foot. It was quite dramatic watching Keith perform, but his playing was no match for George's.

From the night Keith showed up, the music grew louder, the jams went on till dawn, and the party extended to the swimming pool and hotel rooms. Our agent had once again sent us to the wrong place, but this time we were in control and having a blast. West Palm Beach needed a good rock club, but this Holiday Inn wasn't about to turn their lounge into one. Except for the waitresses, I don't think anyone at the West Palm Beach Holiday Inn was sorry to see us go.

When we weren't gigging, I took trips to Texas to deliver merchandise. I had kept in touch with my border-town customers and I sold them perfume packages, to be delivered personally, cash on delivery. I once took Ezra to Texas with me.

Alissa had painted the aluminum bakery truck with stars and stripes in bright red, green, yellow and black (the colors of the Ethiopian and Jamaican flags) with the name Reggae Rockers whooshing across each side in big block letters. It looked like a hallucination from a bad acid trip. The truck had tall seats, and Ezra and I were more noticeable than I would have liked. While driving through Alabama, something hard hit the windshield. We pulled over and saw what looked like a chip from a pellet or bullet in the glass, with cracks radiating out like a spider's web. The chip was right in front of my face. Ezra and I looked at each other, both aware we were in hostile territory. A white guy with long red hair, and a black guy with long black hair driving a technicolor hippy truck in Alabama—definitely not good!

I always felt because I was a legitimate businessman, I was untouchable. It was like I waited for them to fuck with me so I could say, "Ha, ha, I fooled you!" Only this was the real world, and things didn't work like that. When the carburetor needed its regular adjustment, not one station would lend us a hand, not even ones with black employees—we were just too weird. Upon our arrival in Brownsville, Texas, the truck overheated, forcing us into the first service station we came to. The truck was loaded with boxes, and it became obvious that the skinny old attendant who turned on the water for us was a little too inquisitive. Sure enough, within minutes, every police car in Brownsville had surrounded us, with sirens wailing and lights flashing. Like Barney Fife, every cop was sure this was the Big One! Brownsville had seen many illegal aliens and drug smuggling busts, but nothing compared to the two of us. Not one officer believed I was a businessman making deliveries. Ezra was already in the back of a police car, and it took hours for four officers to go through my customers' orders. Finally, after they matched the merchandise with my invoices, we were free to go. We were warned to make our deliveries and conclude our business, a warning that sounded to me like, "Get out of town by sundown!"

We decided to visit Mexico. I had told Ezra about the Mexican girls, but to our surprise none of them would come near him. It was like we were in Alabama again. It was deathly hot the next morning as we drove through the desert towards Laredo. The temperature soared over one hundred degrees, the truck had no air conditioning and we were dehydrated. I expected to see skulls along the partially paved road. Just as we were about to pass out from the heat, we saw a service station where we bought jugs of warm distilled water. Nothing ever tasted so good, and we made it into town alive.

People behaved differently in Laredo. Instead of staring at us like they did in Brownsville, they approached us and asked about the band. At first we thought it was because of the Reggae Rockers truck, but then we realized we were being mistaken for someone else, so we played along. Eventually we found out Laredo was awaiting a concert by Judas Priest, Iron Maiden and a few other heavy metal bands. Naturally, people thought we were part of the show. We found out where the bands were staying and spent the day of the show hanging out with them by their hotel pool. The guys in Iron Maiden thought we were in one of the smaller bands, which was fine with us, but the best part were the Mexican-American groupies. Even down here in Laredo, Texas, groupies were alive and well, and the girls here loved Ezra.

Coop.

Lauren singing "Oh! Darling."
(left to right): Tony Schittina, Lauren Smolkin, Ken, George Mazzola.

Pearl Livingston-Marley.

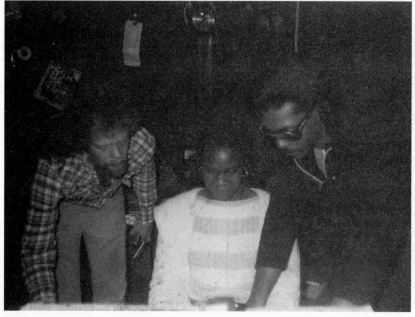

(left to right): Ken, Pearl, Ezra

CHAPTER 22

Dixie Jam

Tony's mother (we all called her Mom) always dreamed of owning her own restaurant. She had worked as a waitress and saved her tips for years, and when the Dixie Diner went up for sale, Mom bought it. The diner was across the street from Miami's famous Criteria Recording Studios.

Tony now had a regular job, because Mom made Tony her cook. While George and I were out gigging, Tony was cooking it up at the Dixie Diner. He hung rock n' roll pictures all over the walls, including all of his pictures of him and Ted Nugent. The recently debuted MTV played all day on the TV that was hanging in the corner of the room. Whenever a group was recording at Criteria they would surely eat at Mom's, and the Dixie Diner gained the reputation for being Miami's premier rock n' roll diner (if ever there was such a thing!).

Tony was either working, or too tired after work to play guitar. He was losing his spirit, and in an attempt to jolt him back to life, George and I talked him into hosting a jam at the diner one Friday night. We dubbed it The Dixie Jam.

We moved all the tables and chairs aside, brought in the equipment, and I set up my video camera to film the whole thing. Tony told us there was an all-female band recording at Criteria, and they were going to stop by after their session with their producer and his girlfriend, who were regulars at the diner. About fifty people came in; the place was packed. We played our usual three-piece set, and at the end of our last song the girls from across the street came in. They got up on stage, introduced themselves as Tin Angel and began to play. As I focused my camera, I wondered how a band as awful as they were had obtained a record deal. I continued filming, and after a few minutes a woman came up to me and said she was the band's manager and asked if I would please give her the tape. I offered to give her a copy, explaining this was a special occasion and I wasn't about to give up this tape. She replied that she'd have to think about it.

After Tin Angel finished playing, she took me over to a guy seated at the counter and introduced him as her fiancé, Jack Douglas. He didn't seem to care if I kept the tape or not, and when our conversation drifted to the topic of Rockland County, Jack told me he too was from Rockland. It was the first time I had met someone in Florida who had grown up in the same county as I did. We started naming our friends and talking about our high schools. He told me he had gone to Tappan Zee High School, but had heard about Skunk Hollow. Even though he was ten years older than I was, we knew a lot of the same musicians. People like Jack were the true revolutionaries and had paved the way for people like me. He had been a bass player for Wayne Cochran and was playing gigs and hanging out in beatnik spots like The Hearth when I was in second grade. I felt like Jack was an old friend, so I invited him over to the house for a home-cooked meal. He said it sounded great and we arranged that I would pick him up at the studio the next day.

George came over and I introduced him to Jack. I said, "George, this is an old friend from Rockland County, Jack Douglas."

George, dumbfounded, just stared at Jack, and I wondered if, at last, George had smoked too much pot. Then, in an awed voice, George asked, "Not the *John Lennon and Aerosmith* Jack Douglas?"

What did George say?

When Jack answered, "Yes," George asked if he'd come into the kitchen to look at a picture of his girlfriend. As they were walking away I heard George, in breathless anticipation, tell Jack, "It must be fate that you are here because my girlfriend is an amazing singer . . . "

Did I hear George say "John Lennon . . . Aerosmith?"

After Jack returned from the kitchen, he said, "I'll see you tomorrow, Ken. Pick me up at Criteria, at six," and he walked out of the diner.

George, still awed, asked me, "Do you know who Jack Douglas is?"

"Uh, a guy from Rockland?" I answered.

"No! I just read an article in *Musician Magazine* about him. He produced John Lennon's *Double Fantasy* album, and he produced Aerosmith and discovered Cheap Trick! I always wished a guy like that would hear Lauren, and now . . . "

George came over with the magazine the next morning and we read the article together. Jack recounted for the interviewer the night he, John and Yoko had just finished up in the studio. Jack gave John a few cassette tapes of the session to take home so he could listen to them. An hour later, still holding the tapes in his hand Jack learned that John had been shot.

The article went on. Jack had not only produced six Aerosmith and three Cheap Trick albums, he also produced or engineered Alice Cooper, the Band, Bob Dylan, George Harrison, the Who, and Mick Jagger. He had worked on the Bangladesh and Woodstock albums. Now I was in awe! George and I got busy planning how I would play the tape of him and Lauren on the night when Jack would be at my house. Alissa cooked a fantastic spinach lasagna with all the fixin's, including homemade bread, and at six o'clock sharp, I was at Criteria to pick up Jack.

The receptionist had me wait.

After fifteen minutes, Karen, the guitar player for Tin Angel, came into the waiting room and asked me, "What are you doing here?"

"I'm here to pick up Jack for dinner," I said.

"No, you're not. There is no way he's leaving!" she said.

"Can you tell Jack I'm here?" I asked.

"No!"

I was about to leave, when Jack popped his head in and asked, "Ken, are you in a hurry?"

I said, "Not at all." Karen gave me a look that burned through me.

After Jack went back to work, Karen said, "Don't keep Jack out more than one hour!" The receptionist hit the button and admitted Karen back into the studio. I sat in the waiting room listening to the buzzer ring over and over as people strolled freely in and out of the studio. I thought about sneaking in, but instead sat waiting impatiently, while at the same time trying not to look impatient.

At 9:30 Jack came in and said, "I'm starved, let's go!" I remembered what Karen had said, and wondered how I was going to get Jack to my house, eat lasagna, listen to the tape and back to the studio all in one hour. Then I thought about Alissa's dinner. I hoped she wasn't asleep, or waiting to attack me when I got home. We were only three hours late! I had been afraid to leave Criteria to find a phone and call her, fearing that Jack would come out, not see me and assume I had gone home. I thought I would never get another chance like this again.

I tried to apologize to Jack, telling him how I hoped the dinner would still be hot when we got to the house. Jack, who seemed to have no conception of time, told me not to worry, and asked why I had waited outside and not come into the studio with Karen. There seemed to be a lot Jack was not aware of.

Dinner was perfect and Jack couldn't get enough. Again, the Rockland County thing clicked, and we all told our growing-up stories. Jack recounted the story of how one morning when he was in high school, he asked all the kids on his school bus to wait at their bus stops at midnight, but he didn't tell them why. That night, Jack and a friend broke into the bus yard, stole a school bus and then drove along their bus route picking up all the astonished kids, who were waiting as instructed. Then the bus full of kids went on a joy ride until they got caught.

For his efforts, Jack and his friend, Eddie, were sent to Rockland State Mental Hospital. While there, they befriended a delusional guy who was in for a drug overdose. At first, they felt sorry for him, then they found out he could sneak in enough drugs for all three of them. When Bret told them he was an actor and that his best friends were Elizabeth Taylor and Richard Burton, they went along with him, and before Jack was released, they exchanged phone numbers.

A few months went by, Bret was released and he invited Jack and Eddie to accompany him to a Broadway show starring Taylor and Burton. Although Jack was leery, he agreed to go. After the show, Bret announced it was time to go backstage. Jack warned Bret it was a bad idea to sneak backstage (they'd probably end up back in Rockland State Hospital), but Bret paid no attention. As Jack mentally rehearsed his explanation about how his friend was crazy, a voice yelled "Bret!" and Elizabeth Taylor ran open-armed to embrace Bret. Jack and Eddie stood speechless. They wondered if maybe the guy that was down the hall from them in Rockland State was, in fact, Superman.

After more than an hour of recalling past experiences, I mentioned that Karen would have my ass if I kept Jack for more than an hour. Jack told me not to worry, and then he told me the story behind Tin Angel, who was managed by Jack's fiancè, Christine. Jack had been asked by Atlantic Records to record a band from New Orleans called Zebra, and Jack said he would produce their album if Atlantic would also sign Tin Angel. It was agreed that Jack would produce Zebra and Atlantic would pay the cost of making a Tin Angel album. Sort of a double deal, one which I assumed was keeping Jack and his fiancé together. I thought, "If it's that easy to get a band like Tin Angel a deal, just wait till he hears George and Lauren's tape!" Jack sat in the living room and listened intently to the five songs.

He didn't seem to get too excited about the tape, but said it was good and he'd consider working with the band in the future. I told Jack that I had money saved, and if he thought the tape was good enough, I'd like to invest in it and do whatever it would take to get George and Lauren started. I could feel the familiar determination sensation kicking in.

Jack at that point advised me to start three corporations: a production company and two publishing companies. He told me there were two societies that monitored publishing payments, BMI and ASCAP, and by having two publishing companies I could be affiliated with both. I didn't understand what he meant exactly, but I was determined to do things right. Jack gave me his phone number and told me to call him in a week, after he was back in New York.

I asked my accountant to start the three corporations. He questioned why I needed three corporations, and all I could think to answer was, "Finally I'm going to be in the record business, and this is going to be the beginning of something big." In my mind it was destiny that led me to Jack and I was ready for what lay ahead. At least I thought I was ready. My three corporations were started, so I picked up the phone.

To my surprise, Jack had given me his manager's phone number. Stan Vincent had no idea who I was, but offered to relay my message to Jack. I told him to tell Jack I had started three corporations and wanted to know what to do next.

A few days later, Jack called and told me he had listened to the tape again and really wanted to work with George and Lauren, but before we got into it, he had something else he wanted me to get involved in. He said Stan Vincent would be calling me. Now, more than ever, my head was in the clouds. Not only did Jack Douglas like and want to work with my group, he had something else he wanted me to get involved in! I thought maybe it was an Aerosmith album or something else big. I anxiously awaited Stan's call.

Stan let me know from the start he didn't understand the attraction between Jack and me, but Jack wanted him to make me an offer that involved a three thousand dollar investment. He explained that if I went to Criteria Studio and paid them the money, the studio would turn the Tin Angel tapes over to me, and then I should fly to New York with them. He said he'd explain the deal to me when I got to New York. I figured three thousand was a small price to pay for what I would eventually gain. Upon arriving at Criteria, I was informed Atlantic Records had refused to pay the three grand needed to release the tapes. I found this news surprising. Why the huge record company was refusing to pay the seemingly small debt was unclear, but I figured it must mean more opportunity for me.

I had been given instructions to carry the tapes onto the plane and not let them go through any metal detector. There were so many tapes, and they were so heavy, I barely made it onto the plane. Stan Vincent was awaiting my arrival at the gate. It was obvious to him who I was, but Stan's appearance surprised me. He looked younger than I had pictured, and much shorter. Jack was sitting in Stan's Mercedes-Benz, which was parked outside the terminal. When we got to the car, Jack moved to the backseat and I jumped into the shotgun seat for the ride to Stan's office in Manhattan.

Stan kept repeating, "I just don't understand how you guys are going to work together, but that's why I'm the manager and he's the artist." All the while Jack sat in the back seat making sniffing noises. I didn't want to turn around. Stan continued to let me know how lucky I was to be there with Jack Douglas, and, no offense to me, but he couldn't understand why Jack wanted to offer this investment to me—something he wouldn't have done.

"But that's what makes Jack, Jack!" he went on.

I tried to defend myself by telling Stan there was something between Jack and me, how we had hit it off, and how I'd invited Jack over for dinner having no idea he was a famous producer. Jack, who had been silent except for the sniffing noises, added, "Yeah, that Rockland County thing."

Stan's office was his apartment on East 80th Street. An array of gold records decorated his living room walls. Stan was also a songwriter, and had written several hits in the '60s and '70s, including "Ooh, Ooh Child," a beautiful song he'd written eighteen years before when his son was born. Stan's girlfriend came out of the bedroom. She looked to be about twenty-two years old, pregnant, and she worked as Stan's secretary; she offered us a drink.

After engaging in more small talk, Stan slowly got around to why I had to pay for and pick up the tapes. The story went that Atlantic Records was upset with Jack for spending so much time on the Tin Angel album, while the Zebra album was unfinished. Both projects were running over budget and Atlantic was losing interest in the Tin Angel project. Then Stan revealed to me that the reason they had me fly to New York was for him to offer me points on the Tin Angel album. For fifteen thousand dollars.

That was twelve thousand more than the money I had already shelled out. From the way Stan was talking I should have been jumping for joy, however, I was a little taken aback. I didn't even like the girls or their music, and I knew they resented me, plus I wondered about George and Lauren. What about them?

Then I realized I had no idea what a point was. While Stan explained about a point being one percent of retail sales, he kept reminding me how lucky I was. When I questioned why they needed the money from me, Stan said it was because Jack needed the money to finish the album the way he wanted, not the way Atlantic wanted. He told me how Jack is known for going over budget, and although the record companies may not have liked his unorthodox style, they loved the millions of dollars his albums brought in . . . and this is where I came into the picture. Regardless of what Atlantic thought, Jack knew he had a big hit with this all-girl group, and fifteen thousand would guarantee its success.

Stan went on, that this was not the first time Jack had seen something in a band. Once while in Madison, Wisconsin, Jack went bowling, and a local band called Cheap Trick was playing at the alley. When Jack saw them, he knew they were going to be big. (He had that same feeling when he first saw Tin Angel!) The following night, Jack returned to the bowling alley with a metronome (a ticking device musicians use to help keep time). After their set, Jack told the band he was from New York and that he wanted to bring some record company execs to Madison to hear them play. Sure, the band had been handed that line before, but this was the first time a guy carrying a metronome around a bowling alley had handed it to them. They had no idea that Jack was a record producer and that he had brought the metronome to see if the band really did play live in perfect time—which they did. The following week, Jack returned with some Epic Record executives, and the rest is rock n' roll history.

Stan pointed to the huge stacks of papers on his coffee table. They were legal documents pertaining to a lawsuit Jack had brought against

133

Yoko Ono for refusing to pay him his share of the *Double Fantasy* royalties (as agreed to in their contract), and then Stan read aloud testimony from a deposition given to Jack by Yoko's lawyers. Jack's money was all tied up in the lawsuit, and that was the reason why they needed to sell the point on the album. He told me Yoko owed Jack over five million dollars.

I asked if I could buy a point on the Zebra album instead, and Stan said that would cost me twenty-five thousand dollars. Stan picked up on my indecision, and said if I was afraid to invest in the album, he had an alternative plan. "Why don't you lend Jack the money, and Jack will pay you back in ninety days, with interest?"

In the back of my mind, I wondered, "Why me?" and "How could I be sure Jack will pay me back?" but there were greater forces leading me, and Stan was very good at what he did. He asked me to look around his apartment.

"Do you know how much it costs me to maintain my lifestyle?" he asked. "Eighty thousand dollars a year, and all I do is manage Jack for 20 percent. Figure it out. If I need that a year, then it's 20 percent of, how much money? That's how much Jack has to make every year . . . "

Then he added that it wasn't his idea to bring me up here, and quite frankly, I was there only because Jack wanted to work with me. I wasn't about to back down, but I had two conditions. One, I wanted a loan agreement (Stan said he'd have Jack's accountant put one together), and two, I wanted my name mentioned on the Tin Angel album. I figured if I was supplying the money to finish it, I deserved thanks, and it would be the first time my name, if not my playing, would be on an album. We all shook hands and decided to visit a neighborhood bar to toast the beginning of our relationship.

We sat at a table, and perched at the bar was an elderly gentleman who was sipping a drink and doodling with colored pencils on a piece of paper. I walked up to the bar and asked the bartender for change for cigarettes. The artist looked at me and smiled. When I returned to the table, Stan informed me I had just met Jimmy Dorrian, a famous artist who hung out there.

A little while later, Mr. Dorrian came over to our table and handed me the drawing he had just finished. He smiled at me and said he had drawn a portrait of me. It looked like a mini Picasso.

Stan was amazed. "I've been coming to this bar for years, and never has Mr. Dorrian so much as spoken a single word to me, much less handed me an original work!" He said I was a good omen for Jack, and we celebrated with another drink.

It was still early when Stan dropped us off at Jack's brownstone apartment on 76th Street. Jack informed me that Steven Tyler, lead singer from the band Aerosmith, his wife Cyrinda, and their baby daughter were also living in the apartment, but Steven wasn't home at the time. There was another apartment downstairs, and I was told I could sleep there.

Cyrinda Tyler and her friend were draped across the living room couches watching TV. Gold and platinum records hung on every wall. The house was a mess, and the child, a toddler, was sitting on the floor. Jack excused himself to go upstairs to find Chris, leaving me with Cyrinda and her friend. They both looked half-starved. Cyrinda immediately asked me if I'd watch the kid while they went to the store.

I said, "Sure."

An hour later, Chris came downstairs to greet me. The first thing she did was to apologize for asking me not to film Tin Angel that night at the diner. She explained how she had to be careful about things like that, and since she was their manager, it was her job to do the dirty work. Then she told me how happy she was that Jack was going to be working with someone from Rockland County and how he needed a friend. She apologized for the mess in the apartment and whispered, "Steven and Cyrinda are such pigs!"

I replied, "Cyrinda went to the store and I'm watching her daughter."

Suddenly, Chris was very angry. "Cyrinda had no right to ask you to babysit. We're throwing her out of the apartment tomorrow!"

She called for Jack, and when he came downstairs she said, "Jack, do you believe Cyrinda just walked out and left Ken to babysit?"

I said, "I don't mind," but she went on telling Jack it wasn't right. Jack, who seemed not to care either way, agreed with Chris they would throw Cyrinda out in the morning. I hoped it wasn't because of me. By this time, Cyrinda's daughter had fallen asleep on the floor and Jack carried her into a bedroom.

That night, Jack, Chris and I sat around the living room, and they continued where Stan had left off.

While still a teenager, Jack hung out in Manhattan and hustled in pool halls around town. Being a musician, he also wanted to be a part of the recording industry, so he began hanging out at Record Plant Recording Studio on 44th Street. He offered to do odd jobs, anything, just so he could be there. When Roy Cicala, the owner of the studio, realized he wasn't going to be rid of Jack, he appointed him janitor. Jack became friends with everyone—producers, engineers, artists—and everyone liked him. During the day he ran errands, but all of his free time was spent watching and learning. It was an innovative time for recording, and Jack was learning the techniques used in making a record. Being janitor, he had the keys to the studio, and at night when everyone was gone he went into the studios and played with the equipment. When he could get away with it he made copies of the tapes and did his own mixes. When his talent became evident, many producers wanted Jack to assist, and he became an engineer.

As an engineer, Jack worked with the Who on the *The Kids Are Allright* LP and hung out with Keith Moon, who snuck the still underage Jack into the discothèques. Jack was also called in to work with George Martin whenever George came to New York to do Beatles mixes. George was like a father to him—a teacher and a major influence.

Jack's first job as a producer came while he was engineering Alice Cooper's *Muscle of Love* LP for producer Bob Ezrin. Bob hated working with Alice Cooper but was committed to do the album. He knew Jack was an able producer so he went home, leaving Jack to produce the album. Jack recalled that everything was going fine until the night before Bob was due back to listen to the mixes. Someone in Record Plant had dosed the water cooler with LSD.

Jack was editing a song when he started to feel strange. He had all the tape cut, and was ready to piece it together. As he worked, it seemed pieces of tape were being moved around. Jack and his engineer finally realized what was happening, and they spent the night carefully trying to piece the tape together while tripping their brains out. In the morning, when they played the song back, they realized it was horrible, but it was too late to do anything about it. When Bob listened to the songs, his first remark was, "That last song is great! How did you do that?" Jack never told him.

We stayed up all night talking, and Cyrinda didn't come home until early the next morning. It was noon when Jack woke me. He and Chris were eager to have me send the money from Florida, so I called Alissa and instructed her to wire the money. "I'll tell you why when I get home," I assured her.

Chris brought my breakfast, and told me how carrying breakfast to the downstairs apartment reminded her of when Steven Tyler had stayed in the apartment while Jack was working on the last Aerosmith album. Every morning she brought Steven a tray with breakfast, a pen and pad, and a cassette player and tape of the band jamming in the studio the night before. While the band was working on pre-production with Jack, Steven had been in rehab. After he was released, Jack had him stay in the apartment, and Jack recorded the sessions each night for him. Steven spent the next day listening to the grooves and writing lyrics.

Jack told me it usually took a year for Aerosmith to complete an album. The first months were spent without Steven while the band laid down tracks. Later, when Steven listened to the tracks, he wrote the lyrics. Usually, things were not prepared in advance, the way they were in most bands, but everything came together, and it was this spontaneity that made the band so special. Like the day they were working on a new song at Record Plant and they decided to take a break and go to the movies at Times Square. They saw the Mel Brooks movie *Young Frankenstein.*

While walking back to the studio afterwards, Jack started imitating the hunchback character. He bent over, turned his face to the guys and growled, "Walk this way!" Before he knew it, they were all playing hunchbacks, and when they got back to the studio, Jack played the track they were working on, and he sang, "walk this way!" at the hook. Steven started singing it, and a classic Aerosmith song was born. Unfortunately, Jack didn't list himself as co-writer or retain any of the publishing, a prudent move that, had he done it, would have eventually made him a lot of money.

Later in the day we went downtown to see Jack's accountant, Mel Epstein. Like most people Jack associated with, Mel worked for famous stars, especially rock stars. Some of his clients included Peter Gabriel and Woody Allen, who happened to be stepping out of the elevator as we stepped in. The money had arrived and Mel had an agreement drawn up dated April 4, 1983, stating I was personally lending Jack's production company, November Music, fifteen thousand dollars to be paid back in full in three months with 10 percent interest.

That evening, Jack and Chris said they were going upstate to see Jack's parents, and they would be back in the morning. They left me the key to the downstairs apartment. Next to the bed was a promotional copy of a book that was written by a friend of theirs named May Pang. May was known as John Lennon's girlfriend, and she was with John the year he and Yoko were separated, the year the press dubbed Lennon's "Lost Weekend." After suffering awful press accounts that Jack told me were spearheaded by Yoko, May made a deal with Warner's to tell her side of what really happened between John and her. The book was great reading and I fell in love with May Pang.

I waited all day for Jack and Chris to return. Then I waited all the following day. I finished the May Pang book, explored the Museum of Natural History and hung out in Central Park. I loved New York, but was anxious for Jack and Chris to come home.

I called Stan Vincent to tell him I was worried because they were supposed to be back two days prior, but he just laughed and told me this was the usual, that sometimes Jack would be days late to sessions and Stan had to cover for him. I realized Stan was telling me about another side of Jack and Chris that I was just starting to become aware of. I was having a hard time believing what I was hearing, especially what he was saying about Chris.

Stan told me if I planned on hanging out with Jack, I should have as little as possible to do with Chris because she was actually ruining his career. This did not sound like the same Stan who, a few nights ago, couldn't say enough about the Great Jack Douglas, but after all, they already had my fifteen thousand dollars. This gave me a lot to ponder. It seemed Stan hadn't liked me from the beginning, so I theorized that maybe he was just trying to scare me off. When Jack and Chris finally got home, they apologized for being late. I acted like it was all right, even though, I was pissed as hell.

I returned to Florida to find George and Lauren furious at me for lending Jack money to finish the Tin Angel album. They kept asking me, "What about us?" I promised them that soon we would be going into the studio with Jack. Then I had to face Alissa. I told her everything I had learned while in New York, showed her the signed loan agreement and assured her Jack would absolutely pay me back.

CHAPTER 23

Somebody Help Me Now

Three months passed, and the loan was due. Every day George, Lauren and Alissa asked me what was going on, and I couldn't tell them because it was impossible to reach Jack. I called and called, and if lucky, I got Chris, who promised me Jack would call me back that evening. She said Jack really wanted to work with me and told me about all the great things they were doing in New York, but Jack never called back, and I was running out of excuses to give George and Lauren. When I felt I was losing control of the situation, I decided to fly to New York and confront Jack in person.

Chris opened the front door, and to her surprise found a very unhappy me standing on her doorstep. She escorted me upstairs to the bedroom where I found Jack lying in bed with one eye open and one eye half-closed. From his mouth hung a cigarette almost burned to the filter, with a long, curved ash about to fall onto a pile of ashes that had collected on his chest. Cigarette butts lay everywhere, plates with bits of old food were scattered around and magazines and old newspapers covered the floor.

I walked in with my guns loaded. "Jack if you have a problem paying me back, tell me. Don't avoid my calls. If I'm the problem, just pay me and I'm gone. I'm not a groupie and I don't expect to be treated like one." All this came out in one breath.

Jack looked up, the ash fell from the cigarette to his chest and he said half-consciously, "Hey, Ken, howya doin'? What are ya doin' in New York?" When he caught on to what I was saying, he said, "Oh no, I've just been working, and involved with the Yoko lawsuit. I haven't been avoiding you."

Once I was alone in the other room with Chris, she asked me to stay. "Jack really needs you here, especially now. He needs to be with someone from Rockland County . . . see how sick and depressed he is? I'm so glad you're here . . . "

I stayed, and found that as long as I was in New York with Jack and Chris, things appeared to be fine again, and when I was in Florida, I felt helpless with no control of the situation. While I was in New York I didn't have to constantly formulate answers to George, Lauren and especially my wife's unanswerable questions, and not only was I able to better understand Jack and Chris, I was becoming a part of their lives. And learning a lot more about their back story.

Jack had married his childhood sweetheart, Lori, a documentary filmmaker. At the height of their success, Jack and Lori bought a house in an upper class New Jersey neighborhood and had two children. Their lives were straight and regimented, but as Jack's success grew, he fell victim to the spoils of his job. With all the most world-famous recording stars recording at Record Plant, the studio became a haven for drug use, groupies, parties and anything else one could desire. As production budgets grew, so did the spoils. A competitive, successful studio left nothing to the imagination, and an artist was denied nothing.

Jack was famous for going non-stop for days, and he did amazing things with his mixes. To help Jack keep his profitable pace up, cocaine, a standard tool of the profession, was readily available. It was only the product he created that mattered, not how he arrived at it, and he was an innovator and a master producer of his time. The studio became his home, so there was little time left for Lori and the kids. Lori didn't change along with Jack, but instead had contempt for the life he was leading. Their marriage was crumbling, and it was a relief for Jack to accept production jobs in other cities where he was away for weeks or more at a stretch.

Jack met Chris in her hometown of Los Angeles. She managed rock bands and was featured in a *Life* magazine article detailing her work on Robert Kennedy's campaign. She was also leading the rock n' roll lifestyle. From the beginning, Chris was infatuated with Jack and the aura surrounding him, and eventually she became part of Jack's life. Being Jack's girlfriend not only gave Chris free access to the music scene and the best drugs around, it was an outlet to advance her own career.

Drugs played a major role in their relationship. Cocaine was used for work, and heroin was used for play. The fantasy became a reality when Jack left Lori and his children and moved in with Chris.

While I was around, Jack and Chris never had any money. They always had plausible excuses and reasons why they were broke. Besides the lawsuit with Yoko, Chris told me CBS owed Jack over five hundred thousand in back royalties for his Aerosmith productions, but he couldn't get the money until David Krebs, the band's manager at the time, had done an audit of CBS's books. Chris continually asked me for small loans, usually twenty dollars, and occasionally a hundred. Each time she borrowed money she'd say, "Oh, don't worry, when Jack gets his money, he's really gonna take care of you! You've saved our lives," then, in the next breath she would ask me not to tell Jack. After all, it was only twenty dollars!

I became aware of Chris's power over Jack. When the three of us were alone, she strongly voiced her opinions of the people associated with Jack's career. If Jack asked her to stay home when he went to work, she protested until she got to go. At the studio, as soon as Jack was in the control room working, Chris wandered around and manipulated band members, studio personnel or anyone else present. Anyone who desired to work with Jack knew they had to stay on Chris's good side, and that meant playing along with her. It was the people who could not put up with Chris who would abandon Jack.

It wasn't for days, until after a Tin Angel session, that I was able to talk to Jack alone. Jack was mixing a song, supposedly paid for with the money I had loaned him. I had to wait a long time for each opportunity to talk to Jack without Chris being there, and I was worried about the loan, worried about all of the uncounted dollars I had given Chris, and most of all, anxious to get started on the George and Lauren project.

Jack said he could not yet repay the loan, but he knew I was anxious to get started on the project. We decided it was time to bring George and Lauren to New York, and Jack knew of a studio in New Jersey where we could get a good rate. We put together a ten-thousand dollar budget, one that included bringing the band to New York, plus recording costs. Finally, my project was about to be launched, and I ran to the phone to call Florida.

Alissa packed our Datsun station wagon with Brian, Rachel, George,

Lauren, all of George's equipment and Lauren's luggage, and they headed out immediately. When Chris was told we were going into the studio,
she appointed herself consultant. First, she wanted to manage the band.
Next, she said we needed pictures, and, George and Lauren would have to
go shopping for clothes and of course, Lauren had to have a new hairstyle! Jack added that we should use Rod O'Brien as our engineer, who
had worked with Jack on Aerosmith productions and was one of New
York's finest. Chris went on about all of the great New York studio musicians we could get to play on the demo.

"You know, Jack, we need this, and we can't go without that," she would
say, and Jack would pay only half attention to her, but never really said
no. It all sounded good, but I had planned for a budget of ten thousand
dollars, and this sounded quite a bit more elaborate. Plus, I had just
signed George and Lauren to both a publishing and a production contract
and had no desire to approach them with a management contract. I was
scared, but Chris assured me that we had a hit act on our hands, and it
would be a mistake to try and save pennies. I met Alissa and the gang in
Rockland County at the Gurowsky's house. George had never been to
New York. He couldn't get over how beautiful the mountains and woods
were and he freaked out over Skyview, but it was early spring and Lauren
was cold, especially in Alissa's parents' house.

There was no way I could let on to anyone about the real Jack and Chris
(not even to Alissa), a task that would prove very difficult. I took George,
Lauren and Alissa into the city to have a meeting with Jack at a coffee
shop near his house. We arrived early. Three hours later when Jack still
hadn't arrived we decided to leave. On the way to my car, we spotted Jack
ambling down the sidewalk.

"Ken, I'm sorry I missed our meeting. Uh, Chris just found out her
mother has cancer, and she was so upset, there was no way I could leave
her." Everyone felt terrible and assured him they understood, then Jack
and I arranged to meet the following day without George and Lauren,
who needed a day of rest.

Alissa and I got a ride into the city the next day with her sister Susie's
husband, David. This would be the first time Alissa would have the
opportunity to hang out with Jack and Chris, and I was nervous. When
we got to the apartment, there was a note on the door that read, "Ken, had
to go out, will be back soon."

We waited on the stoop for five hours. When they finally showed up, they acted like they were ten minutes late. I'd already been through it and Alissa was catching on quick. When I told Chris I was sorry about her mom, she didn't seem to know exactly what I was talking about. (We later found out that her mother did have cancer, but everyone had known about it for years.) As soon as we went into the apartment, Chris zoomed in on Alissa, and together they decided what Lauren's new look would be and made plans for a photo shoot, while I told Jack I had musician friends from Rockland I'd like to use. Jack told me to set up rehearsals and he would come up to hear the band.

A few days later, I took Lauren into the city to have her hair styled and pictures taken. Lauren was less than anxious to have anyone touch her long blonde hair. She knew Chris was going to try to convince her to cut it. Naturally, Chris picked one of the most expensive salons in New York. As she put it, "This is where all the stars get their hair done." The punk scene was happening and all around Lauren were people with spiked hair, shaved heads or hair the colors of the rainbow. Lauren was nervous, but she did allow the hairdresser to trim the ends and put "a little" curl in it. It turned out to be an outrageous curl. I thought she looked great, but Lauren thought she looked like a French Poodle. While walking down the street, she'd catch her reflection in store windows and look like she was going to cry. When we arrived at the photographer's apartment, she scooted into the bathroom to try and tame down her new hairdo.

When Chris picked, she picked the best. While awaiting Lauren, Bob Gruen showed off files of his work. It seemed he had done photos for just about every known rock artist, but his thickest file was of John and Yoko. Bob showed us pictures he had taken of John and Jack during the *Double Fantasy* sessions. He also told us about the night he took John out to a reggae club in his Volkswagen. At the club, some Jamaican Rastafarians thought John looked familiar but refused to believe he was actually John Lennon. They asked, "What would John Lennon be doing here?" In fact, John loved reggae and was a regular guy who liked to hang out. He would have recorded *Double Fantasy* in Jamaica, had Yoko allowed it. (She was pushing for Nashville but they settled on New York.)

Alissa was now bored of waiting for Jack and Chris, just as she had grown tired of waiting in bars while I played roadie. When driving her and the kids to Kennedy Airport, I felt relieved that she was leaving. We were not even close to getting into the studio and Alissa wasn't aware that half the budget was already spent and going over budget was inevitable.

I put together another killer band. Jimmy Finnen played bass, Matthew Hill (the kid playing football my first day at Skunk) played drums, and Marc Davenport of "Reggaenomics" fame played keyboards. They all knew who Jack was, and probably would have done the sessions for free, but I paid them. Jack was pleasantly surprised when he heard them play. It was obvious from the first note that we would hire them. Pre-production consisted of four rehearsals at The Land in Marc's A-frame studio on top of the mountain. Jack listened to all of George and Lauren's songs and worked with the band on the song arrangements. He picked three songs he wanted to record, including a Spencer Davis remake titled "Somebody Help Me Now."

Jack invited George, Lauren, and me to a private party at Studio 54 celebrating the premiere of a 3-D Aerosmith video. At the party we were introduced to the band, all except Joe Perry who had left the band, but his replacement, a guitar player named Rick Dufay, was there. People had good things to say about Jack, and with him they discussed his case against Yoko. Everyone was given 3-D glasses, and at midnight a giant screen dropped down and the video was played. It must have looked like an outer-space scene, with hundreds of people looking up at a giant screen, wearing big plastic glasses shaped like the Aerosmith logo. Aerosmith's manager had made a deal to show the video nationwide as an opening attraction to the Jaws 3-D movie. The contract must have fallen through, because the video never made it to the big screen.

The next day, six people crammed into my Datsun hatchback and we started on our way to the studio in New Jersey. I was driving and George and Lauren sat next to me up front. Jack, Chris and Rod O'Brien filled the backseat, and all our equipment was stuffed into the rear. As we hurtled down the New Jersey Turnpike the car hit a bump, the hatchback flew open and piles of our stuff flew out all over the highway. The guitars were safe, but everything else was spread out across the pavement. I got off at the next exit, circled back and breathed a sigh of relief when I saw my Echo-plex sitting square in the middle of the lane. It seemed to be in one piece, but it was surrounded with crushed knobs and flattened guitar cords. It was a mess. Chris opened the car door and snatched her flattened purse, and as I approached the Echo-plex with the intent to snag it, a bus went speeding by. We watched in silence as the box disappeared under the bus, then, bits of plastic, metal and wires shot out from under the rear bumper with knobs bouncing off in all directions.

There was nothing to do but laugh at the day's entertainment. George, however, was not in a laughing mood. He had a big problem. He had lost all his special sound effects equipment, including his wah-wah pedal. Jack assured him he would find someone in New York from whom George could borrow the effects he'd need.

Marc, Jimmy and Matthew were at the studio when we arrived. Jack spent his usual hours setting up the drums and microphones to insure he would get his famous sound. Everyone was given headphones, so when Jack spoke from the control room, the band was able to hear his instructions. When Jack was ready, he set up a mike for Lauren to sing a dummy track. Her vocals were not going to be used in the final mix, but would be heard through the headphones to help the musicians while they were playing their parts. Basic tracks are the recordings of the rhythm instruments: bass guitar, drums and rhythm guitar. Lead guitar, keyboards, vocals and solos are called overdubs and are added later. Rod and Jack were impressed with the professionalism of Marc, Matt and Jimmy, and the work progressed smoothly.

Besides music, Jack's other passion were weapons. There were all sorts of military and gun magazines around his apartment and he had a reputation for shooting guns in studios. When the studio assistant, Alan, asked Jack about this, Jack laughed and pulled one of the two guns he carried out of his bag. Alan told Jack if any guns were fired in the studio, he, the assistant, would be fired. This only caused Jack to kid him throughout the day by pulling out one of his guns and acting like he was shooting at things.

In Jack's heyday, while working on an Aerosmith album at Record Plant, Steven Tyler came into the studio holding a Mac 10 semi-automatic machine gun. He let Jack check it out, which he did by shooting several rounds into an elevated drum riser. Then Steven took the gun and continued shooting up the riser until Roy Cicala, the owner, came storming in to see what was going on. To everyone's surprise, Roy grabbed the machine gun and continued shooting into his riser until it came crashing down to the floor.

When a band member took a break, Chris accompanied him to the bar around the corner where she'd tell him how impressed Jack was with his performance, assuring him that Jack would almost certainly be calling regarding future projects. When Matthew's session was done, Chris asked him if he would drive her, in my car, to pick something up. At 2:30 in the morning, Jack and Rod were ready to call it. When Rod realized Chris had not returned, he took a cab back into the city leaving Jack, Lauren, George and me to sit and wait for her. There was no lounge in this studio, just a few couches outside in the hallway. Jack was on one, Lauren on the other and George and I were on the floor. We fell asleep waiting for Chris.

The studio had another session scheduled for 9:00A.M. Alan was hooking up microphones for the three gospel singers who were there to record a jingle for their church. I was the first one to wake up. Waiting up half the night, sleeping the other half on a cold, hard floor and being awakened by gospel singers loudly clearing their throats was an entirely new experience for me.

Jack was the last one to open his eyes. We all looked on as he sat up, opened his bag and pulled out a gun. He walked into the control room and assumed a police stance, pointing the gun at the three women at the microphones in the studio. They smiled back at Jack and kept on singing. Jack held his position until Alan, who was kneeling down to arrange some wires, stood up and saw him. Unlike the smiling ladies, Alan had a very different look on his face. At this moment Chris came wandering in and said, "What did I miss?"

I was out of cash. Chris had taken the last of my money when she went into the city with Matthew. After I dropped everyone off at the apartment, I drove to Canal Street to see Murray Rosenwasser, a neighbor on South Gate Drive when I was growing up. Murray was the guy all the kids loved. He used to take me to basketball games when I was nine years old. You could always depend on Murray. When I told him I was doing a project with Jack Douglas, he said he knew Jack and his wife Lori. Jack had purchased a diamond ring from a public television auction to give to Lori on their anniversary, and he hired Murray to pick up the ring with him, (I assumed to verify its authenticity) and they spent the afternoon together. Murray told me how conservative Jack had been. Jack talked with Murray about how everyone in his business had been into drugs, but he and Lori were straight and avoided the scene. I could not exactly picture that version of Jack.

While cashing a five-thousand dollar check for me, Murray warned me that after Jack broke up with Lori, he gained a bad reputation. I thought, "If only you knew the half of it!" Then I realized Jack's reputation must be worse than I had previously thought if I was hearing about it from Murray the jeweler.

Jack said his friend, Rick Dufay (who seemed friendly enough at the Aerosmith 3-D party), would be happy to lend George his guitar effects. George was looking forward to talking shop with Rick, a fellow guitar player, and thought maybe he would come to the studio with us. George even familiarized himself with his work. While at Jack's apartment, George listened to a solo album Jack had done with Rick called *Tender Loving Abuse*.

Jack gave us the address where Rick lived with his girlfriend Myra, who was in charge of booking parties at Studio 54. We knocked on her door around 7:30 at night. Myra answered the door and told us Rick was sleeping. We explained that Jack had told us it would be all right to borrow some of Rick's equipment, and we relayed some of what had happened to George's effects. She said she would wake up Rick, and closed the door.

A few minutes later, Rick, wearing a blanket, opened the door, glared at us and asked, "What the fuck do you assholes want?"

When I started to explain why we were there, he interrupted with, "I don't give a shit, tell Jack I ain't lending any equipment to a bunch of nobodies!" and he slammed the door in our faces.

We were stunned by his rudeness. Lauren felt belittled, George lost his confidence and I figured out what was meant by tender loving abuse.

Jack borrowed Zebra's effect rack, and George not only regained his confidence, he couldn't wait to get started on his leads. George loved working with Jack. He would ask George to repeat solos over and over, and George would nail it every time, putting more of himself into each take. Jack was a producer who knew what he needed from his artist, and George was determined not to let him down. When the guitar overdubs were finished, Marc came in to finish his keyboard overdubs, and on one of the songs, Jimmy was called in to play his stand-up bass. Watching Jack work was like watching a painter. First, he laid down all of his colors, then the shapes, then he mixed everything up, and all of a sudden a beautiful picture sprung to life.

When Chris heard that I had paid Rod O'Brien fifteen hundred dollars, she decided there was no way Jack was going in on speculation. Jack had every intention of doing the demos without being paid a fee until Chris

147

demanded two grand. Then the studio bill came to more than our initial estimate. Every time I tried to regain some perspective I was bombarded with, "Do you realize what we have on our hands? These songs are hits! Any record company would pay us over two hundred thousand for this stuff! We're getting away so cheap . . . " I bit my lip and tried not to feel any doubt. I figured I had come this far and had already paid more than my fair share of dues, so I picked up the phone and called home. Alissa wired more cash. Everyone had to get paid.

George and I called the raspy, mean growl Lauren had in her voice "the raunch." When it was time for her to do her vocal tracks, there were parts in the song where she was supposed to vamp and growl. This was what George and I had been waiting for. Lauren was going to belt it out and we couldn't wait for Jack to hear it, but no matter how hard Lauren tried, she couldn't get it out. George and I couldn't understand. We kept asking, "The raunch, the raunch, where's the raunch?"

Jack, who had no problem with how Lauren was singing, thought George and I were crazy and the whole thing hysterical. He wanted to find the raunch. He stopped the session and said, "Rod, you look outside and I'll look in the office." Then he turned to us and said, "Give me a good description of what the raunch looks like." From then on, whenever it was Lauren's turn to do vocals, Jack would ask me if she'd found the raunch. Lauren complained that she had caught a cold and begged for one more take. Jack gave her the take and was satisfied. He did a rough mix and made a cassette copy for us to take back to Florida. On the ride home, the more Lauren listened to the tape, the more upset she became. We kept assuring her that what she was listening to was only a rough mix and that Jack's real work would come later when he did the final mix. At this point, I could have used some reassuring myself.

I spent much of the coming year in New York. The time I spent at home was time recuperating from the daily trials and tribulations of Jack and Chris. My perfume business was still going strong, and as long as there was a telephone and Alissa was in Florida, I was still in business, so I took on a new mission. I was determined to straighten out the lives of Jack Douglas and his fiancè Chris.

CHAPTER *24*

Straight Ahead

The time had come to throw Cyrinda Tyler out of the downstairs apartment. Cyrinda was addicted to heroin, and any money she could get her hands on went to dope. Chris was worried about her stealing things from the apartment.

Jack and I were walking down Columbus Avenue several days after Cyrinda had moved out, leaving all of Steven's and her stuff behind. We saw her crying into a pay phone, and she spotted us. She sobbed that her daughter was at a friend's house, but that she herself had no money and no place to go. I couldn't believe this was the famous Steven Tyler's wife. Even if he didn't give a shit about his wife being broke and a drug addict, she was dragging his daughter all over Manhattan and that was something I couldn't get past. Jack felt some pity and responsibility towards Cyrinda, so he took her over to David Krebs' office, the manager of Aerosmith. In the cab on the way over, I gave Cyrinda a hundred bucks. She reached into her bag and handed me a picture of her and Steven and insisted I keep it. Then she thanked me and told me Steven would take care of me when his tour ended—a line that sounded all too familiar.

David was just leaving when we arrived. It seemed the one person he wanted nothing to do with was Cyrinda Tyler. David and Cyrinda had it out right in front of Jack and me. David told her there was no money for her and he couldn't give her a dime. She screamed back that she was broke and had no place to stay. It went on for quite a while. I felt I was hearing something I shouldn't have, but no one seemed to care that I was in the room. I wondered how Steven would react to his manager treating his wife like that . . . or perhaps Steven was calling the shots through David?

Eventually David accepted responsibility for Cyrinda, which allowed Jack and me to leave. Jack mentioned that all of Steven and Cyrinda's clothes and personal stuff could be picked up at the apartment, and David said he would take care of it. That's what I liked to hear—a manager who would take care of things!

A few months later, while Jack was on the road with Aerosmith recording live shows, an eviction notice was served on his apartment. Chris and I were staying there when the notice was nailed to the front door. We rented a truck, and to find help in loading it, I walked down Columbus Avenue and asked a couple of street musicians if they wanted to make a quick fifty. With all the furniture and junk in the apartment, the truck loaded up quickly. David Krebs (the manager who took care of things) must have felt that saving the Tyler's personal possessions was of little importance, for all their stuff was still in the apartment. When I asked Chris if maybe we should do something with it, she told the street musicians that all this stuff belonged to Steven Tyler from Aerosmith, and they could have anything they wanted. I had to fight with the guys to keep a pair of ancient, hand-beaded moccasins that I felt Steven would not want to lose. I was later able to give them back to him in Miami.

We drove the truck to Jack's parents' house in upstate New York, about two hours north of the city. His parents' house was full of pictures of Jack, ranging from baby pictures to pictures of Jack working in the studio with John Lennon. In addition to Jack's mother and father, Blake, Chris and Jack's five-year-old son lived there, and he looked exactly like Jack. Chris had told me that when Lennon was killed, she and Jack were so shattered that they couldn't take care of Blake, who was a baby at the time. They brought him upstate to Jack's parents, where he was welcomed and cared for. Chris said she couldn't wait to get the money from the Yoko Ono case because then she and Jack were going to buy a house and take back their son.

I knew Jack was distraught about the situation. Not only did he lose custody of his first two children, now, due to the circumstances, he was unable to care for Blake. Jack was smart enough to put Blake's interests first, so for the time being Blake stayed with his grandparents.

Doing business with Jack as a partner was not easy. I was there to shop the Lauren Smokin (Lauren's real last name was Smolkin) tape, but for one reason or another something always interfered, like Jack's road trips with Aerosmith that left me in New York with Chris for weeks at a time.

I became active in Jack's business affairs. Stan Vincent's only interest was the lawsuit; as far as he was concerned, Jack was a has-been, and he wanted as little to do with him as possible. He definitely didn't want to have anything to do with Chris, so he avoided becoming involved in their personal lives. Chris and I developed a special camaraderie. As negative as people were about her, I felt quite the opposite. She may have been crafty and incorrigible, but she had brains. Many people find people like Chris unsettling, but she was the first person I had ever met whose method was more madness than mine was, and at times when I felt like giving it all up, she was the only one behind me, always pushing me on. I was just establishing my career, and starting out with a producer like Jack was no small feat. Now all I had to do was finish the demo and play it for the record companies.

Atlantic Records showed an early interest in The Lauren Smokin Band. Jason Flom, from their A&R department, came to the studio in New Jersey to hear what we had recorded thus far. Jason gave us, and especially Lauren, the impression he was interested in signing her.

He also told me Atlantic had the power to make hit records, even if the artist sucked. He told us how Laura Branigan (she sang that obnoxious song "Gloria!") got signed. She started out with the A&R department, I suppose with guys like Jason. He said no one took her seriously, but she was "a lot of fun." The head of the A&R department finally signed her and she continued to work her way up the Atlantic bedroom ladder until one day a top exec walked her into Ahmet Ertegun's office. Ertegun, a short, balding gentleman is known as the founder of Atlantic Records. He got his start selling jazz records out of the trunk of his car in the 1930s and '40s, and utilizing his street smarts, he constructed one of the most powerful music companies of his time. Laura Branigan became known as Ahmet's girl. When she was unable to make a hit record, Ahmet called a meeting and threatened to fire the whole staff if they couldn't produce her a hit. The best writers, arrangers and producers were called in. Jason concluded by telling me Branigan eventually married one of Ahmet's attorneys, but she still saw Ahmet around the office, even though their relationship was hush-hush. After hearing this story, I wondered what Jason was trying to tell me—that if Lauren slept with him, it would start the ball rolling? Jason did everything to impress Lauren. She thought he looked like a kid playing the part of a man, and besides, she would say, "He has no chin!" George couldn't stand him. We later found out that Jason's father was an attorney for Warner, Atlantic's parent company.

When Jason heard we were from Miami, he introduced Jack and me to one of his best friends from the town, a cocaine dealer I'll call Mr. C. This guy had all the trappings of a big-time dealer; huge home, Mercedes-Benz, four-wheel-drive Jeep, speedboat and an assortment of guns, mostly machine guns. Mrs. C. looked like Michelle Pfeiffer when she played Al Pacino's wife in *Scarface*. Mr. C. split his time between New York and Miami, spending a lot of time at Atlantic where he was well known, even sitting in on staff meetings with Jason.

We spent a lot of time at Atlantic, and we occasionally ran into Zebra's manager, Mark Puma. Mark, in his twenties, had a good reputation. He looked sharp, handled himself professionally, and most importantly, he didn't snort coke. Mark was also managing the once unknown band named Twisted Sister who had been turned down by every label, including Atlantic. Twisted Sister went to Europe where they became a huge success and were signed by an Atlantic affiliate overseas. When they came back to the states, Atlantic signed them. Getting a record deal this way was called *coming in the back door*.

Twisted Sister received huge financial support from Atlantic, and their record was rocketing up the charts. Jack hoped Mark would use his success with Twisted Sister to help influence support for the newly released Zebra album, while I hoped a successful Zebra album would help get The Lauren Smokin Band onto Atlantic.

I was still spending a lot of money on Jack and Chris. I tried to justify what I was doing by telling myself that Jack was due for a big comeback, and I wanted to be there when it happened—but it was no wonder Jack had such a terrible reputation. He was late for meetings, went over budget, and gossip pegged him a cocaine and heroin addict. This didn't matter to me. I knew a lot of artists with the same reputation who had still made big comebacks. There was no reason Jack couldn't do the same.

Back in Miami, George and Lauren were getting impatient. Jason Flom had been to a Zebra show in Miami and he took Lauren with him to the Tampa show. He desperately tried to sleep with her. She didn't give in and slept in a separate room, yet Jason managed to corrupt her in other ways. Jason implied to Lauren that Jack and I weren't working hard enough for her, and Lauren, who should have known better, took what Jason said as fact. My whole life revolved around obtaining George and Lauren a record deal. If Lauren thought the record company was trying to get her to lose me so they could have her all to themselves, she was wrong. Record companies didn't want to deal with an artist's daily problems. They preferred to have guys like me, to handle it for them.

I had shopped George and Lauren to all the record companies, and when letters started coming in informing me that The Lauren Smokin Band wasn't right for them (*but please keep us in mind for any future projects*), I had no intention of admitting failure. Everyone, from Alissa, Brian and Rachel to our families were pulling for me. I couldn't see letting them down, and, I still had Jack's career to work on. As my relationship with George and Lauren became strained, Jack and Chris started to lose interest in them too, preferring that I concentrate more on Jack's career and less on Lauren's.

Jack's was again receiving quarterly royalty checks for Aerosmith, enough for him and Chris to rent an apartment on West 72nd Street, but when his phone got turned off for non-payment we sat in his accountant's office and used his phone to schedule our meetings. One time, while I was on the phone, Jack drew pictures of The Lauren Smokin Band, showing George with one leg or Lauren with one arm, and we laughed hysterically like two children. After a while everything seemed funny.

I was getting low on cash, and I didn't have enough money to buy perfume deals. My parents lent me money by borrowing against their house and I gave them 10 percent of the profits. Over a year had passed since I had been in the studio. Alissa became frustrated and couldn't understand my relationship with Jack and Chris. I tried to explain to her that they not only needed me, but they were also like family and there were too many ties between us to sever the relationship. They had both promised me that when the Yoko case was settled, we were going to start a perfume import-export company, and I was going to manage Jack's career and his money. Alissa, on the other hand, said, "When Jack gets his money, he's going to forget your name."

CHAPTER 25

It's Over Now

Brian and Rachel attended public elementary school. Rachel did great in school, and had the easy, friendly personality she displayed as a baby, but Brian still had the demanding, curious ways that made caring for him exhausting. He also seemed to have difficulties in school with his so-called behavior. He was poor in reading and couldn't spell simple words, even in the third grade. We were baffled. We couldn't figure out why his teachers didn't recognize how intelligent Brian was, and our once-confident child suddenly began to think of himself as quite stupid. We hunted around until we found a private school with an unstructured curriculum; it looked more like a ranch than a school, with horses and barns and surrounding fields. Brian loved school all of a sudden, but private schools cost a lot of money.

I needed advice, therapy and money so I put Jack on the back burner and turned to good ole' Ross. Ross Cosmetics had grown tremendously. He was manufacturing his own line of cosmetics and facial creams, but was still selling hundreds of closeouts. He moved his warehouse to a building a block long, and then he bought the block. Ross was amused by my stories, even if he didn't have any great advice or insights to offer me, but he did ask me if I was ready to go back to work. I immediately took him up on the offer, as it would help keep me in Florida for a little while and that would certainly help my relationship at home. Ross Cosmetics had just gone public, and he needed to ship a lot of merchandise to make it appear as if he were making huge sales. In a few weeks the trucks were rumbling and the boxes flowing and I was once again selling cosmetics, this time from my rented house in North Miami. I did a lot of advertising. Flea market dealers, jobbers and other wholesalers came to the house and bought cash and carry. I rarely had to go out on a sale or make a delivery. Alissa had time to work while the kids were in school, and our time together, both personal and business was a happy time.

One of my customers was a shy and lonely flea marketer named Mike Varanci. Mike was most impressed that I had gotten my start at a flea market so he came over to the house on a regular basis. He became a close friend of ours, and always offered to lend a hand moving boxes around or packing orders. Ross's shipments arrived regularly and there was always something to do. In a couple of months I needed a warehouse, so when it came time to move I asked Mike if he wanted a job.

Finding a warehouse was easy. Conveniently located, less than one mile from our house, was a small warehouse complex in a wooded area along I-95. Like my first warehouse, the buildings were constructed of cement block with an office in front and a big roll-up door next to the office door. We took the last warehouse on the row because it had built-in shelves that were perfect for boxes of perfumes.

We installed an alarm system and I ventured out to get insurance. I found that insurance companies didn't like the risk of insuring a big-inventory business like mine, and after being turned down repeatedly, I went to the agent who sold me my car insurance. The company was called United Casualty and they were more than willing to insure me. Things were going well—in no time at all we were selling to what seemed like everyone around town. Flea marketers and storeowners kept me busy, but the real money was made selling to the wholesalers and department stores by contacting them over the phone. Alissa worked the showroom, I worked out of the office just behind it and Mike did the packing and shipping in the back. We played rock n' roll music throughout the day, poked fun at customers, and had such a good time it didn't feel like we were working. At 3:00, Alissa went home to care for the kids and I drove the Reggae Rockers truck home later.

Mike told us he lived with his Uncle Sonny and invited Alissa and me to a party on his uncle's boat. Knowing Mike had family in Florida made me that much more at ease with him, as he was in control of what went in and out of the warehouse. His counts were always perfect. Customers never had to call up complaining of missing items in their orders, and by having Mike in control in the warehouse, I was able to concentrate on expanding the business.

The day before the party, Mike told us his uncle was involved in the Mafia. We didn't quite know how to take this information, as Mike was the last person I would expect to have Mafia ties. We remembered our adventure with Pete Scarpachi and wondered what was in store for us this time.

Uncle Sonny was all we expected, and more. He had a crew of tough, young characters working for him on his seventy-foot yacht. There were about twenty-five guests assembled on the lower deck, and they were drinking champagne and eating lobsters and crab legs served to them by girls sporting skimpy bikinis. Sonny sat in a big lounge chair on the upper deck, and Mike stood next to him, steering the yacht up the intra-coastal waterway. When Sonny wished to speak to a guest, he sent one of his boys down to escort that person upstairs. No boat in sight compared to Sonny's boat.

It was my turn to be introduced to Sonny. I felt the effects of the alcohol as I climbed the stairs. Sonny directed me to sit down in the chair next to him.

"So, Mike tells me you are in the perfume business. I think I can help you out. I'll be down to see you during the week." I complimented him on his yacht and thanked him for inviting us. It was a cordial meeting, and because of Sonny's regal looks, I felt like I had just met the Godfather. It was now hard to think of Mike as the same old Mike, but business went on as usual.

When Sonny paid his visit, two gentlemen accompanied him. The first man had a pockmarked face and looked like the leading man in a B prison movie; the other was an elderly man crouched over a cane. Sonny called the older man Uncle Sallie. It seemed everyone had an uncle.

While Uncle Sonny and Uncle Sallie asked me questions about my business, Mike and Mr. Sing-Sing went on a tour of the place. When I walked into the warehouse they were staring up at the roof. Mr. Sing-Sing said, "You know, you need more security in here."

I disagreed. "You know how hard it would be to get into this place?" They both laughed.

Before they left, Sonny said he would make some phone calls and get back to me. I didn't know what he meant by that and he left me with an unsettled feeling.

A few weeks later, Alissa, the kids and I were visiting my parents who had bought a condominium on Ft. Lauderdale Beach. While walking on the beach we heard an explosion. A speedboat, not too far out, was on fire. Within minutes an injured man was carried to shore. A huge crowd of people had gathered around and an ambulance sped away. We watched the scene from afar. On the local news that night we watched coverage of the incident. They showed the injured man's face as he was lifted into the ambulance. It was Mr. Sing-Sing.

Monday morning, Mike told us what had happened. The owner of the boat needed to get rid of the boat so he could collect on the insurance policy. An accidental fire was supposed to burn the boat up, but the plan had gone a little too well. The boat wasn't supposed to have exploded the way it did, putting Mr. Sing-Sing in the hospital. Mike said it was all right, because when someone got hurt they were paid a bonus. Listening to him, I experienced the same eerie feeling I had when Sonny had paid me his visit. I began to wonder why Mike was working for me, so I asked him. He replied that it wasn't for the money; he just dug Alissa and me.

When Mr. Sing-Sing got out of the hospital Mike brought him to work. The left side of his face was scarred from the fire, adding to the bad boy image he so proudly portrayed. Before leaving work that day, Mike asked me if he could borrow my truck. It was still loaded with empty boxes from a delivery, but they said they would drop them off at the dump for me. There wasn't any reason I could think of not to let them borrow it, so I stood and watched as Mike and Mr. Sing-Sing drove away in my psychedelic Reggae Rockers truck.

The next morning when Alissa and I arrived at the warehouse and opened the door, the alarm didn't beep as usual. We turned on the light and saw that the alarm panel had been ripped clean off the wall. I was shaking as I walked through the showroom and office and into the warehouse. It was always pitch-black in the warehouse until you switched on the lights, but this morning, bright rays of sunshine flooded the room, streaming in from a giant hole that had been chopped through the back wall. Almost all of the expensive perfumes were gone, and there was a trail of bottles on the floor that led from the shelves to the hole, and then outside and around the side of the building. I was confused and started to panic. Alissa tried to calm me down, then went next door to call the police.

Mike was due in at 11:30. We both suspected he had something to do with the break-in and we were furious. To top it off, we had lent him our truck, which he probably used to rob us. When Mike arrived, the police and detectives questioned him and included him in their report. He seemed shocked about the theft, and cooperated with the police, but it seemed there was no way to prove that he, or anyone else, had committed the crime. There were no fingerprints or any other evidence. The alarm wire had been cut from outside on the telephone pole. It made little sense to me to invent a monitoring system that could be disarmed by cutting a wire behind the building. It was a detail that the salesman just forgot to let me in on.

The insurance company arrived next. Three guys who looked like detectives walked around conversing among themselves in Spanish, and I had no idea what they were saying. Within a week, I received two letters from Universal Casualty. The first letter informed me that I didn't in fact have a hundred thousand dollar policy, as I thought, and the second letter told me my claim was denied! A few days later Universal Casualty went bankrupt. It was a company that sold car insurance cheaper than all the other companies, and when one of the partners absconded to South America with millions of dollars, the company went bust. I later found out that my policy was the only commercial policy the company had ever written.

Uncle Sonny called a friend of his who was in the insurance business in New York. They put me in touch with a Florida attorney who offered to sue the company in an effort to get them to pay up. We found out the government had taken over the responsibility of paying their claims, so I stood a chance to be reimbursed. For the next month it seemed like Mike, Sonny and their friends were in control of my life. They even knew the certified adjuster who was hired to count the remaining inventory. I couldn't move any merchandise to my house and get back in business until every bottle and eye pencil had been counted.

When the counting was completed, it was determined that I had lost about one hundred forty thousand dollars worth of merchandise. A third of that was on consignment from Ross, and the agent said that the policy did not cover merchandise that was on consignment. After many depositions and a letter-writing contest between my attorney and Universal Casualty, a settlement was reached. FIGA, a government agency that covered bankrupt insurance companies, paid the claim, with my attorney receiving one third, and Ross getting the balance, leaving me with a loss.

Ross and I decided to give business another try. Ross took out his own insurance policy to insure his goods, and I attempted to buy new insurance for mine. Amidst this, I was invited for another cruise on the yacht. Mike said Sonny had a business proposition for me. My first thought was that Sonny either wanted to take over my business or wanted me to work for his organization. Either way, I was prepared to tell him that I was out of the arm-breaking business.

On the boat I was introduced to Freddie, who I was told was an ex-keyboard player from the band Chicago. Sonny asked me for a favor. He told me Freddie had an idea, and he and a few investors were backing it. He wanted me to get Jack Douglas to work for Freddie.

Freddie's idea was to assemble a singing group consisting of wholesome American kids, between the ages of fourteen to seventeen, to be called Kids. He had a television network interested in a Saturday morning television cartoon, and had lined up possible sponsors, including Kellogg's and Pepsi. Phase one of the project was to audition the singers, and the second would be to record the album. Freddie had already composed the songs and they were great. Not only did I like the idea, I couldn't wait to call Jack to tell him I landed a well-paying gig with the potential for a long-running success. This was just the break I had been waiting for—after Jack successfully launched Kids, it would be easy for me to line up other production jobs for him.

Jack was still waiting for trial, but Yoko kept postponing the trial date. Freddie and I flew to New York to fill Jack in on the details. Jack agreed to produce the album for his standard seventy-five thousand dollar fee. It was agreed I would receive a 25 percent management fee. In New York, I stayed one night at Freddie's apartment. Jack had lent me his Gold Studio 54 card and I took Freddie out to the club. The next morning, I couldn't find my wallet, which I thought I'd left on the table next to the couch where I had slept. After searching the apartment, Freddie found it in the bathroom. All of my money and identification was still in it. Everything except Jack's Gold Studio 54 card.

I returned to Miami to continue my perfume business. I found a new insurance company that agreed to insure me. The only stipulation was that I needed to install an alarm with an isolated phone line that, when cut, would activate the system and alert the police. I contracted with Honeywell to install the alarm, and they said it would take thirty days. Meanwhile, they would install a temporary alarm similar to the first one.

I submitted the Honeywell contract to the insurance company and they agreed to insure me. It was an expensive policy, but I wasn't about to stock any merchandise in the warehouse until I was fully insured.

Ross resumed sending down shipments. When I told him many of the items were junk, like the thousands of dozens of fluorescent nail polishes, he told me "Don't worry. Just keep it there." I put the boxes on the shelves and forgot about them. I was more concerned with the arrival of a large shipment of expensive perfumes that would put me back in business.

Jack flew in to help Freddie audition and pick the models for Kids. Hundreds of applicants were interviewed, and each one sang a song. Jack was staying at the house, and the auditions were held at TK Records. At this point, Mike took on a heavy-handed attitude toward me. First, he came to the house and said, "Sonny doesn't like your Jack Douglas; he hears he does a lot of drugs." Then he wanted me to reduce Jack's fee to half, completely disregarding our signed production contract. Jack had already been given a small advance and expense monies, and was to receive the balance of the first 50 percent before the album was started. The final payment would be made once the album was completed, and I had not yet received a penny.

As I expected, Jack was furious. At the same time, Mike was now telling me I owed Sonny this favor. Freddie didn't like my being involved, and thought if he had Jack to himself he could persuade him to reduce his fee. One morning, Mike, who was no longer working for me, came into my office and said, "Sonny doesn't want you to come to the studio any-more, and he wants Jack to stay with Freddie in his hotel room." Mike also told me Sonny wanted me to be more involved with my other busi-ness, which sounded more like, "Sell perfumes and stay away from Jack." Mike spent a few hours at the warehouse and was there when the ship-ment of expensive perfumes arrived from overseas.

In the morning I went to work as usual, and was confronted with deja vu. During the night I had been robbed. Same scenario; the hole in the back wall was in the same spot, except this time it was new concrete lying in chunks all over the floor. The alarm wire had been cut and the panel was ripped from the wall. There were big spaces on the shelves where the night before big boxes of perfumes had sat. All the new ship-ment was gone, although the thieves did leave the load of fluorescent nail polishes.

I was horrified. I didn't know who was robbing me or why. A million scenarios flashed through my mind. The most obvious scenario was that Mike's gangster uncle was either trying to put me out of business or muscle in on what I was doing. Then I thought it could have been Freddie who arranged this with Sonny. I thought maybe they were trying to weaken me and get me away from Jack, and I even suspected my competitors and my neighbors. I was paranoid, and everyone was suspect.

The insurance company declined my claim, saying the policy was not yet in effect because the new alarm had not been installed. After a lot of panicking and a little thought, I hired the same lawyer who settled my first loss. This time, the claim was settled for less than the actual loss and the attorney took a third. Ross had his separate insurance policy to cover his goods, so paying him wasn't an issue, but he no longer was interested in doing business with me. He came to Florida, and Alissa and I stood in the parking lot and watched as the last of his goods were carted out of my warehouse and loaded into a truck.

We reminisced about the morning, not so long ago, when we received two deliveries—a new baby, and then our first truck bulging with boxes of opportunity. Life held so much promise; we could never have imagined in our wildest dreams things could go this wrong. As we watched the truck drive away with the last remnants of our cosmetic business, we wondered how, where and why it all went wrong. There was no going back to fix things, and for the first time in my life I faced the future without a plan. More than losing my business, I was saddened by the loss of hope.

So, I took stock. I had lost a successful wholesale company, but I still had a production company and two publishing companies. Kids was a disaster, and going back into the cosmetic business was not an option, so I decided I would step in as Jack's personal manager. My first move was to get Jack back in the studio. I arranged for George and Lauren to record some tunes for Atlantic, who agreed to provide one of their studios free of charge, but George told me they were not sure if they were ready to go into the studio again. I surmised they were in the midst of negotiations for a production deal elsewhere; the Atlantic opportunity soon passed.

Jack was hired to record Zebra's second album. I was staying at his apartment and things were pretty much exactly as I had left them. Any money Jack received from Aerosmith royalties or the Zebra advance vanished immediately. Managing money was never one of Jack's or Chris's talents.

Jack was making a conscious effort not to arrive late to Zebra sessions or create any havoc. In the past, when Jack was producing one of his classic albums, he never worried about being on time or going over budget, but now the labels preferred that producers save pennies rather than be creative. Jack was aware the industry was changing. The suits that were in control were no longer interested in guys like Jack. They brought in younger producers who would copy Jack's work, leaving little originality in their sounds, but were always on time and precise with their budgets. A lot of new groups appeared who looked and sounded like Aerosmith clones, but Jack was never called in to produce any of these groups.

CHAPTER 26

Jack and the John Lennon Sessions: The Aftermath

John's untimely death had left Jack a cripple. Chris was there to comfort him and together they drowned their misery in drugs, but what was also unbelievable to Jack were the events that followed John's death: Yoko refused to pay Jack his 4 percent royalty as per their production agreement. Jack knew Yoko didn't need his money. So why was she trying to worm out of paying Jack his fee?

During the making of *Double Fantasy*, Jack and John had become very close. Jack used to tell me it was like John had been reborn. John was happy to be forty years old and to be working again. He was becoming independent of Yoko, and no matter how hard she tried, she was losing control of him. Yoko constantly threatened Jack that he had better stop taking John out at night, and she wanted to know everything that happened when she wasn't there. Little did she know that Chris was setting John up with beautiful models and actresses (one of them being Goldie Hawn). Yoko was also unaware that as John regained his confidence, he was speaking openly about leaving Yoko.

Now John was dead, Yoko was in control, and unfortunately for Jack, she was making his life miserable. She claimed that Stan Vincent somehow tricked John and her into signing the production contract; that instead of Jack receiving a straight 4 percent of sales, his standard producers cut, Jack was entitled to a mere 4 percent of the Lennon's 18 percent share. This would have left Jack with only pennies per each album sold.

I was told about a heated affair Yoko was having with the Dakota carpenter, a guy named Sam. John had not cared too much about it, as he was already talking about leaving Yoko and he was having the time of his life working and playing with Jack. I was always amazed when I was told about the real John and Yoko. Believing news stories, like most, I pictured John at home, happily baking bread, while Yoko bravely strode off to work each day to support her happy family. It was hard, at first, to believe the awful truth about the abuse John suffered at the hands of his wife, but after being around so many people who knew John intimately, it had to be true.

I was told that shortly after John died, Yoko ran off with Sam, to Hungary as I recall, where they secretly got married. John Lennon dies and Yoko runs away to marry the Dakota carpenter. I wondered how that never made headlines.

If all this were true—had Yoko known John was aware of her affair, and that he was becoming an independent man again and thinking about leaving her—the timing of his death would have had to be in her best interest. With John dead she became owner of the bulk of their huge estate. Had John not died, and had he divorced her, she could have lost her wealth, power, and fame.

Jack was about to meet Yoko on the battlefield. He was in the studio working on the second Zebra album when the trial started. Yoko tried to avoid appearing in court by having her lawyers appear on her behalf. She went so far as to fly to England when the trial was about to start for the purpose of dedicating a park in honor of John's memory. This angered the judge, and he told Yoko's lawyers that if she wasn't in front of his bench personally on Monday morning, he was going to award Mr. Douglas everything he asked for.

I was in New York for the first few days of the trial. Jack told me about one particular day after court when Yoko's lawyers invited him to the Dakota to talk about settling the case. He was told to come alone. Yoko and Sam met him inside the apartment. Yoko explained to Jack that she didn't want to fight him; that together there was so much unfinished work for Jack and her to complete. Then Yoko asked Jack to follow her to another room where some people were waiting to talk to him. She led him into a room where her lawyers were assembled.

They made a proposal. If Jack agreed to take a sum of cash (Jack was led to believe it was upwards of one million dollars), they would announce publicly that they had agreed to settle the case for one hundred thousand dollars. Jack would receive the bulk of the cash secretly, meaning he would only have to pay his lawyers their share of the lesser amount. Jack didn't want to rip off his lawyers. He refused their offer and was escorted out the door.

The next morning in the judge's chambers, Yoko's lawyers told the judge that they tried reasonably to settle the case, but when Jack arrived at the Dakota he was drunk and all drugged up. They implied Jack had made a scene and was violent. The judge reprimanded the lawyers. He said that after seeing Mr. Douglas in court day after day, he found it hard to believe he would behave in that manner. Yoko was furious at the judge. A short time afterwards, the judge was at a party where he opened a bottle of champagne. The cork hit him in the eye, blinding him, and a new judge was appointed to take over the case.

The trial seemed as if it would drag on forever, so I flew home. One morning a few weeks later, after Alissa sent the kids off to school, she turned on the television to watch *CNN Headline News*. The first story the newscaster announced was about Yoko Ono losing a case brought against her by record producer Jack Douglas. Mr. Douglas was awarded three-and-a-half million dollars. Alissa woke me up and we watched the story repeated on the following news cycle. Jack had won, and finally, the waiting and the hoping were over! Everything would be all right.

When I returned to New York, a lot of new people were hanging around. Jack was in the limelight again, and people who had avoided Jack and Chris before the trial, had mysteriously re-appeared. Rick Dufay, the guy who gave us a hard time when we needed to borrow guitar effects, was one of many who couldn't wait to help Jack spend his money. Jack owed me almost forty thousand dollars—that I could account for—and he promised that as soon as Yoko's check cleared, he would pay me. There were plenty of uncounted dollars, but I wasn't worried.

Alissa and I agreed we wanted Brian and Rachel to grow up in a house of their own, to be able to keep the same friends and go through high school without always worrying about moving from one rented house to another. Alissa and I had grown up that way and we wanted our kids to experience the same security. Now that Jack would be paying me all the money he owed me, Alissa and I went house hunting. We found a gorgeous four-bedroom, three-bath house with a sparkling blue swimming pool on a grassy acre full of orange trees. After looking at what seemed like hundreds of houses, we both knew from the moment we pulled into the driveway we had found a real home for us and the kids. The down payment was a whopping seventy-five thousand, but with my insurance settlement plus the money Jack would soon pay me, we could afford it, so with great excitement we paid a deposit and signed the contract.

CHAPTER 27

Sex Twins and Rock n' Roll

I had just returned to Florida from New York after meeting with Jack. He had said that the Yoko money should come any day. Alissa and I were celebrating at our favorite spot, The Button South nightclub. We were feeling damn good about life. We anticipated living in our new house with the kids and shared our pride in Brian and Rachel, who were growing more beautiful each and every day. I told Alissa I planned to manage Jack's money and career and that things were coming around for us. We agreed I would continue to work with Jack, and concentrate on established artists, not those whose rent we end up paying when they're broke. At around 10 P.M. we decided to leave. When we got outside, I realized I had left my cigarettes on our table. As fate would have it, I went back inside to get them.

I entered the club just as a new band was beginning their set. When I walked past the stage I couldn't help but notice the attractive, redheaded lead singer. What caught my attention most was her outfit—a sexy, extremely low-cut leotard, black lace tights with holes cut out exposing creamy skin, a thin shawl, wide studded belt and rhinestone high heels. The audience clapped and cheered as she belted out a popular top 40 tune. As I turned and picked my cigarettes off the table, I looked up and saw that she was now at the other end of the huge stage. This seemed peculiar because I had only taken my eyes off her for a second. I blamed it on the liquor and again fixed my eyes on this wild woman rocker. Then I glanced back to the other side of the stage and there she was again, singing as before! She wasn't that fast, and I wasn't that drunk.

On the stage were twins. Identically clad redheaded twins, singing and dancing in unison . . . it was too much! I ran outside and got Alissa. We stood and watched in awe for forty-five minutes as the girls got nasty, tearing at each other's clothes and whipping the wall of guys in front of the stage into a frenzy. The beautiful twins sang, danced and slithered around, making sexual gestures at each other and the audience. They would lie on the stage and entwine themselves, then pull each other up by fistfuls of thick red locks. The band was as hardcore as the girls, and with two screaming guitar players, they had a psychedelic edge to their sound. When the set ended, Alissa and I did not need to speak. We tele- pathically knew what the other was thinking.

I assumed the band would be elated as I approached them to tell them who I was and what I could do for them. One of the girls stood by the edge of the stage talking to her entourage of male groupies, so I made my way through the crowd and stood in front of her; she looked as good as when she was performing. When I managed to get her attention, I told her I had really enjoyed the show and that I worked with a producer in New York who might be interested in hearing their demo. She told me to go talk to her soundman, "the guy in the sound booth that looks like Ron Wood." She was anxious to lose me and return to her admirers.

At twenty-three years of age, Pam and Paula Mattioli, the hard-rock- ing, sexy twins of Gypsy Queen, had more than paid their dues. They grew up in Buffalo, New York, the daughters of a police officer and a top- less dancer. At the age of fifteen, the sisters packed a suitcase and head- ed south. They landed in Daytona Beach, Florida where they learned the reality of street life working at clubs and hanging around with bikers. Paula was the first to harden as the result of her drug abuse. Pam was the naïve one, and more interested in clothes and make-up.

They did share the desire to be loved by rock n' roll boys, and fanta- sized about being rock n' roll stars. Their first gig was singing with a local black band, not singing Led Zeppelin and Aerosmith tunes as they had hoped, but singing top 40 funk tunes. The lead guitarist tried to pimp the girls, and a motorcycle gang tried to purchase them for four thousand dollars. Pam and Paula ran from Daytona to Miami where they worked as waitresses or hotel maids. They sang with other musicians' bands and they did some session work for TK Records. Then they sought out the musicians who would become Gypsy Queen.

It was easy for them to find willing players. A good lover was just as important as a good guitar player; Pam's boyfriend, Augie Treto, became their bass player and Paula's boyfriend, Pedro Riera, was an equally gifted guitarist. Bryan LeMar was brought in to play second guitar after Pam broke up with Augie and became Bryan's lover. It was a family-style band except for Jay on drums. I never heard who he slept with to get the part.

Gypsy Queen composed their own material with the hope their originality would lead them to a recording contract and stardom. Like most rockers, they dreamed about money, fame and power, but the reality was, in order to keep the rent paid and the band together, they had to play top 40 hits at local clubs. To keep the dream alive they wrote lyrics and composed songs in their spare time. Paula and Pedro were the most prolific writing team, but Pam and Augie contributed their fair share.

The girls were accustomed to men propositioning them. It was a familiar scene—some guy would approach them after a show and tell them he was in the business and he had the power to make them stars. The girls had heard it all before. I made my way to the sound booth where I found the Ron Wood clone. Actually, he looked more like a Ron Wood skeleton, deathly pale with spiked black hair. Augie gave me the phone number of their manager in Orlando. No one in the band knew or cared who Jack Douglas was, and I realized it would be difficult to obtain a tape, so I took it upon myself to make my own.

I arrived the next night armed with my video camera and filmed the band's performance. After the set they invited me backstage. Instead of demanding that I hand over the tape, the girls wanted to talk to me. I told them I was going to take the video to New York to play it for Jack Douglas. They had heard of the groups Jack had produced, of course, but could not believe it was that easy. Paula said, "You're a nice guy, but you shouldn't go around telling people things like that," and Pam said, "God, if only it were true!"

Augie told me that after the gig I could follow the twins home and pick up a cassette of their original music to bring to New York. When the last set ended, I waited outside the dressing room. Pam yelled that she wasn't going home, and Paula yelled that she wasn't going to let some strange guy follow her home. I was tempted to say, "Fuck it," but I had an airline flight in the morning and already had told Jack that I had a surprise for him.

169

Paula finally agreed to have me follow her to their apartment, and I waited in the parking lot while she went to get the tape. Before she went up she said, "My boyfriend is in the apartment," and then paused a moment to make sure the message had sunk in. By the time she returned with a tape, the first rays of dawn were brightening the top floors of the apartment buildings and it was almost time for Alissa to drive me to the airport.

Jack and Chris were awaiting my arrival. When we got to their apartment Chris said, "Now Ken, please tell us it's not another band." A smile slowly crept across my face and Jack knew it was another band. Before I let the cat out of the bag, Jack implored, "Well, at least tell us it isn't another female singer!"

"Uh, well, no, it isn't *a* female singer," I said, and Jack responded "Good!"

"It's double female singers!"—And I played the video.

Jack and Chris laughed as they watched the twins' antics on stage, especially when they grabbed bottles of beer from guys in the audience and sprayed it all over each other. Chris, who had spent months convincing me to forget about Lauren and instead concentrate on Jack's career, thought the band was great and was already talking about the girls' haircuts. Jack kept rewinding the tape to the beer fight and wondered how hard Pam was really pulling Paula's hair. After he'd seen the performance it was hard to get a serious response out of him.

The next morning Jack sat on his living room floor and spent hours listening to all the songs on the cassette. It was a self-produced, four-track homemade demo. Jack preferred to listen to homemade demos. He always said, "A good song is a good song. You can recognize good songwriting even if it's played out of a paper bag." It was his job to do the producing and all he was interested in was the song, and whether the band could play in time.

Jack knew how excited I was. After he finished listening to the tape, he gave me the go-ahead. I was to arrange for the girls to fly up to New York and meet him. Chris was worried about the girls hitting on Jack. She told me that all the girls who worked with Jack wanted to fuck him; she cited Patti Smith as an example. Jack had to reassure her that he made it a rule not to get involved with his female artists, and I personally never saw him with another woman.

Paula, Pedro and Augie were at the apartment when I called with the good news. Augie answered the phone. He had recently been hospitalized with complaints of stiffness in his skin and joints, so he couldn't play his bass, forcing the band to replace him. Joey was young and hot-looking, qualifications that were sure to win the twins' votes, if not more. It was Augie's desire to remain a part of Gypsy Queen which got him out of the hospital. He had been diagnosed with scleroderma, a terminal disease that hardens the connective tissues in the body, and it was now Augie's living nightmare. He had just lost kidney function and was on dialysis. He had also lost most of his body weight and his skin had a tight, waxy appearance. If you didn't know he was dying, you would assume he was a drug addict. Augie became Gypsy Queen's soundman, a position he could handle. He also took it upon himself to deal with booking agents, club owners and guys like me.

When I identified myself, I heard him say to Paula and Pedro, "It's that guy who was at the gig," and before I had the chance to say anything more, he asked me, "Hey, what's the name of that producer you know, and what album did you say he produced?"

I replied "Jack Douglas, and the album is *Double Fantasy*." He asked me to hold on while he went to look for Paula's cassette copy. I tried to tell him that producers names weren't normally listed on cassettes, but he was gone before I had a chance.

When Augie returned to the phone, I thought I was speaking to a new person. It was as if he'd had an epiphany during the time it took him to search out Paula's tape. I could hear screaming in the background, and Augie had trouble speaking a full sentence. He had just seen Jack's name on the cassette alongside John and Yoko's names, and for the first time since I had met the band, they believed I was more than just another local wing nut.

I called Alissa. "Augie will be picking up money to fly himself, the girls and their manager to New York," and I instructed her to take fifteen hundred dollars out of the account.

Alissa reminded me, "The closing on the house is in less than two months. When is Jack going to pay us?"

I told her, "Yoko hasn't sent the check to the lawyers yet, but don't worry. Jack told me he would pay us as soon as she does."

We put Augie, the girls and their manager up at the Mayflower Hotel on Central Park West. At dinner, we found their manager Bruce to be somewhat of a bore with little knowledge of the business. He certainly was not the manager type. The twins seemed a bit nervous at first but turned out to be delightful. At times it seemed they shared the same mind. When they talked, they drew close to one another. I wondered if their knees were touching under the table. Occasionally, they would communicate with their eyes, telepathically answering questions. While one spoke, the other filled in gaps in a sentence without missing a beat. If not for them wearing different outfits it would have been impossible for Jack, Chris or me to tell them apart. Even their poses were identical.

Bruce told us that a few months earlier he had sent publicity photos of the twins to several magazines. *Playboy* responded by inviting Pam and Paula to California to stay at the *Playboy* mansion where they were asked to pose for the centerfold of their anniversary issue. Playboy offered them fifteen thousand each to bare all. It was a tough decision for the girls, especially when they considered their present financial condition—broke! It was a tug of war between the thrill versus modesty, plus their concerns about how it might affect their career. While deciding whether or not to become bunnies, they were told the magazine was also planning a layout titled "Women in Rock." Although there was no fee involved, the girls opted out of the centerfold and into " Women in Rock."

They told us about the picture shoot. Paula was so nervous that she made herself sick. She arrived at the studio with a fever of 102 degrees, and Pam broke out in pimples. The photographer told them not to worry, he would make them look perfect. The photographer tried his hardest to get them to bare all, or all that he could, which wasn't much. Though Chris seemed relieved, Jack and I glanced at each other with a hint of disappointment in our eyes.

We also discussed the group, their songs and recording an album. Jack said he would arrange to come to Miami to see the band perform live sometime before Christmas, and we left it at that. They headed back to their hotel while we took off in the other direction towards Jack and Chris's favorite newsstand. The new *Playboy* had just hit the stands, and on the front cover it said "Women in Rock."

There was more than one photo of the girls from Gypsy Queen. In one, the girls were wearing black bikini bottoms and open leather jackets. In another they were bare-breasted. It did look like their breasts had been airbrushed, and Chris kept saying those weren't really their breasts . . . they looked too good!

Pictured along with Pam and Paula were Stevie Nicks, Tina Turner and

Pat Benatar. They bared nothing, but left little to the imagination in their suggestive attire. There were also some unknown female artists, and they bared all. It appeared the less famous you were, the more you showed. Jack and I got a kick out of the pictures and decided the spread would neither help nor hurt the girls' careers. If anyone inquired about their posing in *Playboy*, they could gloss over it by mentioning what an honor it was being featured with such greats as Tina, Stevie and Pat. We knew in the long run they would sink or swim only on the quality of their music.

When I returned to Florida I received the star treatment. Word of who I was spread quickly throughout the South Florida music scene, and before I could blink an eye, everyone wanted me to hear their demo tapes. I was invited to all the clubs, and bands were setting up showcases in my honor. People assumed that due to my association with Jack Douglas, I had worked with him on all his productions. Hell, I wasn't even an Aerosmith fan, but I knew enough Aerosmith stories to keep everyone amused.

Gypsy Queen waited impatiently for Jack to pay his visit. Knowing Jack and Chris as well as I did, I kept in close telephone contact with them the day of their expected arrival. At the same time, the band kept calling me to make sure they would be prompt. It seemed as if they, too, knew about Jack. When Chris called and said they had missed their flight but would catch a later one and meet us at the club, I knew I was on shaky ground. I had no choice but to explain to the band that Jack couldn't make his flight and would try to get a later one. Pam and Paula had planned a special performance at The Button South, and they were horrified at the possibility of Jack not showing up. Even the local media awaited Jack's arrival, and everyone was asking me if I was sure he was coming that night. No one answered his phone so I assumed he was on his way.

Nine-thirty came and went, and the band played their first set. At midnight they played their special set in case Jack arrived in the middle of it. I was sitting at our reserved table and the girls kept giving me inquiring glances, hoping I would nod or smile to indicate Jack had arrived, but there was no such luck. As it grew late, it became obvious to me that Jack wasn't coming. It was no surprise to me, and from past experiences I knew how badly the band must have felt.

As Jack's representative, I did my best to cover up. While I gave everyone the picture of Jack and Chris stuck at Kennedy Airport waiting for a flight, I had my own mental image of Jack lying on someone's couch with one eye shut and one eye half-open and a cigarette butt hanging out of his mouth.

I tried to make excuses but Pam and Paula still took it hard. They figured Jack didn't really care about them. The guys seemed to understand, and tried to explain to the girls that this was the way the business worked. I had the band members doing my work for me, so I must have been doing something right.

When Jack finally made it down a few days later, it was with problems. He missed his first flight and had to take a taxi to another airport to catch a later flight out. At 9:00, to everyone's surprise, he walked into Summers on the Beach, the Ft. Lauderdale club where the band was performing. Again, everyone was on hand to greet him. Jack stood by the bar as the girls performed a great show complete with costume changes, brilliant comedic antics and seductive moves and expressions. After the show we made plans to sign the band to my production company, Fantail Productions. Jack and I also entered into a limited partnership in which Jack would produce one Gypsy Queen album a year for five years.

I contacted the Miami Herald and the Sun Sentinel newspapers and arranged for stories to be written about the band and my signing them. Jack told the interviewers he planned to produce albums of original Gypsy Queen music, and that he believed the twins had the potential to be a major hit. He explained about their music being multifaceted, hard-rocking, and there was no denying that their sexuality was the main attraction, particularly when multiplied by two. He also said that when he saw the live show it was more than he had expected. When the band read what Jack said about them, they were euphoric—until it was time for me to tell them what Jack had told me when the reporters were not around, which was that he hated the band's rhythm section—the bass player and drummer. Before we could move any further he wanted me to replace them. Joey and Jay were enjoying their moment of fame with the rest of the band—their last moment of fame. I knew soon I'd have to deflate their euphoria.

The local newspapers wrote feature articles with titles like "Sex, Twins, and Rock n' Roll." With the January issue of *Playboy* still on the stands, many headlines read, "Twin Rockers of Gypsy Queen Get National Exposure from Playboy." The girls were doing radio, television and newspaper interviews, and the band was offered more gigs than they could play. For a while it seemed the Gypsy Queen twins were everywhere. The clubs ran radio advertisements heralding, "Playing tonight! The twins as featured in *Playboy* magazine!" The girls were petitioned by the magazine to go to different newsstands in the afternoons and autograph copies of their issue.

The hype that turned Pam and Paula into local celebrities was a thrill at first then it became annoying to the point they wished the *Playboy* thing would just go away. They asked the clubs to stop advertising their appearances with cheesy slogans. They were accustomed to the star-struck groupies who hung around the stage doors, but now they were receiving sexually explicit phone calls. I couldn't believe their phone number was still listed in the phone book. The girls said they liked receiving flowers and gifts from their admirers, until the day a huge box of clothes arrived with a note that read, "These are all the clothes I own; I want you to have them." The box was stuffed with men's clothing, complete with socks, underwear and shoes. We pictured a guy walking the streets naked, telling everyone, "I gave my clothes to those women of Gypsy Queen!" Although humorous, it did prompt Pam and Paula to move to a different apartment and get an unlisted phone number.

While the girls were being treated like celebrities, the guys in the band were experiencing quite the opposite. No one was interested in the music, and the press seldom mentioned Pedro, Bryan and Augie. They had been professional musicians long before the twins entered their picture, they wrote and arranged most of the music and put up with the twins. They were not a back-up band—Gypsy Queen was one entity, and until now they had shared the limelight equally, but now even the female groupies were more interested in the girls.

Augie and I became close friends, and while he was filling me in on the behind-the-scenes news about the band, I slowly let him in on what it was like dealing with Jack and Chris. We trusted each other and supplied each other with useful information. Augie was the first one I went to when I had to go about replacing Jay and Joey. The band was working almost every night, so we had to figure out how to replace the rhythm section without losing too many gigs or getting everyone upset.

I felt like an assassin. First I spoke to Pedro and Bryan, and although they felt badly about axing their friends, from a professional standpoint, they were both in favor of the change. Next I had to break the news to Pam and Paula, and not only did they take it to heart, they didn't understand why. They reminded me that Jack had told the reporters about how much he liked the band and I explained to them that in public one never says anything bad about the band, no matter how dire the situation might be. Augie, Pedro and Bryan tried to make them understand that it was a business decision—Jay and Joey had poor timing, weren't playing tight and made the band sound terrible. As Pedro put it, "They suck."

I flew to New York to make plans with Jack, and while I was there Jack's lawyer called with the news that Yoko had appealed the judgment, but they suggested trying to negotiate a settlement rather than take the case to an appeals court. Jack was again spending money, mostly money he was borrowing from me, but with the huge judgment in his pocket I felt he was a good risk. Alissa was the only nervous one—we were supposed to close on the house in less than a month.

Rick Dufay, along with everyone else around Jack and Chris, were constantly snorting from small bags of white powder they called opium, or from small bags of white powder they called blow. Late one night I decided to snort a line of coke that was left on the console, but as it went up my nose, Chris exclaimed, "Ken, you just snorted a line of opium!" I thought she was kidding until I started to feel dreamy. I spent the rest of the night sitting on the couch next to Jack, both of us with one eye open and one eye half-shut, cigarette butts hanging out of our mouths. I was fading in and out of hazy, euphoric dreams, and occasionally heard Chris say, "Jack, is Ken okay?"

In the morning, Rick couldn't wait to tell me I had snorted heroin. Rick often bragged about going cold turkey, so I asked him why he would always start doing heroin again after going through the pain of withdrawl. He replied, "What the fuck do you know about anything? Just because you got high once doesn't mean you know shit!" I may not have known shit, but I did know I wasn't about to become addicted to heroin.

Now more than ever, I was determined to change the course of Jack's downward plunge. His children in Wisconsin, his son in upstate New York and his parents all knew of his supreme talent. They wanted him to be successful again, and I was going to be his Messiah and lead him to the Promised Land. Chris became my ally as well as my foe. We spent hours covering up for Jack and planning his comeback, yet as much as Chris loved Jack, her drug addiction overpowered her. She knew she was blamed for Jack's downfall and agreed if Jack were to ever be taken seriously again, she would have to stay away from his business affairs.

I went back to Florida to help the band find a new drummer and bass player. Jay and Joey thought I was joking when I told them they were fired. I had to convince them it was for real. Jay was shattered, but Joey said he planned on rejoining his old Latin disco band and that helped ease my guilt a little.

CHAPTER 28

Something Very Simple

The girls took on a bad attitude and gave me the cold shoulder. "Who are you to disrupt our band, and where is Jack?" they asked me. I realized that working with this band wasn't going to be easy. Jack was in New York, and never had to deal with the band and their frustrations. While in Florida, I became shrink, swami and social worker for seven egotistical and broke musicians, and when in New York I was shrink, swami, social worker—and bank—for Jack and Chris. The only sane times I had were in an airplane, high above the clouds.

It was necessary for the band to take time off so they could audition bass players and drummers, decide on who to hire and then teach the new players the songs. I hoped this would be accomplished quickly, because as their executive producer it became my financial responsibility to pay the salaries of the entire band whenever my business decisions interrupted their gig time.

The band had their own ideas about who they wanted to audition, but Jack insisted on sending in a bass player named Paul Ill (yes, that's Ill, as in sick). Paul had worked with Jack in the past, and now he was hanging around Jack just like everyone else. During these times, Jack sometimes talked about Lennon. While listening, I often imagined what it was like when it was John Lennon sitting there getting high with Jack and telling Beatle stories. Now it was Jack's turn. He was my mentor, but to Rick and Paul he was also the one with the drugs. Their relationship was mutual; they needed the drugs and Jack liked the company.

During the *Double Fantasy* sessions, John hung out with Jack and the assistant engineer after everyone left the studio. John spent hours talking about the old days. Jack had hidden a tape recorder, and he taped many of the conversations. From these talks, Jack gained insight into how John felt about his ex-Beatle bandmates Ringo Starr and George Harrison. John loved Ringo and looked upon him as if he were a younger brother, but he still had unresolved differences with George. Jack told me that during several later sessions, George had visited John at the studio and the two of them were able to work out some of these differences and resume their friendship. John alludes to his opinion of Paul's musical abilities on a cassette tape John had given to Jack as a gift. The cassette is of a rehearsal John conducted with the group Elephant's Memory in preparation for his historic New York City concert. As he was teaching a musician a part, John exclaims, "It's something very simple, otherwise Paul couldn't have played it; he could only play basics!" In return for this gift, Jack had planned to present his secretly made tapes to John, but he never got that chance, so after John died, Jack sadly gave the tapes to Yoko.

Paul turned out to be a burnt-out bass player with a bad heroin addiction. The guys in Gypsy Queen accepted Paul, but the girls immediately took offense to his scruffy look and receding hairline. The band had taken one week off so Pedro could teach Paul the songs. I wrote Augie a check for twenty-two hundred dollars, equal to the amount a club would have paid the band for a week's gig.

To save money, Paul stayed at my house. Soon after his arrival I realized he was running low on drugs and I had no idea where to purchase heroin. Jack promised to mail down enough for the week, but the package never arrived. It turned into one hell of a long week. Paul was about to go through cold turkey. I was the only one who knew and it was my job to keep it a secret.

By Thursday Paul had developed a bad case of the shakes, and on Friday, the night of Gypsy Queen's first performance without Joey, I couldn't imagine him getting out of bed much less playing a gig. But to Paul's credit he got out of bed, took a shower and put on his stage clothes. Carrying his bass, he walked beside me into The Button South and wandered backstage. Moments later I spotted Joey sitting at the bar. With his long black hair, he was young and sharp and full of energy and self-confidence. I wondered if maybe the twins were right, that I indeed had no right to interfere with their band. I took a seat beside Joey. There were no hard feelings. Along with the rest of the audience, Joey was anxiously waiting his first glimpse of the new Gypsy Queen addition. I sipped my Stoli's and cranberry and thought back to the night I had sat at this exact same bar with George and Tony waiting to hear Johnny Depp play his first gig with The Kidds. I prayed that Paul would prove himself as worthy a player as Johnny had, but I soon found what I really needed was a direct line to God.

For me, there is no such thing as a quick and easy disaster. They always come slowly and they're painful. First Paul started out in the wrong key, then he went into the wrong song. He was missing notes while running back and forth and almost bounced Pam off the stage. Amidst this confusion, the rest of the band managed to maintain a professional appearance. The crowd was oblivious and erupted into applause after each song, thinking Paul's antics were part of the show. I hoped I was the only one in the club who knew how bad Paul was, until I saw Joey's bemused expression. Then I turned my gaze to the stage; twelve razor-sharp eyes stared me down.

On my way home from taking Paul to the airport the next day, I knew we desperately needed a good bass player. I racked my memory in search of one until, suddenly, a light bulb lit up over my head. The Pat Travers Band had spent a lot of time in Miami, and their bass player, Mars Cowling, who played on George and Lauren's first demo, had made his home here.

An Englishman in his forties, Mars was content with his decision to retire from rock n' roll. He was working in a bait and tackle shop and had recently purchased a twenty-five-foot fishing boat. It couldn't possibly be a good time to ask him to venture out of retirement and into a new musical project, but if there was one thing he knew, it was how to play the bass. He had devoted his life to a business that never repaid him. Throughout the years he had been a salaried bass player, and since he wasn't a songwriter, he was not entitled to the big bucks Travers had made. He had no love for Gypsy Queen, and for sure he hadn't quit playing with Pat Travers so that he could join a local band, but since Jack was producing the album, he agreed, for a price, to work with us.

Mars had a short fuse. It wasn't easy to talk to him, as he was arrogant, stubborn and always said exactly what was on his mind. However, we developed our own special relationship; I made him nervous and he gave me a headache.

Next we had to hire a drummer. The band held auditions at Bryan LeMar's house. Each drummer warmed up with an easy Led Zeppelin tune, then Pedro and Bryan showed him a few originals. If he made it past the originals, it was time for the sudden death round. Gypsy Queen had an original called "Who Are You?" with a very fast and off-the-wall drumbeat. No drummer could play it and keep the timing. I even flew Matthew Hill down from Rockland County for an audition, but like the rest he didn't survive the sudden death round.

Pam and Paula had a girlfriend whose ex-boyfriend was a drummer in a country and western band in Orlando. Everyone thought it a waste of time to audition him, but to be polite to the twins' friend, we set up a time for him to try out. I had pictured a guy with a cowboy hat and boots. I had to laugh when Keith came in with straight jet-black hair and a black leather suit. After playing four songs the band launched into "Who Are You?" and Keith was right with them.

Mars and Keith became the new Gypsy Queen rhythm section. At first the twins didn't like the idea of their bass player being in his forties, and they weren't sure if Keith's shoulder-length hair was long enough. They were more interested in being backed up by David Lee Roth look-alikes, but Pedro, Bryan, Augie and I knew we had created a monstrous rhythm section. (Plus, I was happy not to be shelling out any more twenty-two hundred dollar paychecks!)

After gigging for a couple of weeks, the band became impatient to start work on the album. Jack had just finished the second Zebra album, so I convinced him it was time to start work on the Gypsy Queen album.

The day Jack was due to arrive I got a message from him saying he'd just been hired to produce a Cheap Trick album and he had to go to Wisconsin, but he wanted us to begin without him so he was sending Lee DeCarlo down to start pre-production. Not only was the band laying in wait for Jack, I had notified the *Miami Herald* and *Sun Sentinel* newspapers and Channels 7 and 10 Evening News that Jack Douglas was to arrive in town and had dedicated himself to launching Gypsy Queen's rise to fame. Being the great promoter that I was, I had the media following the continuing saga of Gypsy Queen and now I had to explain why Jack was sending his engineer instead. I hoped that by saying Jack was producing a Cheap Trick record everyone would be left sufficiently impressed.

Lee DeCarlo was best known for the work he had done as Jack's engineer on John and Yoko's *Double Fantasy* album, and he had also had his share of confrontations with Yoko. While working in the studio, Lee liked to sip Jack Daniels. Yoko had a strict policy about no liquor in the studio and the only food she allowed was sushi. No one dared to defy Yoko, but John told Lee not to worry. One night, Lee arrived at the studio to find that John had arranged to have a big potted plant placed on the floor at the end of the console where Lee sat. Buried in the dirt was a silver flask with a thin straw sticking up. Every time Lee wanted a sip, he would cough, lean over and have a drink. Yoko once mentioned to Lee that he had better take care of that cough.

Another time, John told Jack and Lee he was tired of eating sushi. From that day on, there were hourly bathroom breaks where John excused himself, then hurried to the maintenance room and stuffed a Big Mac or a slice of pizza down his throat before Yoko questioned his absence. Eventually, the maintenance room became a junk-food cafeteria for everyone in the studio, and Yoko wondered why there was so much sushi left at the end of the night.

Jack picked out the tunes for Gypsy Queen and had booked time at New River Studios in Ft. Lauderdale. The night of Lee's arrival, Mars and the twins waited at the studio while Augie, Pedro and I went to the airport. Augie and Pedro had bought a gram of cocaine as a welcoming gift for Jack, but since he wasn't coming we decided to make the best of the situation and snort it up ourselves. We started out early because we didn't want the rest of the band to know what we were up to. As we drove along, someone suggested we stop at Wendy's. I took the drive-thru and ordered at the microphone.

When I pulled up to the window, the girl said "That will be fifteen dollars and forty-five cents." I gave her sixteen dollars, received my change and drove away. A few minutes later and several miles down the road, Pedro asked for his Coke.

"Augie, give Pedro his Coke," I said.

"I already did," Augie said, as he tried to get the last of the coke out of the bag and up his nose.

A few minutes later, Pedro again asked for his Coke. Augie told him there was no more coke left, and then we realized I had driven away from Wendy's without getting the food.

At the airport gate, all types were disembarking from the plane. We had no idea what Lee looked like, so we took turns guessing as the passengers walked past us. No, he wasn't the elderly man with the cane nor was he the little guy with the briefcase. Finally we saw one last straggler. He was large, over six feet tall with blonde, shoulder-length hair and unshaven. He had on a colorful, loose-fitting Hawaiian shirt.

I walked toward him, hand extended and said, "Lee, welcome to Florida."

On the ride back to the studio, we filled Lee in on things. When I mentioned that Mars was in the band and waiting at the studio, Lee insisted we stop at a 7-Eleven where he picked up a six-pack of Heineken beer.

Mars had worked with Lee three years earlier in Miami when Lee was producing a Pat Travers album. After several weeks in the studio, Lee decided there was too much cocaine and too little work being done, and he wanted off the project. Instead of wasting time explaining this to Pat, Lee told everyone he was going to the store for a pack of cigarettes. On his way out the door Mars asked him to bring back a six-pack of Heineken beer. Lee took the order, then proceeded directly to the airport.

When we arrived at New River Studios Lee snuck up behind Mars, tapped him on the shoulder and held up the beer. "Hey Mars, here's your six-pack!"

Mars was dumbfounded but managed to ask, "Is it still cold?"

Lee DeCarlo may not have been Jack Douglas, but working with him was an enjoyable experience. As far as Lee was concerned, he was acting producer and while he was behind the board he was going to produce hits. He even filled in for Jack and did interviews. He did an interview with a reporter from Channel 10 News named Susan Candiotti. Susan looked to be less than five feet tall. After the interview, Lee said that she would make a great spinner, and explained that he had an ex-girlfriend he used to spin around while making love to her. Many years later I named the second nightclub that I opened, "Spinners," and Susan Candiotti went on to work for *CNN Headline News*.

Although Cheap Trick had not worked with Jack for years, opting instead to work with other producers such as George Martin, Todd Rundgren and Tony Platt, they felt Jack could capture something the other producers had missed. The band had to convince their manager, Ken Adamany, to use Jack, and Ken had to convince Lennie Petze, president of Epic Records, who warned that if they hired Jack, the production would go over time and over budget and there would be a lot of drug use. Ken proposed to fly Jack out to Wisconsin where he could keep an eye on him. Jack loved the idea of working in Wisconsin because he could see and be near his children there. I saw this as another break we had been waiting for, because if Jack could produce hit songs while staying on time and on budget, he'd be on his way back to the top.

Lauren Smolkin.

(left to right): Jack Douglas, Rod O'Brien.

Aerosmith 3D video party.
(left to right): George Mazzola, Lauren Smolkin, Jack and Chris.

Lee DeCarlo.

Paul Ill arriving at The Button, and Alissa.

Jack and Chris.

CHAPTER 29

Brokedown Palace

It was the day before we were to close on the new house. Alissa was packing the last of our belongings and getting the kids ready for the move while I was trying to get Jack on the phone. Having received a recent CBS royalty check plus the Cheap Trick advance, Jack promised he would send my money on time for the closing. I couldn't reach Chris or Jack and Alissa was in a panic. She had been packing for weeks, the lease had run out on our present home and the landlord had already rented it to someone else. I realized that if a check did not arrive within twenty-four hours we would be homeless, and we'd also lose the five grand we had put down as a deposit on our new house, so I did the only thing I could think of. I started to panic.

In the morning, just as Alissa was about to make the phone call to cancel the closing, a Federal Express truck barreled into the driveway. The driver practically threw the familiar blue and white envelope at me, and I signed for it. I ran into the house and we both ripped it apart. In it we found a white envelope, and in the envelope was a cashier's check from Jack. We dashed off to attend closing, and that day the Geringer family moved into their new house.

We shouldn't have cared what the Seimers thought of us three months prior when we went to see the house they were selling, but it was obvious from our first meeting that Linda Seimer didn't like us. She was impolite and acted as if we were wasting her time as she took us on a tour of her gorgeous home. Yet we very much hoped to fit in, and we wanted Brian and Rachel to have lots of friends just like in the old neighborhood where a pack of kids was always running in and out of our house.

A few days after we signed the contract to buy the house, we made the mistake of bringing Augie over to see it. Although Bob Seimer was sincere and friendly, I could see Linda grimacing distastefully as she backed away from the thin and haggard Augie. The next time we came to meet with the agent at the house, two young neighborhood girls ran up to Alissa and asked, "Is it true you have a friend who has purple and green hair sticking out of his head everywhere?" It was a perfect illustration of how children learn prejudice from their parents. If Augie had been black, we probably would have been welcomed with a burning cross as a housewarming present.

We decided the best route to acceptance, once we actually settled in, would be to make a good first impression on all the other neighbors. A few days after the move, I ran into Ian Lewis, an old friend of mine from my reggae days. Ian was the bass player for the band Inner Circle, who later put out the song, "Bad Boys" ("Whatcha gonna do when they come for you; bad boys, bad boys"), a song that later became the theme song of the TV show COPS. Alissa and I went to his studio to visit him. Soon after, Ian, who was bigger than a mountain and very black, with a multitude of thick, waist-long Styrofoam tubes, came over the house with Pearl and they stayed the night. Early in the morning, as our curious new neighbors drove by the house, they caught sight of Pearl, in a nightgown, and Ian (who was wearing only shorts), standing in the middle of our front lawn.

Having a house out in the country meant that Brian and Rachel would grow up in a clean, safe environment with good neighborhood schools and plenty of children to play with. It also meant that we would have lots of room for Ian, Pearl, Jack, Chris, Lee and Rick, not to mention all future rock n' roll crazies (and there would be plenty) to come, lay around our pool and sleep in the separate guest quarters. Well, for the first few days, Alissa and I tried to fit in. Really we did!

Except for Stephanie, our next-door neighbor, not one other woman gave Alissa as much as the time of day even though Alissa always greeted them with a friendly "Hello!" when she saw them on the street. However, there wasn't one husband who wasn't as sweet as could be. They always waved to her as they drove by, or stopped to chat for a minute. There may have been a personality disease on SW 57th Street that affected only the wives, but I guessed they were just jealous of Alissa's looks.

CHAPTER 30

Caught in the Web of Our Fate

Brian's computer habit started when he was eight years old. We bought him an Atari system and he started with Space Invaders and Asteroids, then graduated to Pac-Man and Donkey Kong.

One time while living at our previous house we went away for a few days and asked a neighbor to watch the place. She didn't remember when I said we'd be back, so when she noticed activity at the house she called the police. Brian was home alone when the police arrived. He was sitting in his room furiously playing a computer game when his door was flung open. He turned around and found himself looking down the barrel of a gun. What did he do? He turned right back to his game!

That night when he told Alissa what had happened, she was amazed. "Weren't you scared?" she asked him.

"No."

"But Brian, there was a policeman in your room pointing a gun at you!"

"I don't care! It was my best game ever!"

By age ten, Brian was a full-fledged game-playing junkie and Alissa and I tried to break his habit. We bought Rachel and him all-terrain vehicles, sent them to karate classes and tried music lessons. Rachel loved the lessons, but Brian lost interest after a few days and went back to his games. It was useless. He was hooked.

He had recently moved up to a Commodore 64 computer, and I promised to buy him a color printer for his eleventh birthday. A local Jefferson Ward department store was going out of business, and at their final clearance sale I bought an Okidata color printer that said "Commodore 64 Compatible" on the box. While hooking up the printer to Brian's computer, we noticed that not all the pieces were in the box. Without them, the printer would not print. When I tried to exchange it at Jefferson's they told me they were out of printers and I couldn't have my money back, as all sales were final. The store manager sympathized with me, and gave me Okidata's phone number so I could call them. I went home and called the number, and the representative gave me two choices. I could either ship the unit to the company and they would send me a new one, meaning Brian would have to wait three weeks, or I could exchange the unit at one of their other authorized distributors. I decided to exchange the printer. By doing this, the distributor could send it back, we would have a new unit, and everyone would be happy. I was given a list of a few other local stores and planned to exchange the printer as soon as possible.

Lee had basic tracks done on five songs when Jack called from Wisconsin and put a halt to the sessions. Cheap Trick was booked to play several north Florida and Georgia gigs, and Jack had arranged for Gypsy Queen to be their opening act. We had been in the studio with Lee for over a month. He wanted to finish some guitar solos before leaving, which meant that Lee, Pedro and I would have to camp out in the studio for awhile.

After three days of non-stop work, Lee was finished and ready to go home. We had the weekend off before the Cheap Trick gigs, and the band and I were determined to get some sleep before we hit the road. Pedro and Augie took Lee to the airport, and I waited at New River Studios for Alissa to pick me up.

When she saw me she couldn't believe how tired I looked. It was ten o'clock in the morning and I couldn't remember when I had last slept, showered or changed my clothes, but before I went home to sack out, I wanted to exchange Brian's printer at Zayre's, an "authorized Okidata distributor."

I drove south on I-95, and as we approached the Stirling Road exit where we normally exited for home, Alissa asked if I was sure I wanted to go to Zayre's; maybe it would be easier to do it later on. I knew that later I would be sleeping, so we sped by Stirling Road and got off at the Hallandale Beach Boulevard exit. It felt as if a part of my life still existed alongside that exit ramp. As I sat and waited for the always-red light to turn green, my gaze drifted to the warehouses that ran alongside the highway. I looked at the same unit that had housed my first East Coast Cosmetics. Every time I got off at this exit, my mind went into a trance as I saw the people and heard the voices of my past. I asked myself, "Why am I not in the perfume wholesale business?" and wondered what my life would be like had I stuck with it. Then I wondered what my life would have been like had I taken over Dad's drapery business. Would I have been happy? Would Alissa have been happy? Were we happy now? I looked at my wife sitting patiently beside me and thought of all I had put her through: The Reggae Rockers, George and Lauren, Jack and Chris, and now Gypsy Queen. For me to succeed she put aside her own dreams and sacrificed her security. Without her, I wouldn't succeed. I cast about desperately in my mind for something I could give her—something she had always wanted but never had. Then it hit me! I'd take her on that honeymoon to Hawaii . . . and I could afford it, as soon as the Gypsy Queen royalties started rolling in. I opened my mouth to tell her, but the light turned green, and I realized that now was not the right time. As soon as I got back from the Cheap Trick gigs I'd take her out to our new favorite dinner—Japanese sushi—and surprise her. I steered left, drove two blocks to Zayre's and pulled into the parking lot.

We entered the store together and I was holding the printer. We passed a large man dressed in a suit and tie who was talking angrily to a lady who looked like a customer. We made our way to the service counter at the front of the store. There were two ladies waiting to be served in front of us, so as I awaited our turn, I turned my attention to the man who was still shouting at the customer. His back was toward me so I couldn't make out what he was saying in his Jamaican accent, an accent I was quite familiar with.

There is no pleasure in standing in a department store line early in the morning, especially for someone as exhausted as I was. I hoped to exchange the printer without being required to explain the entire Jefferson's story. I just wanted to go home and to bed.

Alissa grew weary of waiting and wandered off to the shoe department to look for sneakers for Brian. When it was my turn, I explained to the young girl behind the counter I had a printer that was missing parts.

"Do you have a receipt?" she asked.

I was about to explain when she added, "Because if you don't, we cannot give your money back. You'll have to exchange it."

Great! Things were going my way and this would be quick and easy. The girl pointed me to the brand name department and told me there would be someone there to help me. She also said if there was another unit on the shelf, I should leave the old one there and bring the new one to her.

I walked to the counter in the brand name department where they keep the cameras and electric shavers and said, "Hello!" No one answered, but on the shelf to my left sat two Okidata printers. This time I was going to make sure all the parts and pieces were enclosed. I took both units off the shelf and opened them one at a time. While I was examining the contents of each box, I noticed a young man watching me. When I looked his way he quickly turned his head and pretended to be looking at the merchandise on the shelf in front of him. Who he was or what he was doing held no interest for me, so I continued to look at each printer to see if one appeared to have all its pieces. When I was satisfied that they looked complete, I put one unit back on the shelf along with my deficient unit. Just then Alissa came over from the shoe department.

She commented on the young fellow who was now staring directly at us. "I know he's there, but who cares?" I said. Then Alissa asked me why I had left my printer on the shelf. I replied that the service counter girl told me to leave it there, and we decided we should tell her exactly where on the shelf I had left it. We went back to the service counter and got on line. As we stood there, we could see that the mysterious man had followed us to the front of the store, and was involved in an intense conversation with the big man in the suit.

When we got to the counter the young girl was gone, but there was an older lady in her place. I was somewhat aggravated that I would have to recount the entire tale of the Okidata printer to this new person. As I talked, she kept nodding her head in agreement, until I told her I had been instructed to leave the old printer on the shelf. Then she said, "The girl you spoke with is new here. She should have taken the printer from you and held it at this counter."

"I'd be happy to go get it and bring it back here," I offered.

"That won't be necessary," she replied, and she put the new printer in a bag, stapled a receipt to it and handed it to me. "Thank you for shopping at Zayre's!"

The big man was the first to approach as we were about to exit the store. "You cannot leave this store. Give me that bag!"

Then he and the young man became engrossed in a conversation.

Alissa couldn't understand their Jamaican accents, but I could make out their words. I tried to translate for her while defending myself against what was being said.

"The man take them computer thing and open them..."

"I wanted to make sure all the pieces were in it!"

" . . . Ya man, they steal them computer thing and put it in them bag . . . "

"No, the lady at the counter put it in the bag for us."

Our voices grew louder and people started to congregate, hoping to catch a glimpse of what was happening. I proceeded to get angry. This was not amusing, and Alissa was almost in tears. I wasn't sure how they could be accusing us of stealing because I had a bag and a receipt, and my returned broken printer was on their shelf. We were in the right and I wasn't going to allow these guys to humiliate us any longer.

"This has gone far enough. You are publicly embarrassing us, and if you don't stop, someone is going to be liable!"

The two Zayre's employees laughed at me. The big one, who had been addressed as Mr. Jones said, "The man say 'stop' when *him* steal tem computer, ha! And *him* say I be liable. Ha ha ha!"

They laughed and Alissa's hand tightened around mine. I could feel her tension.

I started to tell them again about the printer I had left on the shelf, but Jones went on to say, "I am not a stupid man! Don't tell me no lies, I see you come into store wid nothing in tem hands, and you walk out wid my computer!"

I suggested we go into an office where it was quiet and I could explain what happened.

I never did find out what Mr. Jones' official title was. He was in charge of security, and was acting as store manager that day. The other man was part of Zayre's Loss Prevention Team. His name was Mr. Smith, and neither Smith nor Jones (their real names!) would listen to me. They refused to go to the brand name department to get my printer off the shelf. Instead, Jones picked up the phone and called the police.

They tried to frighten us by looking at Alissa and saying, "You going away for a long time—tis not de first time we put white trash like you in jail!" To them it was a big joke, but Alissa was scared and pleaded with them to let us go.

"I have children at home waiting for me," she said, and Jones laughed. "You should have thought of that before you steal dat computer!"

Alissa was panicking. She told them that we were friends of Bob Marley's mother and sister, but this only amused Jones and Smith. They called her a "damn liar!" and laughed again. They were proud of their capture and determined to prove we were thieves. The only thing I found comfort in was the fact that soon the Hallandale police officers would be there.

The police arrived after forty-five minutes of our being harassed and frightened by Jones. Two officers walked in, one older and one younger. Everyone started talking at once, and there was a lot of noise.

The two officers tried to separate us and listen to our stories one at a time. After Alissa and I told the officers what had happened, I added that a young girl had been at the counter and she told me to put the printer back on the shelf. I suggested we go there and retrieve it. I thought if they saw the broken printer Alissa and I would be exonerated.

"They be liars!" Jones said. "There be no young girl at my counter. I swear I see dem walk in de store wid nothing and walk out wid de computer! You have to arrest dese two thieves!" He kept calling the printer a computer.

Alissa was crying, convinced that she was indeed going away for a long time. I tried to convince Officer Hazzard, the younger officer, to go and get the printer off the shelf, and even though Jones protested vehemently, Hazzard agreed.

When he returned, he had two units. As he opened them in front of us, I noticed that Brian had forgotten to take out one of his own disks from the printer. I pointed it out to Officer Hazzard, and while Jones was yelling, "The man is a bloody liar!" the officer pulled the disk out and looked at it. It had words scrawled across it in Brian's childish handwriting.

Both officers were now cordial and diligent. "Are you sure you saw these two people walk into the store with nothing in their hands, Sir?" they asked Jones several times. "Are you sure you are not making a mistake?"

Jones was adamant that we were thieves, and he insisted we be arrested. Officer Hazzard placed us under arrest and read us our rights, then escorted us to the patrol car. We had to walk through the store in handcuffs. Everyone stopped what he or she was doing and looked up. They stared at Alissa, who was understandably terrified. In the car I told Alissa not to worry. I said that once we got to the police station, away from Smith and Jones, they would listen to me, and realize there was no reason to arrest us.

I also got the funny feeling from Officer Hazzard that he didn't want to arrest us. It seemed he believed me, and he knew we didn't belong in the back of his patrol car, but when we got to the police station Officer Hazzard walked us to the counter and disappeared. No one behind the counter was interested in why we were there, and certainly they had no reason or time to hear our story. We were caught in the web of our fate, and it was beyond our control.

We were not fingerprinted, they took no pictures and we didn't get a phone call. We were put into two separate cells. There was a metal shelf in my tiny cell that served as a bed. There was no place else to sit. The shelf had dried blood on it so I stood in the middle of the floor. I managed to get the attention of an officer as he passed by. He told me that the building we were in was only a holding station, and soon we would be picked up by a sheriff and taken to the Broward County Jail. I felt sick when I heard we were going to a real jail, and I was worried about Alissa. I imagined how scared she must be, and how worried she was about Brian and Rachel.

Sitting in the back of the police car in the steel cage while the Broward County Sheriff drove us to jail, I thought about how I was caught in the system with no way out, for something I did not do. I was locked in the back of a police car wearing hand and ankle cuffs, and worse, my innocent wife was next to me wearing bracelets that matched mine.

Nothing like this had ever happened to Alissa. I knew she wasn't as strong as I was and that she was blaming me for putting her in this predicament. I felt guilty for causing her sorrow and I felt we were in a hopeless situation. There was nothing I could do or say to ease her pain. The officer who was driving took a liking to Alissa, calling her Babe and Honey, and when I spoke, he told me to shut up. He kept looking at her in his rear view mirror, and when we got to the jail, he took her out of the back seat and handcuffed her to himself. "How does if feel being chained to a real man, Honey?" he asked her. She didn't answer.

We were taken into the building and escorted to a small room with a desk. Behind the desk was a lady sheriff. She asked us our names and addresses. When I tried to speak for Alissa, the lady snapped, "Shut up!"

"Can't you see she's worried about our children?" I said. Again I was told to shut up, and then I was taken to a small holding cell. The last thing the sheriff said to me was, "You should have thought about your kids before you decided to go shoplifting!" This was the second time this had been said to me, and I was pissed. I thought we were innocent till proven guilty, but apparently in Broward County, Florida, all someone had to do was point the finger and you were guilty.

Time loses meaning when you're locked up in a room. I walked back and forth, hit the wall, kicked the wall, called for a guard, counted from one to a hundred, then back down to one. I sat on the floor, tried to unravel the puzzle, got up, walked back and forth, hit the wall, and then did it all over again.

Eventually I was retrieved and taken back to the question-and-answer table. Alissa was nowhere to be seen, and I imagined her ahead of me on this journey into hell. I was informed that after I was processed I would be allowed a phone call. Processed? I envisioned myself on a conveyer belt being prodded, pinched and branded like they brand cattle.

There was no time to straighten my messy hair or adjust myself in any manner; they just ordered me to sit in the chair and look into the camera. I stuck my chin out and put on the meanest face I could come up with. No picture could convey the pain I felt, but this one came damn close. After my fingerprints were taken, I was escorted down in an elevator to a big room that had rows of desks along one wall, and rows of cells lining the other three walls.

Some of the cells had labels above them that said Misdemeanor, Felony, or Violent. I was put in the cell labeled Felony with four other felons. I took a seat on the bench. Whenever an officer walked by, each prisoner tried to get his attention. The prisoner sitting next to me jumped up suddenly and ran to the bars, attempting to catch the eye of a passing guard.

"This is bullshit! I'm supposed to be in Misdemeanor!" he shouted, but the guard strolled by, ignoring him and everyone else. The man continued his tirade, kicking the bars as if each kick would grab the guard's attention. He probably would have continued if the powerfully built guy next to him hadn't said, "Sit down and shut the fuck up!"

When he sat down next to me, I asked him, "What's the difference between misdemeanor and felony?"

"Felony means you get a finger stuck up your ass!"

Oh!

After a short wait, I was taken into a small room where a man in a white doctor's coat sat on a swivel stool. The two officers who brought me in stayed to make sure I cooperated. Doc' told me to undress, turn around and bend over. He donned a rubber glove, and yes . . . I am now a member of the exclusive felon club!

When I had my clothes back on I looked at this man and asked, "How did you get such a distinguishing job?" I was humiliated, but I tried not to laugh at this poor fool who had the job of sitting in this room all day poking his finger up felons' asses.

I spent the next several hours in a big cell with an assortment of criminals. Part of the time I paced, part of the time I sat on the floor, and part of the time I stretched out on the bench. When the cell became crowded, the best place to sit was on the floor. I was kept occupied listening to everyone around me relate their arrest stories. There was quite an array of offenses, but the most prevalent charge was drug dealing. Most of the guys accused of dealing were black neighborhood street dealers caught with enough dope to be charged with a felony. I wondered why, if the cops wanted to arrest the real drug dealers, they didn't go down to the rich, white high school where the kids can afford the expensive stuff?

I was asked, "What are you in for?"

"I returned a printer to Zayre's. They said I was stealing it, but I was just exchanging it!" I answered.

My cellmates had a great time making fun of me. "Sure," said one guy, "I was just walking down the street, and they put drugs on me!" I was embarrassed at not having a better story to tell.

From my cell I caught a glimpse of Alissa as she was led by, as did every male prisoner on the floor. Whenever a female prisoner was brought in, loud whistling and lewd remarks emanated from the cells, and Alissa received some of the most creative. The uproar was so loud that I wasn't able to get her attention. She looked miserable.

Soon after this, I got to make a phone call. I called my lawyer Lou Supraski, the same attorney who had represented me for my two insurance claims. He said he would call my parents, and work on getting us bail. After I was done with the phone, I was moved upstairs to the Broward County Hotel for Criminals where there were rows of cots and dozens of prisoners. I stretched out and fell asleep for the first time in days.

It was near dawn when my bail was met and I was released. My father was waiting downstairs for me. (How embarrassing!) He told me Alissa had been released a few hours ago and was at home.

He said, amazingly enough, Brian and Rachel had not been worried about us in the time it took before he and my mother had gotten to the house. Rachel had been at a friend's house and had just assumed we were home, and Brian was always so engrossed in his video games he didn't care if we were home or not.

The next day I went to the Hallandale Police Station to see if I could talk to Officer Hazzard. I had to find out where the printer was that I had returned. I needed it to prove we had not gone into the store empty-handed. I knew if the cops had left it in the store with Jones, neither I nor anyone else would ever see it again.

When I walked into the station I was greeted by a couple of officers who asked me how my wife was doing, which was not very well. Officer Hazzard appeared, shook my hand and said he was glad to see me out of incarceration. I felt I was making a better impression, as I had slept, shaved, showered and was dressed well.

Then he said in a quiet voice, "I am not supposed to be talking to you, since I was the arresting officer, but just between me and you, I don't believe a thing that guy Jones had to say. It was only because he insisted, it was my duty to arrest you."

I couldn't believe what I was hearing, and wished that I had a hidden tape recorder.

I asked him the 2.2 million-dollar-question. "Where is the printer that I had returned?"

Hazzard answered. "I think it is here, in the property room. We confiscated two units." He told me there was no way that I would be allowed to see the printers. They were being held as evidence—evidence to help convict us.

This was war, and I was right, and to prove it I would need to hire a criminal lawyer. Louis Supraski was the only attorney I knew. He was a business lawyer, but he shared his office with a criminal attorney named Henry Volpe. Lou called him "Volpe." I had seen him in Lou's office, but until now my only contact with Volpe had been a brief handshake. He had a halo of red hair and a red beard, and he always had an expression on his face that looked as if he were mad at someone. He reminded me of a mad dog ready to attack.

My first formal encounter with Volpe was at my house. It was early Monday evening, and as a personal favor, Lou brought Volpe over after work. Both of my parents were at the house when Lou and Volpe arrived. After the handshakes and introductions Volpe got right to the point.

Rather than allowing me to calmly explain what had happened, Volpe preferred to ask questions. I felt as if I were on trial. He had two questions to every one of my answers.

As the meeting progressed, our voices grew loud, and Volpe's face turned bright red. It got to where Alissa couldn't stand it anymore and she went into the bedroom and slammed the door. Volpe seemed more like an enemy than a person who was there to defend us. With Alissa gone, I felt weakened. I was left alone with my parents, Volpe and Lou. Like downing a player on a chessboard, they had rid the game of Alissa and only I was left to defend myself. Was it my imagination—or did they all think I was guilty?

Volpe was ready to tell us his evaluation of the case. He wanted to try a plea bargain. He said he could probably make a deal with the district attorney, which would involve our doing community service. We could plead no contest, which is like saying we admit we are guilty, while asking the judge to be lenient.

No way! Those bastards at Zayre's were not going to get away with accusing me of stealing, by having me admit I was guilty. Volpe could see that my mother had also weakened, so he directed his argument to her, telling her it was my decision, but if I didn't take a plea bargain I could be facing a long jail sentence and a criminal felony record. He said he had seen cases like this where the judge had taken away the convicted felon's children!

Alissa must have heard Volpe say this because she came into the room in tears. "I'd rather do community service then go to jail and lose Brian and Rachel!"

Volpe had gotten to her, too, and now everyone was against me—it seemed even Alissa believed we were guilty! Now I hated Volpe and wanted to throw him out of my house. The meeting ended with Volpe saying he would schedule a meeting with Brad Collins, the assistant state attorney handling the case, and that his fee would be twenty-two hundred, apiece. There would be nothing to do now, but wait.

That night Alissa and I hardly talked about what happened. We hardly talked, period. All she said to me was, "I want you to leave me alone." In the morning I would be leaving for the Cheap Trick gigs and I should have been anticipating returning to a celebratory dinner, and a surprise for Alissa, but instead of giving her a honeymoon in Hawaii, I had given her a trip to jail.

CHAPTER 31

Surrender

As we sped down the highway in a caravan of cars and a twenty-six-foot U-Haul truck with windows open and hair flying in the breeze, I felt like I was fifteen years old again. There is a magic to being part of a band on the road, and everyone in the caravan felt it. Whether as a player, manager or roadie, the road always held a special attraction for me.

Our first gig was in Daytona Beach. Motorcycle week had just ended and spring break was gearing up. We would do a few days in Daytona, alone, then meet up with Cheap Trick in Gainesville. Gypsy Queen were instant celebrities. Pam and Paula's old hometown was filled with college students, and it was vogue to party after hours with the band. None of the guys in the band went back to the hotel alone, not even Mario the sound tech, who was at least one hundred pounds overweight. Party supplies included plenty of beer, food and occasionally cocaine, which usually entered by way of the groupies. Once in a while, Pam or Paula would join the party, but they had their own private parties to attend to. Daytona was a blast, but when it ended we were anxious to meet up with Cheap Trick.

We arrived in Gainesville early in the morning and ate some great burritos (a favorite rock n' roll breakfast) before driving straight to the club, a small place called Joe's that couldn't have held more than one hundred and fifty people. We spent the entire day setting up the equipment, but to our mounting dismay, there was no sign of Cheap Trick. By the time sundown rolled around we still hadn't heard a word from them. We were scheduled to play both an eight o'clock and a midnight show, with Cheap Trick performing one show that was advertised to start at ten. They were the stars, and unlike Daytona, Gypsy Queen was just the opening act. All afternoon we hoped to at least meet their road crew. The club was so small we worried about where and how they would set up their equipment.

At eight o'clock we were huddled in the tiny dressing room and the twins were so worried they were about to lose it. "What if they don't show? This is being advertised on the radio, you know!" All of their anxiety was being unleashed on me. "We are not going on stage until we know Cheap Trick is in town!"

At nine there was no stopping the show. Between an overzealous crowd and a nervous club owner, I talked the band into going on. The guys began to play the first song of the set without the twins, a standard top-40 tune. When the second song started, two angry twins hit the stage, and the crowd roared. It may have been a tiny room, but by the sounds of this crowd we could have been playing Madison Square Garden.

Halfway through the set, the Cheap Trick caravan pulled up. The band stayed in their bus while their crew poured out of another, led by their ringleader, the rough-looking, six-foot-three road manager named Big Paul. He hurried through the packed club followed by his warrior crew and pushed aside everyone in his path. There was no time for greetings. He stormed the dressing room where a couple of the Gypsy Queen crew and a few groupies were hanging out. Paul gave no explanations. He just said, "Clear the room. Now!" and "Get all this shit out of here before I throw it out!"

Gypsy Queen was finishing up their set and had no idea that their guitar cases, clothes and whatever else was being transferred to a table behind the stage. I took the lead and tried to get everything out of the dressing room and into one place without losing anything. As the Gypsy Queen gear was being moved out, guitars were being carried in; the dressing room quickly became the place to house Rick Nielsen's amazing guitars. There were about fifteen of them, each one propped up on its own stand. It looked like a classic guitar show, with all shapes and models, colors and sizes.

When Big Paul finally spoke to me, his instructions were, "Keep your fuckin' band out of my face, and oh yeah—tonight we'll use your set-up. Tell your soundman our guy will come up and run sound, and we're not setting up any drums either. Bun E. will play on yours." I didn't want to rock the already swaying ship. I told Big Paul I'd work it all out.

I was relieved that Cheap Trick had made the gig, and even though no one liked their stuff being moved out of the dressing room, they were thankful the band had showed up. Besides Big Paul, who had gotten into everyone's face, this wasn't so hard to deal with after all, and the band members, in contrast to their road manager, were relaxed and friendly.

Rick Nielsen was the first to introduce himself, and he invited me to come into the dressing room after their set. Big Paul and his crew stayed in the hall to make sure no one crossed the line into Cheap Trick territory, including Gypsy Queen and their crew. I met Robin Zander, lead singer, Bun E. Carlos, drummer, and Jon Brant, bassist. Rick said Jack had told him all about me, and that he was glad to meet me. Robin, who was more interested in meeting the twins, apologized for Big Paul, explaining that eventually he would grow on me (I hoped not!). Bun E. was quick to tell me about Jack and Cheap Trick stories. Jon Brant said he had always wanted to work with Jack; that of the three albums he had done with the band, this one would be the most memorable for him. I was pleased the band was confident to be working with Jack again, and felt optimistic that Jack's career was making a turn for the better. Over the next few days I became good friends with the guys, especially Rick, who was married and had three sons. Rick liked to look at the girls, but like me, he would never touch. That was Robin's M.O. Robin would fall in love with a different girl every night.

One night after a gig, we were sitting in Rick and Bun E's. room. Robin said he was going to his room, and left with a pretty, blonde girl he had just met at the hotel. After forty-five minutes, they came back to see if they had missed anything. Then Robin said he was going to walk the girl to her car and he'd be right back. A few minutes later, Robin burst into the room holding the side of his head.

"I just got punched in the face!" he announced. We jumped up to alert Big Paul, who was most likely in his room reporting back to his boss in Wisconsin, but Robin said don't bother and proceeded to tell us what had happened.

While he was walking through the lobby holding hands with his girl, a guy approached them from behind, pulled the girl away and punched Robin in the face. Before Robin could react, the boyfriend grabbed the girl's hand and dragged her away. Then they stopped walking, and the girl waited while the guy turned and walked back toward Robin. As the man got closer, Robin braced himself for a fight, but instead, the guy shook his hand and . . . apologized! "I didn't know you were Robin Zander! I love Cheap Trick!"

I had two weeks to spend at home before I had to go to New York to assist Jack as he finished the Cheap Trick album. Alissa still didn't want to talk about what had happened at Zayre's or the charges we were facing. Her silence was aggravating, and not only did I want to have the charges dropped, I dreamed about getting even with those who were responsible for doing this to us. My life with Alissa was coming apart and I wanted someone to pay.

Alissa may not have wanted to talk about our legal problems, but she had something to say about everything else I was doing. She hated everything I did and spoke negatively about all I had achieved in the past. She felt I had blown it by leaving the cosmetic business, I had no right being in the music business, and no matter what I did or what I was trying to do, I was sure to fail. I started to dread being home, and I couldn't wait to get back to New York.

Rick Nielsen, Robin Zander and Big Paul were in New York when I arrived. Robin loved to walk the streets of Manhattan and enjoyed it when fans spotted him. Big Paul's job was to keep Robin out of trouble, while I couldn't wait to get him into trouble. Robin was as much fun in the studio as he was out. When he thought his vocal performance was lacking, he puffed cigarettes and swilled Jack Daniels. It was a trick he said Steven Tyler taught him, to give his voice a harsh edge (the raunch?), but all we got was a coughing and drunk Robin.

Jack was consumed by work. He was creative, and his mixes were genius, but drugs were being delivered to the studio on a daily basis. I could see trouble brewing. Big Paul knew nothing about recording albums, but he was the type of person who involved himself in situations where he really wasn't needed. He would construct a situation in which the band was in danger, and then rush in to save the day. After that, he'd run to the phone and call his boss, Ken Adamany, to remind him of how indispensable he, Big Paul, was.

One day I overheard him on the telephone talking to Ken, who was in Wisconsin. "Ken, Jack is so fucked-up he doesn't know what he's doing.

This album is never going to get done if you let Jack continue working on it."

I tried to warn Jack that there were forces working against him. I told him Big Paul was being allowed to see and know too much, but Jack said this is how he always worked, and no one had ever complained before. Rick defended Jack. He told Ken Adamany that he didn't see what the problem was, and he liked the way Jack was producing his songs. When Jack finished recording Robin's vocals, Robin decided to fly home to Wisconsin and take Big Paul with him. Once rid of Big Paul, work on the final mix could commence without interruption.

Rick and I were staying with Jack and Chris in their apartment on 72nd Street. Jack was immersed in mixing the album, sometimes going for days without stopping. Rick and I took turns sleeping on the one couch in the studio. Even the studio engineers had a hard time keeping up with Jack. When it appeared he was finally nodding out, he'd suddenly jump up and say, "Stop! Play that again!"

When Jack went home to the apartment, he often put on one of his laser discs—_Citizen Kane_ or _The Natural_—and we'd sit in front of the television telling stories until, eventually, Jack's eyes closed, and he'd be out. Rick told us about his wife and his sons. I liked that side of Rick, but what I really wanted was to see him without his baseball cap. I thought it was glued to his head because he fell asleep and woke up with it on, yet whenever he came out of the shower, the hat was dry.

Yoko's lawyers were still appealing the judgment, but Jack's lawyer felt confident the case would be settled soon. Chris fantasized about all the ways they would spend the money—houses, cars, trips around the world—but I had a feeling I knew where the money would go.

When Jack was nearly finished with the Cheap Trick album, Yoko dropped her appeal and the lawyers agreed on a settlement. Jack was to receive three million dollars, a deal he was very happy with, and he couldn't wait to receive the money. Everyone had been extending him credit, including his connection. Stan Vincent was very happy, too. Before Jack received a penny, Stan took his six hundred thousand dollar share. The lawyers took their million, plus another eighty thousand for handling the appeal. After Jack paid his accountant, Mel Epstein, he was left with over a million dollars.

The Cheap Trick project quickly turned into a disaster. Jack continued to mix the songs after Rick flew home to Wisconsin. He worked non-stop. We didn't know it, but Ken Adamany and Epic Records were in the process of pulling the plug on Jack's mix. They called in another producer, Tony Platt, to re-mix parts of the album. Jack had spent extra time on a song he planned to release as the record's first single. It was a fast, hard-hitting tune called "Rock All Night." Tony tore apart Jack's mix of that song, and Epic released a mild ballad called "Tonight It's You" as the first single. When Jack found out Tony had been called in behind his back, he was furious. As Jack's manager, I went to a meeting with Leonard Petze, the president of Epic Records. I took tapes of the Cheap Trick mixes to play for Leonard, but before he heard even a note, Leonard said the album was overproduced. He wished Jack had never been hired, and felt Epic had thrown away their money on the high producer's fee. It was apparent to me that Jack would now be blacklisted at Epic in addition to all the rest of the companies that refused to hire him.

Jack wanted and needed to make a comeback more than ever. I thought if Jack was to have a second chance, I would have to be sure he was on time for appointments. I handled all of his scheduling, and Chris and I again agreed that she would stay away from his business. For a while she busied herself running around with real estate agents looking at million-dollar estates. She'd come in to show Jack brochures, and Jack always found time to look at them. He looked at the pictures carefully and asked if this one had a pool or if he could build a studio in that one, but I knew Jack wasn't anxious to buy another house—he had already lost one in his former marriage.

I assumed that if Jack were relieved of his money woes, he could concentrate on work, but I couldn't have been more wrong. Chris and Jack rented a house in Snedens Landing, a tiny, exclusive area in Rockland County nestled in the shadow of the Tappan Zee Bridge. Katherine Hepburn, Bill Murray and Mikhail Baryshnikov were Jack's new neighbors. Together with the Manhattan apartment, he was paying eight thousand a month in rent. Before long, Chris found another house for rent on Long Island's Montauk Point. They wanted a house on the ocean for the summer months, she claimed, and this house, owned by a friend of theirs, was famous for its parties.

Chris said, "We have to get this house. Jack's always wanted it!" They rented the house, and the money Jack was paying in rent doubled. Really, all Jack ever needed was a room with a bed. Whether in Manhattan,

Snedens Landing or Montauk, Jack locked himself in his room, turned on the TV, got into bed and remained there until it was time for the next session.

CHAPTER 32

You've Got to Protect the Innocent

Our criminal trial date was drawing near. We had to attend a pre-trial hearing in front of the judge, along with assistant state attorney Brad Collins and Volpe. Alissa and I sat in the hall on the bench while the rest of them went at it. I couldn't hear what was being said until I heard the judge say, "You have fifteen minutes to confer with your clients."

In the hall, Volpe explained that the judge had agreed to a plea, and Volpe and Alissa tried to talk me into taking it. I wasn't as surprised at learning the lawyer had constructed a deal behind my back, as I was at finding out that Alissa knew about it, but hadn't told me. Even though I was spending so much time in New York with Jack and Chris, I never thought Alissa would think I'd agree to this plea bargain bullshit.

Volpe was as furious with me as I was with him. Our argument grew loud, and the bailiff came barging out of the courtroom to tell us we were interrupting the judge's proceedings.

Armed with this ammunition, Volpe said "Now you've made the judge mad. If you don't accept this deal he's offered, I wouldn't be surprised if he throws the book at you!"

"You can take that book and shove it up your ass!"

Alissa gave me a look that told me it was time to shut up and control myself. She hated lawyers and courts. She begged me to take the deal so we could go home and forget the whole thing. I could not do that, and said as much to her and our lawyer.

We marched into the courtroom and Volpe went in front of the judge. "Your Honor, against my advice, my clients have decided not to take the deal, and to go to trial."

The judge looked at us and then asked Volpe if he had advised us of the significance of the charges. He said, "Yes indeed, Your Honor."

The judge looked at the state attorney with a smirk and said, "I will set this case for trial."

Where was the justice in our justice system? Here sat two innocent people, and no one cared! They were angry with us for upsetting their conveyor belt of justice that speeded cases along by making deals. Whether guilty or innocent, everyone in front of the judge was expected to take the deal or suffer the consequences. I was alone but determined not to let them beat me. I couldn't live the rest of my life knowing I had admitted to doing something terrible—that I had not done! I cleared my mind of Jack and Chris, Gypsy Queen, my fucked-up lawyer and my angry wife, and concentrated on how to prove we were innocent.

My only ally was Officer Hazzard, the man who had placed us under arrest. The next day I called Volpe and explained to him that Officer Hazzard knew I was innocent. I couldn't explain how Hazzard knew this, but I insisted he had to be contacted. Volpe said that it was irrelevant what the arresting officer thought, and that any contact with him would make matters worse.

It became apparent to me that if there was going to be an investigation, I would have to do it myself. I tried to reach Hazzard on the phone, but failed. I tried sitting in my car in front of the Hallandale Police Department hoping to catch him coming or going. I went to The Button South to see if he was working the front-door detail. I told the officers at the door that Officer Hazzard was a friend, and gave them my phone number to give to him, but to no avail. I could not find Officer Hazzard. Our trial date had been set and I felt hopeless.

A few weeks later Rachel came into my bedroom and whispered, "Dad, Rick is on the phone." I thought it was Rick Nielsen or Rick Dufay, so I picked up the phone and said, "Hey."

"Ken, this is Rick Hazzard. Your daughter sounds so cute. How old is she?"

I sat up like a shot. "Officer Hazzard, I cannot believe it's you! You can't imagine what I've been going through trying to get in touch with you!"

"I know you've been trying to contact me, but I couldn't talk to you until

I cleared it with my sergeant, and then he had to talk to the department lieutenant."

I was numb. They knew something, and whatever it was, it was in my favor.

"If I can get the lieutenant's permission, I will meet with the state attorney."

I had to know more. Questions were popping into my head, but I stayed focused. "Please, you have no idea what we've been through. Can you tell me what this is about?"

"No, but I can tell you we have reason to believe Mr. Jones is not telling the truth. If I were you, I would get my lawyer to investigate Mr. Jones."

I thanked Rick from the bottom of my heart, hung up the phone and called Volpe. He was so angry that I had spoken to Officer Hazzard, he advised me to seek other counsel. When I asked him if he would refund the money I had already paid him, he told me that even if he dropped out of the case now, I'd still owe him more money.

I was on my own and needed to work fast. I jumped into my car and sped to the Broward County Courthouse in search of any records they might have on Mr. Jones, or Zayre's, but I was told that I needed case numbers in order to request files. Again, I needed to talk to Officer Hazzard. I drove directly to the Hallandale Police Department; by now I was well known there.

I had to wait for Officer Hazzard. When he came out to the lobby he apologized for having me wait, and said he had to get permission from his lieutenant to speak to me. I got the distinct impression that Hazzard was doing this for me because he had to clear his own conscience. He must have known from the start that we were innocent, and how he knew this, I was about to discover.

He gave me three case numbers. I thanked him, jumped into my car and raced back to the courthouse.

I felt like I had discovered gold. I had waited and prayed for months for evidence to surface that would help me prove Jones was a liar, and now I held in my hand the police report that proved it. On the paper I read the following: "Black male seen by Mr. Jones leaving the store with a camera." When the arresting officer asked Mr. Jones if he witnessed the man put the camera under his coat and walk out with it, Jones replied (and the report quoted him as saying), "No, I did not see him, but I will say *I did* see him do it, if it will *convict* him." The officer asked Mr. Jones if he would testify that he saw something, he didn't actually see. His reply was, "Of course I would, because I know he did it, and this is what I have to do to convict a man!"

The officer asked him again. "You mean you would lie?" Written on the paper, right in front of my eyes, was Mr. Jones's response. "It is not a lie when you know the man is guilty!"

I had two more police reports of similar cases. Mr. Jones admitted he did not see the actual offense, but since he knew it had happened, he would lie to prove it.

Officer Hazzard had written one of the reports, and I knew this was why he was motivated to lead me to them. For years Jones could have been having innocent customers at Zayre's arrested. And like the officers who thought they could get away with arresting Pearl for standing on a sidewalk, there was no one to stop him.

I went home and called Brad Collins. He said that he couldn't discuss the case with me without my lawyer being present.

I told him, "Mr. Volpe is no longer representing me."

"Until the court records reflected the change, Volpe is still considered your attorney-on-file!" I was dying to prove to Mr. Collins we were innocent and he was prosecuting the wrong people. It was Jones and his assistant who should be brought up on charges, not us.

I humbled myself and made an appointment to see Volpe, deciding it would be easier, and cheaper to put up with him than to start all over with a new lawyer. Volpe seemed to like reading the reports and I waited to hear him say something like, "It's obvious you are innocent, sorry we made a mistake, go and get on with your lives," but all he said was, "I'll set up a meeting with Brad Collins to discuss this case."

A few days later, Volpe called. He had had the meeting with Mr. Collins and was excited to inform me of the new offer.

"Ken, if you and Alissa plead no contest you won't have to perform community service."

Volpe was shocked when I told him, "Don't you get it? We didn't steal anything. An admitted liar called me a thief, and we are not copping any plea!"

We had to go to more hearings in front of the judge, and we were never allowed to show the judge the police reports. I felt like yelling out, "Jones admitted he would lie to convict a person!" but I would have been in contempt of court.

At our last hearing before trial, Mr. Collins stood up and said, "Your Honor, after meeting with the Hallandale Police Department and the attorney for the Town of Hallandale, we are willing to drop all charges, providing the Geringers will sign a release against the Town of Hallandale and Broward County."

My first thought was, "You've been dragging us through the mud all these months when all of you knew we were innocent, and now you want us to sign a release to protect your rights? What about our rights?" But I wasn't mad at the Hallandale Police Department. I was grateful. It was Officer Hazzard and his lieutenant who had gone out on the limb to help us—and I supposed they could have swept the whole affair under the rug. Their attorney advised them to get a signed release from me so I wouldn't hold them liable for arresting us under false pretenses; we signed the releases and were free of felony charges. This time Jones had picked the wrong guy, and I was already flexing my newly found muscles in anticipation of my get-even fight.

CHAPTER 33

The Big Get Even

Within days of being exonerated, I was busy working on the Gypsy Queen album. Jack heard the tracks Lee DeCarlo recorded and he decided to shelve them and start from scratch. When Jack was in town, I took full advantage of the opportunity to promote both him and Gypsy Queen. I had him giving interviews between sessions, and he and I were always planning his comeback.

Besides making plans with Jack, Chris and Gypsy Queen, I was also planning my attack on Jones and the Zayre's Corporation. Stan Vincent recommended Skip Taylor, an attorney friend of his in Miami. Alissa was not keen on seeing another attorney. She was hoping to forget the whole mess, and I practically had to drag her into Skip's office. She didn't share my burning desire to get even, preferring to leave it all in the past. That was easy for her, but I couldn't accept my life having been interrupted as it had.

As we waited in the lawyer's office Alissa said, "There is no way I am going to give these assholes any more of my money!" I wasn't sure if she meant the attorneys, Jack or Gypsy Queen. Then she told me she thought that since Stan Vincent was the one to recommend this attorney, some way, somehow, it would cost us something. And sitting in his posh Coral Gables office, I got the feeling Skip was expensive.

Skip was surprisingly pleasant. As interested as he was in what had happened to us, he was also interested in my relationship with Jack and

Stan. I was careful not to say anything bad and almost had to kick Alissa, who would have loved to tell Skip what she thought about his friend Stan Vincent. Skip was thorough and took notes as we described our ordeal. I talked fast, but Skip had the patience to politely slow me down without insulting me.

What a difference it was talking to Mr. Taylor after Volpe! Skip told us he would review the information and make a decision on whether or not he would take the case, and the meeting was over.

Several days later, Mr. Taylor called us into his office. He had decided to take on our case, and to our surprise, after we had signed the contracts, he told us that his friend, Tom Morgan, would be handling the case. Skip was a criminal lawyer, but Mr. Morgan had reviewed the case and was very interested in representing us. Skip told us that when handling a law-suit of this type, the lawyer makes a fee only if he can collect money, and that made Alissa feel safer about initiating a lawsuit against Zayre's.

Unlike Skip, Tom was impatient and always wanted to get to the point. He asked the questions and we provided the answers, with no time for idle talk. Tom reminded me of Gregory Peck in the movie *To Kill A Mockingbird*, but without the southern accent. He put on his wire-rimmed glasses and leaned back in the chair while hooking his thumbs into his suspenders. He looked almost too sharp and polished, so this took a little getting used to.

Alissa seemed to feel comfortable with Tom, and our meeting with him appeared to spark a desire in her to seek restitution from Zayre's. In the elevator after our meeting, Alissa told me not to worry about Tom. "If he intimidates you, imagine how he's going to make Jones feel!" I could cer-tainly go along with that line of thinking.

Tom was quick to point out that Alissa had been through a trauma. He insisted she see a psychiatrist, and taking his advice, we found one. After Alissa had a few appointments (which she detested) Dr. Albert asked if she could meet with me alone. Up until now, our only contact had been cordial greetings when I accompanied Alissa to her office. This was the first time an outsider was to look into our lives, and I wanted to protect what few crumbs remained of our once magnificent life.

It was my turn to sit in the patient's chair across from the doctor. As I looked around the room I tried to imagine Alissa sitting here each week, in these surroundings, which were familiar to her. The nervousness I had felt before the meeting started to go away as I eased back into the big brown leather chair. The doctor began by asking me about myself, and I told her about growing up in Rockland County, Skunk Hollow High School, and the story of how Alissa and I met.

Dr. Albert said, "I can see you love your wife very much." Hearing her say this made me feel good, and for a moment I had forgotten about the real problems between us. I wanted to continue talking about the far-distant past, when we couldn't in our wildest dreams imagine such things happening to us.

I was brought back to the present with the doctor saying "I am aware things now are not as good as they were back then." Dr. Albert explained that since the arrest, Alissa was looking inward, not wanting to deal with the outside world, which included me. She explained that Alissa no longer felt the security she had felt in the past, that it was not my fault what Alissa was going through, and I would have to be strong and understand what she was dealing with. Dr. Albert told me she was prescribing Xanax, a mild tranquilizer (which Alissa promptly handed over to Chris).

One day we both got called in for a conference. Dr. Albert sat us down, and after a few preliminary remarks she suggested that we put Alissa in a mental hospital! Dr. Albert wanted to further medicate Alissa and put her under observation for a week. If Dr. Albert did any good, it was at that moment. We looked at each other, got up and walked straight out of Dr. Albert's office. I called Tom and told him Alissa was not going to a mental hospital, and we were through with Dr. Albert.

I couldn't believe Jack and Chris had gone through all of their money in such a short period of time, but they had. I thought back to the year before when I was at their Montauk house with Rachel, who was about eight years old at the time. After a day of yachting and dining, Jack had to go into the city. After he left, Chris realized he had all the money with him.

Chris had promised Rachel and Blake ice cream. She called a limo service in Manhattan and ordered a limo out to the house. Three hours later the car arrived, and Chris beseeched the driver to lend her ten dollars. He answered that he only had a hundred-dollar bill. Chris said that would be fine, she had an account with the limo company, so she would add a hundred bucks to the bill and give the driver an extra large tip. All he had to do was to take Blake and Rachel into town and to the ice cream parlor.

The kids were besides themselves with excitement, and I watched my daughter and Blake, who were jumping up and down in the back of the stretch limo, being whisked away. Chris and I laughed for days at the thought of the limo pulling up in front of the ice cream parlor, the driver, wearing a tuxedo, opening the car door, and two little kids getting out and buying ice cream cones with a hundred-dollar bill. But I also thought it completely irrational for someone to spend a thousand dollars to get a kid ice cream, until I learned it was a drug delivery as well as an ice cream run. Then it made perfect sense.

Jack and Chris never took the time to enjoy their money. There was never any planning. The money was there to satisfy their whims. They had accounts all over New York—posh hotels with twenty-four-hour room service, limos, restaurants and all the best department stores. I don't know exactly how much money they spent, but I do know that within a year they were right back where they started, which was . . . broke in New York.

When Jack asked if he could borrow five thousand dollars, I thought he was kidding. I told him I was broke, thinking all he really had to do was reach into one of his bank accounts. I assumed that Mel had set up funds for Chris and him, similar to the trust funds Jack told me he had started for his three children, but he hadn't. Rather, when the money ran out before all the accounts were settled, Mel got tired of Jack coming to him with bills, and he quit. Even Chris doubted they were really out of money, and begged Jack to tell Mel to give them money.

It really did seem like the money was gone. The toys were gone, the cars were gone, the houses were gone, the unlimited drug supplies were gone along with all the partying friends. We set up a new loan agreement, and again I was lending Jack money. Things got worse—worse than they were before the settlement. At least back then they had an apartment in Manhattan. Now they were homeless.

After being evicted from the Snedens Landing house they found refuge in Rockland County with one of Jack's high school friends. Not only was Mary Ann Jack's friend, she was also Jack's ex-wife's best friend. When Jack was down-and-out, he could always rely on dependable Mary Ann. She had a son the same age as Blake, which was convenient for Chris. When Blake visited, she had Mary Ann take care of him. Mary Ann had one problem. She did not know how to say no.

When Chris sensed that Mary Ann was getting annoyed with her house-guests, she pressured Jack to either go upstate to Jack's parents, or down to Florida. This time, Chris was unprepared for what was about to happen. It might have been because Jack had fallen asleep with a cigarette in his mouth almost setting Mary Ann's house on fire, or it may have been because Chris said "I'll be right back," only to disappear, leaving Blake behind, that Mary Ann reached her breaking point. She called me at home and said, "I've had it. I want them out of my house!"

Mary Ann and Chris were alone in the house because Jack was in jail for buying heroin on 4th Street. I was expected to go to New York, bail Jack out of jail, get him and Chris out of Mary Ann's house and get them to Florida, all without the press finding out about Jack, or Mary Ann killing Chris. That would be easy. It would also be easy to tell Alissa that Jack and Chris were moving to Florida. The hard part would be they were moving in with us.

But I told her, and I got Jack out of The Tombs and put Chris and him on a plane, and once again, rock n' roll crazies invaded our peaceful country neighborhood.

We were recording the Gypsy Queen album in three of Miami's finest studios, until one by one they started to catch on. Criteria was first—they were the strictest. We did the best we could to record as many songs as possible, even asking an engineer who was impressed with Jack if he'd let us in to work at night when the office was closed. We were becoming professional bullshitters, and for a while it worked perfectly. Sometimes people would get suspicious, as we were constantly borrowing money for cigarettes or soda from whomever was around, but usually people thought we were just cheap. No one knew the truth. We were broke.

Jack kept on recording song after song. This time, I had Jack right where I wanted him, and the only thing that could stop us from finishing the Gypsy Queen album was if every studio put a stop to the project. It had been almost five years since the George and Lauren days, and there was no way in hell I was going to throw away all those years of dues-paying for something as silly as a lack of funds!

Eventually we had to leave Criteria because our unpaid bill amounted to seven grand. Though Jack had recorded there with many bands, including the likes of Aerosmith, the studio had a strict cash-on-delivery policy. This meant we could not take our finished masters with us until they were paid for in full.

New River Studio was next. Everything went fine until they heard the rumor we had been kicked out of Criteria for not paying our bill. Then they started to ask questions. It was a touchy situation for them, as they were a new studio and having someone the caliber of Jack recording there was good for their image. But was Jack working there because he was kicked out of Criteria for not paying the bill, or was it really like we told them—that Criteria felt stale compared to New River's new room? It was hard for them to break the news to us. Though they were very polite, and I did my best to talk them out of it, we were told we had to come up with money if we were to continue.

Lastly, we went to Quadradial Studios. Bob Ingria, the owner, was so impressed with Jack he practically paid us to work there, but after enough time went by and our bill grew sufficiently large, he began to hint at needing cash to pay his own mounting debts.

The only way to get money was to shop the band, and we couldn't shop the band until we bailed our masters out of lock-up. We considered initiating a search for an investor, but before putting together a proposal for potential investors, Jack and I decided it might be more lucrative to get him a real, paying job.

We decided we'd have a better chance of finding a gig if we sent letters directly to various artists, bypassing the record companies who were not exactly clamoring to hire Jack. I told Jack to give me a list of all the artists he'd like to work with, and I'd get in touch with them through their management. I wrote a form letter, and then customized it for the individual it was being sent to.

In the letter to Mick Jagger's managers, Tony King and Sir Rupert III, we mentioned that Jack and John Lennon had planned on opening their own recording studio, and one of their initial projects would have been a Mick Jagger solo album. The letter went on to say that John had also planned on doing some of the producing himself, but had never had the chance to tell Mick, so Jack wanted to honor John's dream and produce the album in his stead.

Jack told me that he and John had a joke: if they were ever unsuccessful, they would buy a hot dog stand in Manhattan. He had me close the letter with "If the solo album is unsuccessful, Mick and Jack could always open a hot dog stand in Manhattan." Tony King responded with a letter that said "Mick appreciates the offer, however, he is already working on a solo album, but he would consider working with Jack in the future." There was no mention of the hot dog stand. They must have thought we were crazy.

We came close to putting a deal together with Jeff Beck through his manager, Ernest Chapman. After a series of phone calls to London, Ernest informed us that Jeff wasn't ready to do a solo album; he was rehearsing for his guest appearance on Mick Jagger's solo album.

We did get a commitment from Jeff Beck to play on a Buddy Guy album we were trying to put together. With assistance from Buddy Guy's manager we also got commitments from Eric Clapton and Jimmy Page, who felt they wanted to repay Guy for the tremendous influence he had on them in their early days. I was setting up the session, but was having problems obtaining a commitment from Jimmy Page, who was in New York performing. He cancelled twice. We were told by an insider that he was so fucked-up, he was hardly able to play his own shows. We were upset, but it was a real disappointment for Buddy Guy and his manager.

A few of the artists we were in touch with were Bob Dylan, Simple Minds, the Cult, Ringo and Julian Lennon. Our search for Julian was relentless. Jack was disappointed that Phil Ramone, who had produced Julian's album, made Julian sound identical to the way John sounded on *Double Fantasy*. Jack believed Julian should have his own image, and he wanted to make a Julian Lennon album, not a copy of his father's album. The closest we came to Julian was talking to his manager and roommate Dean, who promised us that Julian was interested in working with Jack, and that he would call us, but he never did. I thought it could have been the controversy between Yoko and Jack that kept Julian from calling.

Because of their past affiliation Stan still got stray calls regarding Jack, and through him, Jack was hired to produce a new group signed to Warner Brothers called Rough Cutt. I stayed in Florida to work on our prospectus for potential investors while Jack flew to Los Angeles to produce Rough Cutt's album.

The album was coming along fine until Chris decided to fly to L.A. for a visit. Wendy Dio, the band's manager, owned the limo company that Warner's hired to chauffeur celebrities. Chris had Jack arrange for her to use the limo for a couple of hours so she could visit her sick mother.

Chris didn't come back. The limo was AWOL, and for the first twenty-four hours Jack was bombarded with phone calls. Everyone from Wendy Dio to Lenny Waronker, a Warner executive, wanted to know what had happened to the limo. The missing car took precedence over the album. Everyone was in a panic, except Jack. All he was concerned with was getting back to work. After day one, and no Chris, Wendy Dio and Warner's had second thoughts about their decision to hire Jack. They probably wished they had taken heed of the rumors and hired a different producer.

When I heard of the missing person report, I was horrified, and not because I was worried about Chris, but because I was worried about destroying the last shreds of Jack's reputation. Before Chris left Florida, we had a little talk about the importance of this job. Since Jack's reputation in New York was ruined, we agreed L.A. would be a fresh start. She originally had agreed to stay away from Los Angeles, but short of locking her up, there was no way to stop her from going. As she put it, she was "only going for a few days." Her mom had cancer and she wanted to visit. She promised to steer clear of Jack's work.

Once in the limousine, Chris had to talk the driver into taking her to Palm Springs. She told him how important Jack was to Wendy Dio and Warner's. She made it sound like, if he wanted to keep his job, he'd better cooperate. Chris was good. She was able to talk him into using his corporate card to charge all her expenses to Warner's.

Chris didn't expect to return to an uproar. In New York, no one ever got this excited over a small thing like a little limo ride, so she blamed everyone around her for being upset. She said she couldn't believe how cheap Warner's was acting, and if Wendy owned the limo company, and she expected to have celebrities like Jack working for her, she had better get used to it. Chris's attitude made things worse. Wendy, along with Warners, deducted all of Chris's expenses from Jack's fee, plus twenty-four hours of limo service at the normal rate.

Jack continued work on the project, but now his New York baggage had caught up with him. Before Chris arrived, Jack was making deals to do some Warner productions with producer Ted Templeman. Ted had asked Jack if he would be interested in working with David Lee Roth. I wasn't surprised, or disappointed, when nothing came of it.

Warner Brothers was not excited about the Ruff Cutt album and it received minimal promotion. Like Jack's quarterly royalty checks from his past productions, the Ruff Cutt money was quickly spent. For a short while Jack and Chris were able to play in New York, but soon we were all back in Florida, searching for an investor.

We met a fan at one of the Gypsy Queen gigs who told us he was a pilot for a small independent airline that made frequent trips in and out of Columbia, South America. Benny Rodriguez expressed an interest in investing money in our project, so we made him a proposal, and he said he would get back to us after returning from his next run. Benny seemed genuine and we had every confidence he had the money, however, we did n't know if we could hold things together until he returned.

CHAPTER 34

Strike It

I think everyone at one time or another has had the experience of a nosy neighbor. The kind that not only has to know everything going on in your life, but also insists on taking part in, and advising you on everything you do. When Alissa's friend Stephanie moved out of the house next door, Robyn and her family moved in. Robyn, the wife of a doctor, was fascinated with us from the moment she learned we were in the rock n' roll business. It quickly became evident that she was bored with her life. She had a live-in maid to clean the house and tend to the kids, and that left her with nothing to do all day. It was fun for her to come over to our house because there was always something exciting going on, and she constantly tried to find out about, and become a part of, everything we were doing. We tried not to encourage her to come over, but when she came knocking, we were polite.

Alissa came up with the idea to ask Robyn if she knew of anyone who would be interested in an opportunity to get involved in the record industry. It seemed like a natural, as Robyn was acquainted with all the doctors in the area, or at least all their wives, and we knew that doctors were always looking for creative ways to invest their money. We were hesitant about getting involved with Robyn, but these were desperate times, and situations like ours called for desperate action.

Alissa and Chris knew exactly how to approach Robyn. All we had to do was allow Robyn to come over and hang out, and when Robyn realized she could use our house as a place to do all the forbidden things her husband disapproved of, she practically moved in. She once told us, "You'll never believe it. I know where to buy pot from a guy who wears a yarmulke!" We did find this pretty funny.

When she overheard us discussing our seeking an investor, she knew just who to take us to. Robyn was confident that her friend Coleman Schwartz would be interested in a proposal such as ours.

Coleman's plush office suite was in a high-rise office building in Fort Lauderdale, and Robyn could not possibly have prepared us for our first meeting. Sitting in Coleman's office observing him operate was like seeing a king run a small country. Jack, Robyn and I sat on a couch and watched Coleman, who was seated behind his giant desk at the opposite end of the room, manipulate three phone calls at once while shouting orders to his staff throughout the suite.

We soon became aware that Coleman had expensive tastes. The only times he'd acknowledge us was when he'd look up and say, "Watch out! That is an original Faberge egg!" or "Please use the other ashtray—that one belonged to Humphrey Bogart!" Before we had our first words with Coleman we learned he had a chauffeur, a Rolls Royce and a Duesenberg. A man wearing a chauffeur's uniform came into the office, dropped the keys to "the Rolls" on the desk, and asked if he should "take the Duesenberg in for service today, Mr. Schwartz?"

Although we couldn't figure out exactly what Coleman did, we could gather from his conversations on the phone it was something to do with oil. He kept referring to his 'wells' with remarks like, "I'll shut that well down if those bastards don't cooperate with us!" By the time Coleman acknowledged us, I felt like I had just seen a promotional video about Mr. Coleman Schwartz. Either this man was the smoothest operator I had ever seen, or we were being lured into a trap. The latter didn't seem likely, as we were there to sell to him, we had no money, and even though for a moment it felt like we were being set up for a fall, there was nothing at the time I could think of that would make us worthy.

Coleman was in his late sixties. He seemed full of energy, but it was apparent that he was run-down. Dressed impeccably, he was short, thick in the middle, bald, and had large, black, liver spots on his head that looked like lunar maps. He acknowledged Robyn by saying to her, "Are these the guys in the record business you wanted me to meet?" but before she could answer, he yelled, "Stuart, get in here!"

Stuart rushed in. He was a younger version of Coleman, except he was dressed like a slob. Unlike Coleman, Stuart was unpolished. He stumbled into the room looking like a cross between a bumbling professor and an overworked accountant. It was amusing to watch the two of them interact. Coleman was the overbearing father and Stuart the rebellious son. We had been in Coleman's office for half an hour, and neither Jack nor I had yet to say a word.

The scenario went something like this:

Scene One
Coleman's Office

COLEMAN. Stuart, these gentlemen are in the music business and they want to do something with us. *(Looking up at us for the first time)* Do I got that right, boys?

(Jack and I look at each other and nod, as neither of us is about to risk speaking)

COLEMAN. Stuart, I checked up on these boys and they produced the Beatles. You know who they are, don't you?

STUART. *(With a big smile on his face)* Of course I know who the Beatles are, Coleman!

COLEMAN. Well, take them upstairs, and see what this is all about. (*To Jack and me*) Gentleman, Stuart has my permission to make a deal with you, as long as I have the final say, right Stuart?

STUART. *(With a bigger smile on his face)* You're the boss, Coleman!

COLEMAN. That's right, and I'm the one with the ulcers, Stuart, and by the way, did you get that $50,000 deposit from Mr. Fairchild?

STUART. I got it under control, don't worry!

COLEMAN. *(in a roar)* Don't worry!!! Who the fuck does he think he is? He wants us to start drilling, and he hasn't even given us a deposit! Stuart, you listen to me, I told you he was a no good sonofabitch and we could have sold that well to Saul, the president of the Barnett Bank! You know he's been bothering me about a well. Dammit Stuart, you just don't listen! If it weren't for Marshall . . . *(Looking at Jack and me)* That's Stuart's brother; he's one of my lawyers . . . Stuart, I'd throw you the fuck outta here! Now, take these guys upstairs and let me do some work before we all go broke, and Robyn, stay down here, there's something we have to go over.

Robyn, who had been beaming the whole time, sat up like a bee had stung her in the ass and cooed, "Okay, Coleman!"

At least she was able to get two words in. Jack and I had still not uttered a word, and we felt awkward as we followed Stuart out of Coleman's office.

Scene Two
Stuart's Office

(Once in the elevator, Stuart takes the lead)
STUART. So, you guys produced the Beatles. That must have. . .
KEN. No, Jack produced John Lennon's last album.
STUART. Oh. (pause) Um, well, he was IN the Beatles, right? So that's enough credentials for me.
(As we follow Stuart down the hallway, Jack and I try not to laugh out loud at Stuart, who waddles like a penguin when he walks. Stuart sits behind his desk, leans back in the chair, places his feet up on the desk, and lights a cigarette)
STUART. Well gentlemen, tell me about this deal we're putting together, and about all the millions we're going to make.

With a line like that, it was hard to tell if we were being taken seriously, but Jack and I were curious. We had to see where this was leading.

Stuart asked all the wrong questions, which advanced my theory that he was stupid, or playing a game with us, or both. I started to explain our relationship with the band Gypsy Queen, and how we were looking for an investor to finish the album and sell the masters. As the meeting continued, Stuart was more interested in telling us about his past as an accountant and all of his celebrity encounters. We were not exactly fascinated, but anxious to get back to the bottom line.

Jack appealed to Stuart's knowledge as an accountant, explaining to him the procedure and expenses involved in finishing an album, and the point structure for royalty distribution. When we began to talk numbers, Stuart became animated. He wanted to know the sales figures of Jack's most successful production. Stuart was leading the conversation, and by equating Gypsy Queen album sales to one of Jack's other productions, such as Aerosmith or *Double Fantasy*, he was envisioning all the millions we were going to make with him and Coleman. At this point, all I could do was sit there and try to figure out how the tables got turned. Instead of us selling Stuart our deal, without his knowing anything about Gypsy Queen or hearing their music, he was selling us—our deal!

The numbers we were asking for didn't seem to frighten Stuart. To the contrary, he said our proposal was small and he wanted more. Stuart suggested we start our own record company. Jack and I were all ears.

Driving back to the house, Robyn was in raptures, but not about the company we planned on starting as much as the fact that she and Coleman had put together their own little agreement. She told us Coleman had gotten her into a deal that had already been closed. All she had to do was give him thirty thousand dollars and Coleman would sell her an interest in the oil well that he and Stuart had been discussing in front of us.

Jack and I were shocked! Robyn was about to turn thirty grand over to these guys for interest in an oil well she'd never seen. I wondered how her husband would take the news, and I couldn't help but have a bad feeling about Coleman Schwartz. I wanted to believe he was for real, but no kidding . . . oil wells?

Stuart and Coleman drafted the papers. Jack, Coleman, Stuart and I would each own 25 percent of an umbrella of companies that would be called The Jack Douglas Entertainment Group. The group would consist of a record company called Wildcat Records, and two publishing companies called Black Gold Publishing and Strike It Publishing. Jack and I were to transfer all of our interests in the band over to Wildcat Records. When the band was told they needed to sign contracts with a record company, they were happy, until we told them we were the record company. It was hard to get them to go along, but they were anxious to get back into the studio, and this made it possible.

Getting money out of Coleman was harder than pulling teeth. He never agreed to anything himself; rather, he had Stuart make the deals with us. When we went to him for money, he would invariably call Stuart into his office, call him an idiot and threaten to end the whole deal.

"Stuart, what kind of a moron are ya? Next time you negotiate a deal with a studio, ya let me do it, okay? I CAN GET THIRTY PERCENT OFF ANY DAMN STUDIO IN THIS TOWN . . . " and on he went. Jack and I were promised a weekly salary of a thousand dollars apiece, and Jack was moved into a waterfront home in Ft. Lauderdale at a monthly rent of twenty-five hundred. It all sounded great in theory, but every time we approached Coleman for money to pay for studio time, Jack's rent or our salary checks, Coleman wouldn't part with a dime. Instead of giving us the money, he asked us to hand over the bills. He would say, "I don't care who these people are! Just tell them that Coleman Schwartz is your financial backer and see where that gets ya!" We did, and it got us nowhere. Only when Jack and I reached the boiling point did we have a confrontation with Coleman, but we soon realized we should forget any hopes of seeing a paycheck. Our salaries turned into back monies due from the first monies received from the sale of the album. Instead of wasting time worrying about salaries we knew we weren't going to get, we concentrated on getting the studios paid so we could complete the album.

It wasn't long before Jack and I figured out what Coleman's real occupation was and how he accomplished filching money from investors. Without us knowing it, the first day Jack and I met with Coleman we were props in an elaborate charade. He was setting Robyn up for the sting. The telephone calls, name-dropping, cars, antiques and yelling at Stuart were all part of the show. Coleman's victims were moderate-to-wealthy people who were readily impressed with his success and what appeared to be his vast wealth. He was smooth and well practiced, and everything, including his interaction with Stuart, was all in the script. People actually believed Coleman Schwartz was one of the *rich and famous*, and by giving him some of their money they too would become wealthy in the oil fields of Texas.

Jack and I had this all figured out, down to the magazines in Coleman's office that featured the world's most famous cars and their owners (of course, Coleman and his Duesenberg were included in one issue). What we couldn't figure out was why he wanted to get involved with us and finance a record company. It wasn't until Benny Rodriguez tried to contact me that we were able to put the last piece of the puzzle into place.

When Benny returned from his trip he called my house, but I was at the office and Jack was in the studio. Alissa gave him the office number, and when he called and asked to speak with me, Coleman intercepted the call. It is possible that Benny had been asked the nature of his call and he mentioned an investment, or, that Coleman was intercepting all our calls. For whatever reason, his call was forwarded to Coleman's office.

When it came to squeezing information out of people, Coleman was a master. Without meeting Benny or knowing why he was calling, Coleman went to work. Once Benny offered information about his intent, Coleman informed him that he was the senior partner of our record label, Wildcat Records, and he quickly set up a meeting with Benny. Neither Jack nor I were aware that Benny had called, and it wasn't until weeks later when we met him at The Button South that he told us what had transpired.

Coleman had met with Benny and told him that he already owned the band Gypsy Queen, but there was a new deal he could get into, and to sweeten that deal, Coleman would toss in ownership of a small percentage of the band. He evidently told Benny anything he wanted to hear, because Benny turned over a whopping three hundred thousand dollars into Coleman's bank account. When Jack and I found out about the deal, the certified check had already been handed to Coleman—which was the same money Benny had earlier determined he would give to Jack and me! At around the time Coleman got Benny's money was the same time he started to pay some of the Wildcat Record bills, including our back salaries and Jack's rent.

When we dug deeper, we found that before Robyn brought us to Coleman's office, she and Coleman had already been discussing an oil-well deal, and to clinch it he offered her a percentage of the big money-making record company he told her he was planning to start with Jack and me. Robyn fell for the deal and now she was showing up at gigs and at the studio, telling Pam and Paula and the band that she too owned a piece of them.

We were indirectly financing our own record label by being the bait Coleman used to attract investors. He would carve The Jack Douglas Entertainment Group into little slices and use them to close deals that benefited only Coleman. This new information hardened us, and we became very demanding.

Once the album was finally finished, the first step in selling the master was for Jack and me to fly to Los Angeles and meet with all the record company moguls. We envisioned a bidding war, and when Jack and I sat with Coleman and Stuart we talked about how much the record companies would have to pay us if they wanted anything to do with this production. Jack and I agreed we would ask for a three-record deal, the first Gypsy Queen album going for at least $250,000, and $100,000 for each subsequent album.

By using Jack's name it was easy to make appointments. We were able to meet with the select few who dominated and controlled the business. We had a product and they had the power to make it sell—it was that simple. Gypsy Queen was teetering on the brink of stardom. The whole world would soon know about these twin rockers; it would be the beginning of my career, but more important it would be a pivotal moment in Jack's comeback.

First we went to Geffen Records, a natural choice since David Geffen's success had been in large part due to John and Yoko's *Double Fantasy* album. I was able to book an appointment easily and thought it a cinch for us to be picked up by Geffen. David was cordial when he greeted us.

"Jack, it's good to see you again. I'm glad your fight with Yoko is over."

I don't know whose side of the Yoko lawsuit David had been on, but we were very happy with the way he received us. He was not what I expected the founder of one of the biggest and most powerful entertainment companies in the world to be. He was laid back to the point of being shy and awkward. He gave us a tour of his offices and studios.

Jack let him know that Gypsy Queen was a special project and that he was the first one we thought of presenting it to.

Instead of being flattered, as we had hoped, David said, "Jack, I am no longer making decisions concerning music. I'm involved full time with my movie company, and I don't have time to work with bands."

I wasn't interested in his movie company. All I wanted was for David to hear the tape. Impatiently waiting for this to happen, I thought about the fireworks that were about to explode after David heard our band. I was about to get a first-hand view of the birth of a star. Two stars—no, three! The twins, along with me, were about to be discovered, and I was right there to light the fuse.

If the fuse ever did get lit, it was burning under my seat alone. David didn't dislike the music, but he didn't react to it in the way I had expected. Instead of fireworks, David told us it sounded good and asked us to leave some copies of the tape for his A&R department, which was headed by John Kalodner.

When David said the name John Kalodner, the fuse stopped just short of the explosion. Wasn't John Kalodner the guy with the big beard, dressed in drag, in the Aerosmith video "Dude Looks Like a Lady"? The A&R guy from Columbia Records who brought Aerosmith to Geffen after Columbia threw them off the label? The guy who was determined to keep

Aerosmith away from anyone (Jack?) who had anything to do with the band in the past? My stomach started to hurt.

When we got out of the meeting and into the elevator, Jack sensed my anguish. "Don't worry. David loved it, and he's just the first. Wait until everyone else hears it!" And every record company in Los Angeles did hear Gypsy Queen. I made sure no company was spared.

All the moguls were polite, and there was a lot of reminiscing about the past. Herb Alpert and Jerry Moss of A&M Records gave us a strong indication they both liked the music, but the idea of signing twin sisters was something they'd have to think about.

Warner Brothers said they liked the idea of twin sisters, but they weren't sure the songs were strong enough.

At MCA Records, Irving Azoff, while passing us in the hallway, apologized for not being able to meet with us personally and directed us to his A&R staff.

Eventually, we were put in the hands of every A&R department of all the Los Angeles record companies.

With a lot of interest but no offers for either a label deal or a distribution deal, we decided it was time to bring the band out to L.A. to do a live showcase. No one could say no to a band who put on a live show like Gypsy Queen! Coleman, who by now was aware we were onto his oil-well schemes, was happy to come up with most of the money, and I coughed up the rest.

We rented a night at The Ritz, a popular showcase club, and hired a publicist to send out invitations to the Los Angeles elite. The club was filled to capacity. The band played a perfect set. Pedro and Bryan were hot, Mars and Keith were a tight rhythm section, and Pam and Paula were phenomenal. The club roared with appreciation as each song ended. It was apparent that everyone in the crowd was blown away by the great live performance. The reviewers raved about the "Twins from Florida," and compared their set to a choreographed Broadway show. We were very excited by this, and couldn't wait to hear what the labels had to say now.

What we thought would surely push us over the edge and win us a record deal haunted us instead. The phrase *Broadway show* placed a stigma on the twins. Instead of seeing them as a hard-hitting rock band, they were perceived as a choreographed novelty act. An image like that could only lead to the death of a group like Gypsy Queen, but there was no time to sit and wait for rejections. If we were going to hold the band together, we had to act, and fast.

With little hope of signing the band to an American label, and with Stuart and Coleman gradually growing frustrated with our lack of success, we decided to shelve America and seek world distribution. It was a big world out there, and it was time for the whole universe to hear our band. We would leave the U. S. alone for now.

During the next seven months, I discovered Europe. Our record company expanded into France, and we formed a joint partnership with Link Records, a small independent French label whose claim to fame was the signing of a new heavy metal group for French distribution named Metallica. Our new partners would be Danny Terbeche, president of Link Records, and his investor, Joe Ricci, Jr., whose father had recently left him an inheritance of forty million dollars.

CHAPTER 35

Miami to Midem

In January 1986, we were preparing for our first Midem, the yearly convention of record labels, distribution companies, publishers and bands as well as other music-related companies throughout the world. It was held at a giant convention center in Cannes, France, and it was the music business equivalent of the movie business' Cannes Film Festival.

At Midem you presented your product to different countries independently, unlike signing a deal in America where you signed one contract and the company owned you the world over. A company could make separate deals with separate countries. For example, if you were shopping a finished master (as we were), you could make a distribution deal with CBS Japan for a possible fifty thousand dollar advance. That would lock you into Japan, but you could still make deals with the rest of the world. A successful group at Midem could land a deal with RCA in the United Kingdom, Polygram in Germany, CBS in Japan, and so on. The total amount of money could be far greater than signing one world deal in America, and a success in any one territory would make it easier to go back to the American labels and not only get signed, but command a much higher price.

For unknown reasons, few artists know of Midem. They spend small fortunes making demo tapes or masters, and after being turned down by the American labels, they give up. I often wonder how many great artists would have been discovered had they shopped their music at Midem. I guess the problem lies with the fact that Midem is not cheap.

In 1986, the record industry was undergoing a time of uncertainty and change. The long-playing record was celebrating its fortieth anniversary, and the compact disc had recently made its debut. New technology, new markets and a new euphoria prevailed. By attending the 21st Annual Midem we were participants in this new interactive marketplace and witnessed the crossing into a new frontier.

While Jack put the final mix on the Gypsy Queen album, I made a deal to sign a group called Hugger to the label. Bob Ingria, the owner of Quadradial Studios, had recorded an album's worth of songs and was preparing to shop them. I explained Midem to him and he was anxious to work with us. Hugger, named after the lead singer Andrew Hugger, had just shot their first video featuring *Miami Vice* star Don Johnson. The television show *Miami Vice* was at the peak of its popularity, and even though the video seemed more marketable than the music, we agreed that possessing a video starring Don Johnson lent us additional credibility.

In addition to signing Hugger to Wildcat Records, we signed Rick Dufay who had been trying for years to make it as a solo act. By this time, even I felt sorry for Rick. Joe Perry was back in Aerosmith, and Rick was out. He was as strung-out as always on heroin, still in New York, and trying to write songs for the album he and Jack were still talking about recording. The album had always been just talk, but Rick was hopeful now that Jack and I had a record company, he would be able to finish it. Jack took him into a studio in New York where he put three songs together and Rick was signed. After spending time in Alissa's pool-side rehab center, Rick was clean, tanned and healthy, and as hot on the guitar as ever.

What started as a simple plan became an uncontrollable monster. When word got out that we were going to Midem, the sharks came swimming in from all sides.

The fastest swimmer was Stan Vincent. When Jack called him for advice on exhibiting at Midem, Stan turned the conversation around to himself by explaining to Jack that there was no way he could successfully do this without Stan by his side. No matter how hard I fought him, Jack was determined to arrange a meeting between Stan and Coleman, a meeting that resulted in Coleman giving Stan a ten thousand dollar check for his services, as well as accommodations in Cannes and free round-trip airfare. Stan also finagled his friend Gary Lazar into the trip. I think he had something to do with managing groups in Detroit, although I never quite knew exactly what he did. Next into the tank was Alan Jacobi, South Florida's most powerful entertainment lawyer. Alan was a dog in heat—he could always smell a deal, so he wrangled himself into our entourage by offering us legal services pro-bono. Coleman, in an attempt to drill a little deeper into Benny Rodriguez's wallet, offered him a trip to Cannes, in addition to offering him (behind our backs) more stock in Wildcat Records. The next one in was Bob Ingria. He made it clear that if Hugger were to sign a deal with us, he was going to accompany us to France.

At the last minute we included my bungalow-days friend Neil Levine, who had started his own promotional company. Record companies hired him to work on their up-and-coming acts, and Neil helped chart the record by making sure the record stores were setting up displays and that the songs were getting airplay. He also was selling masters of rap groups in New York. We hired him as our head of promotion. The only person we managed to leave firmly behind was Robyn.

Things continued to spiral out of control and our expenses grew to astronomical proportions. And that was before we decided to take the entire band with us, as well. Many labels used Midem as a proving ground for new acts, so we thought it a good idea to have Gypsy Queen perform at the exhibition. We were able to secure a time slot on the premier night alongside an act billed as "Russia's Hottest New Rock Group."

Naturally, we had to provide room and board for everyone involved, and with the addition of the band, our troupe had just doubled in size. Our hotel choices were limited to two: the Carlton or the Martinique. The Martinique had a bar that was open late into the night. Stan told us that deals were not made inside the convention center; they were made over drinks at the bar in the Martinique, and the Carlton was an expensive four-star hotel where all the important executives camped out.

Stan had just produced a popular Japanese group, and he made claim to the fact that he could secure us a strong Japanese distribution deal. That is, as long as he could stay at the Carlton where, as he put it, he would be "close to the action" that "we" needed.

For the rest of the Wildcat team, I found a ten-bedroom chalet up in the hills overlooking Cannes. We arrived to find a picturesque mansion that had two master suites, one for Jack and Chris and one for Alissa and me, a huge living room with an amazing view from one wall that was made of glass, and a gourmet kitchen. All eight remaining bedrooms were mini-suites.

The house was full of magic buttons, and like children, Jack and I ran around pushing them all. When I pushed a button on the wall, the giant glass wall in the living room began to move. It slid down into the floor, leaving the house open to a spectacular view of the surrounding hills and the Mediterranean Sea. A Vietnamese couple lived in the little cottage out back, and they were the housekeepers. Except for Pam and Paula, who were to stay at the Martinique, the band was put into a no-star hotel within walking distance of the convention center.

We had an attractive exhibit with Gypsy Queen as our main event. A colorful twenty-minute VHS tape played the Gypsy Queen video, select interviews with the band and Jack, and the Hugger video with Don Johnson. It looped automatically all day long on a rented monitor. Alissa was in charge of running the booth, which was always crowded with people. While all of us (except Stan and Chris) put in time at the exhibit, I spent most of the day walking the show and talking with each exhibitor about our acts. I arranged meetings with all interested parties in our booth, and I played them tracks from the masters. We handed out hundreds of cassette tapes and CDs, and were swamped by interested parties from all over the world. I was in touch with every country present at Midem.

Chris took Pam and Paula shopping, had their hair done, and then paraded them around the convention center by day and the Martinique lounge at night. By the time the showcase rolled around they had stirred up quite a sensation. Everyone at Midem had seen or heard about the fabulous twins, and they were waiting for the chance to see them perform.

From the outside, everything appeared to be moving along smoothly, but by the night of the showcase the politics were again running rampant. The guys in the band were pissed off that while they were staying in a hotel that turned out to be a dump, the twins were at the Martinique and the rest of us were in a mansion in the hills. Gypsy Queen's performance was bumped off the closing slot by the Russian rock band, almost starting another World War, and Keith, our drummer, never made it to Cannes at all.

The set was performed with the girls singing vocals live and the band playing their guitars without them being plugged in, while a tape of the music played. I sat in on drums. The performance went over well, but in the morning papers there was a front-page picture of the drummer from the Russian band and me exchanging drumsticks, with no twins in sight. This did not sit well with Gypsy Queen.

Before the week ended, we organized a catered party at the chalet for Saturday night and invited all the people we felt were interested in Wildcat Records. What started as a classy catered affair grew into a wild open house, with hundreds of people crashing in during the course of the night. Even Coleman made a dramatic entrance, fresh off the plane from Paris. Everyone had a great time, except the Vietnamese couple who spent the night cursing guests in Vietnamese. Herman, the drummer from the group the Scorpions, showed up with M-80 firecrackers, and after an argument with the Vietnamese couple, he and Bob Ingria laid plans for a bombing attack on their cottage. Jack and I became negotiators, stopping what could have been the start of another Vietnam War.

Midem was over and I was exhausted, yet I felt a sense of pride and accomplishment. Midem had been one of my biggest challenges and it seemed a success. The band had left Cannes and were either scattered across Europe or on their way home. Alan, Neil and Gary had left to attend to their own prospective deals. Only Jack, Chris, Stan, Alissa and I, remained at the chalet Sunday morning.

Before Stan left, he sat Jack and me down. "I just want to tell you that everyone did a great job, and I'm sure you guys are going to score some big deals, but I hope Kenny didn't fuck anything up." Then, Stan turned to me and said, "By talking to everyone without having the experience I have, you made our (!) company look like shit." He was inferring that if big deals didn't come our way, it would be because of me.

I was shattered. That afternoon, Alissa and I flew to London where we met up with Jack and Chris. Jack knew that Stan had gotten to me, and he tried his best to make me feel better. We were on vacation, but instead of celebrating, I was miserable. Jack said, "Stan is jealous of you and your relationship with me. We were naïve to think that if we hired Stan he would be a team player, while all along he was playing his favorite game—divide and conquer." Chris added that Stan hated the idea that I was getting additional mileage out of Jack where he couldn't.

Alissa and I rented a car and drove to the French Alps for three days before leaving Europe and returning to Florida. Following that, Jack and I decided we needed to spend some family time with the kids before getting back to the business of music. We rented a Winnebago and took off for the Florida Keys for the weekend. Jack, Chris, Blake, Brian, Rachel, Alissa and I and our two dogs, as well as a designated driver (Chris flew her brother John in from Los Angeles) had a blast all the way down to Key West and back before returning to the reality of Wildcat Records.

There was nothing to do but sit by the telex machine with Stuart and Coleman and wait for the offers to come rolling in. The telex machine held our destinies, and for a while it just wouldn't tell . . .

In a few days, the telex began to spit out paper. It seemed apparent that Midem was the success we had hoped for. Offers poured in from all over the world. There were offers from Germany, Japan, South Africa and Spain, as well as a twenty-five thousand dollar advance offer from EMI London. This was the largest cash advance thus far—the other offers held cash advances of five to ten thousand dollars. All of the companies wanted the Gypsy Queen master, making no mention of either Hugger or Rick Dufay.

We evaluated each offer and made a decision. Before we'd agree to any distribution deal, we first tried to obtain either a better advance for Gypsy Queen, or a commitment for the release of Rick Dufay and Hugger along with Gypsy Queen. We did agree to take the EMI deal without making a counteroffer. Just as we were about to contact EMI with our acceptance we received the telex from Link Records, offering a seventy-five thousand dollar advance! It was hard to believe a company in France would offer such a large advance, as France was not populated with enough rock n' rollers to sell that many records to. A second telex detailed the terms of the offer. They wanted all three acts, and not just for France, but for the entire world—including the U.S. At first Jack and I were against forfeiting additional territories to any one company, but Coleman wanted to accept all offers. If the decision had been his to make, he would have given Link Records the world for seventy-five thousand, EMI London for twenty-five, as well as taking all the offers from the other countries for five or ten thousand dollars. As far as Coleman was concerned, when there was money on the table you took it. Details, such as granting exclusives, were something you worried about later.

Neither Jack nor I could remember having met anyone from Link Records. Danny Terbeche signed the telexes, and we couldn't place a face with the name. Unlike the other companies, which took days to respond, Danny Terbeche responded almost instantly. He was probably huddled around the new-fangled telex machine, same as we were, countering our offer with a counteroffer. He was determined to close a deal with Wildcat

Records, and because he was willing to pay for his terms, we came to an agreement.

The deal was for a term of three years. The first year we would deliver to Link Records the finished Gypsy Queen master plus a finished Rick Dufay album for an advance of one hundred thousand dollars. For the second and third years, Jack would produce three acts of our choosing for an advance of fifty thousand per act, payable upon delivery. The deal also included Jack's production fee of the same amount per act. Wildcat Records would keep all American rights and Link would own the rest of the world. The deal was agreed to by all parties, except, surprisingly, Gypsy Queen, who was expecting a blockbuster international distribution deal with CBS, Atlantic, Polydor or any one of the major labels. Learning that Link Records in France was going to be their international label was bad news, and it was of little consolation to them that we still held rights in the United States. Once Midem was over, the band expected that the big companies would fall all over themselves competing for the rights to Gypsy Queen, and when that failed to happen, the band resigned themselves to their fate.

Danny Terbeche sent a final telex that read, "Joe Ricci, Link investor, will arrive in Fort Lauderdale (date, time and flight). Mr. Ricci will bring a check for seventy-five thousand dollars. Please have Gypsy Queen masters ready." We had been anticipating a wire transfer of funds from Link Record's bank to Wildcat Record's bank, whereupon we would ship the masters and cover photographs to France. Instead, we were going to trade money for masters.

At the airport, Mr. Ricci and his friend Guilliume were as surprised to meet Jack and me as we were to meet them. They were teenagers wearing expensive suits. I, suit-less, was not what they expected the president of Wildcat Records to look like, and Jack, in faded jeans and long-sleeved denim shirt, was even more of a surprise. Each side was expecting men in suits. We got boys in suits, and they got us.

An audible sigh of relief greeted the appearance of Coleman's chauffeured Rolls Royce. Now they were getting their money's worth! We proceeded to Coleman's office where he lay in wait, like a dragon in his lair.

Coleman was in heaven. Not only did he receive a check made out to Wildcat Records in the amount of seventy-five thousand, Jack and I had unknowingly delivered what was to become Coleman's biggest conquest. During the course of his meeting with Coleman, Joe Ricci, Jr. mentioned that his father had recently passed away, leaving his entire forty-million-dollar estate to his only son, who was now sitting across from a gifted swindler. Coleman found he liked being in the record business more and more with each passing day, and while Coleman was busy scheming, Jack and I were busy getting bills paid, including our past-due salaries and outstanding recording studio bills.

Midem ad.

(left to right): Pam Mattioli, Randy Jackson (Zebra), Paula Mattioli.

Neil Levine at Midem.

Gypsy Queen at Midem.

CHAPTER 36

Across the Great Divide

Johnny Depp was back in town, having just finished filming the movie *Platoon*. Soon after Johnny had taken over George's place in The Kidds, the band moved to Los Angeles, and it was at an L.A. rock club that Nicolas Cage noticed Johnny the Kidd performing on stage. After the show, Nicolas approached Johnny. "Have you ever done any acting?" he asked. "You have a great look. Here's my agent's number — I think you should call." Johnny took the advice. His call led to a role in the movie *Nightmare on Elm Street*, then a starring role in the television series *21 Jump Street*, and next a part in the film *Platoon*. I like to imagine that if George had not quit The Kidds, he'd be starring in *Platoon*, but in all reality, if George hadn't quit the band, Johnny Depp, the actor, would not have been discovered that night.

Johnny came over to my house with his friend Sal, and he told Jack and me about his experiences in filming the movie. The actors went through a simulated boot camp to toughen them up and to get an idea of what war was like. He was wearing the scuffed army boots he wore in the movie, along with beat-up blue jeans and a blue bandana on his head. He was still starring on *21 Jump Street*, but he wanted out of the series. Johnny hated being a teen idol and refused to do interviews that perpetuated that image. Like John Lennon, he was a hard rocker at heart, and on this night his clothes portrayed the real Johnny Depp.

I woke Rachel, who at the age of nine was a fan of *21 Jump Street*, and a bigger fan of Johnny. She came out of her room bleary-eyed, and walked into the living room where Johnny stood. She looked up and said,

244

"You're not him!" We laughed. He certainly didn't resemble the whole-some character he portrayed on *21 Jump Street*.

From the moment Johnny saw Rachel he idolized me for having her. "Man, do you know how lucky you are?" he said to me. "One day I hope to have a daughter as beautiful as yours. You must not have lived life until you've had kids. One day, I'll live life too!" His words sent a chill down my spine. Here I was, looking at the guy who seemed to have it all, but Johnny made me realize that I was the lucky one. I was living life while he was just going through the motions. His words reminded me how fortunate I was to have not only Rachel, but Brian and Alissa as well.

Gypsy Queen had made a big impression at Midem, and the telex machine continued to spit out offers. Any distribution offers from outside the United States were referred to Link. We also referred the EMI offer to them. When the album was released in the United Kingdom, the liner notes on the album cover read "Produced by Jack Douglas for Wildcat Records, Link Records, EMI."

With distribution in place, we were offered tour support. A German promoter named Jurgen Meyer, whom I had met at Midem, sent Jack and me tickets to fly to Germany where we would discuss putting together the Gypsy Queen tour.

This would be the first of many European trips taken on behalf of Wildcat Records. Besides our salaries, Jack and I received no other com-pensation except frequent trips to Europe, and they were usually first class. Everyone was spending money on Gypsy Queen, and before the band, Jack, Wildcat, Link, EMI or I made any profit, all of the monies that had been spent had to be recouped. It became evident that if anyone were going to make a dime on our Gypsy Queen album, the record would have to sell as if it were indeed a Beatles album.

Jack and I were on the overnight train rumbling across Germany on our way to meet Jurgen Meyer at his village home atop a mountain. Every few hours the train would stop at a station long enough for us to step outside and look around. At each stop, German soldiers patrolled the platforms. Jack sensed how awkward it was for me to travel through Germany on a train, especially when the armed guards walked past us, and he started to kid me about it.

"Don't let them know you're Jewish!" he would say in an exaggerated whisper.

It was funny and we laughed, but I did experience an eerie feeling. Everything around me was old; the trains, the stations, the buildings, and the scenery, and the soldiers looked like authentic Nazis. The only thing missing were swastikas on their uniforms. I couldn't help but think what it would have been like if it were forty-five years before instead of present day. Was I traveling the same tracks that took millions of Jews from their homes to die in the concentration camps not so long ago?

We were asleep when the train came to a halt. Jack prodded me awake and told me to look out the window. I could barely open my eyes. There were soldiers and barking dogs—big Doberman pinschers—on the platform. A passenger in our car said it was a passport check.

After awakening, I had to relieve myself. As I rose, Jack grabbed my arm and said, "Wait till we get moving before you go!"

"Ha-ha," I said. "They might think I'm Jewish!" I pushed my way past Jack and tiptoed down the aisle to the latrine. "Ahhhhh," I was quietly thinking when the door to the latrine burst open. A soldier dragged me out into the aisle and roughly threw me down on the floor where I was immediately surrounded by soldiers and snarling dogs. A rifle was shoved into my back and when I turned my head to look up, gun barrels were jammed against my face. The soldiers were yelling at me in German as they dragged me to my feet, pushed me into an empty compartment and strip-searched me. When I was taken back to my compartment a search of Jack and our belongings was in progress.

The soldiers were sure that Jack and I were carrying drugs, and the reason I had chosen to use the bathroom at that moment was to flush the drugs down the toilet. Even fearless Jack had a frightened look on his face. Lucky for us, our passports were in order, we had no drugs and it was…1986.

Our meeting with Jurgen was successful. He agreed to arrange a tour for the band scheduled to coincide with the record release. Jack returned to Florida for a while, and I went on to meet Danny Terbeche.

If I was surprised at meeting Joe Ricci, Jr. and his friend Guilliume in Florida, I was in a total state of bewilderment when I first laid eyes on Danny Terbeche. At Charles de Gaulle Airport, I assumed I was waiting for another well-dressed, soft-spoken businessman, when all of a sudden, like an apparition out of a heavy-metal nightmare, Danny appeared. He was well over six feet tall and had a poodle hairstyle of long, black hair. Danny looked and acted like a younger version of Howard Stern. There was nothing soft-spoken or businesslike about Danny, and I had to laugh. Our European partner looked and acted more like one of our rock n' roll crazies.

Danny worked out of the small apartment he shared with his wife and teenage son. There was a third bedroom that served as the official headquarters of Link Records. Danny's wife was petite and quiet, and although his beautiful fourteen-year-old son looked and behaved like his mother, he shared his father's tastes in music. They were both huge Jack Douglas fans.

My room was the living room couch. The first morning of my stay, I was awakened by the wonderful smell of breakfast cooking. While I sat at the kitchen table sneaking glances into the kitchen, Danny and his son proudly showed me every record that Jack had ever produced or engineered. They had them all. I was more interested in the smell coming from the kitchen—the aroma of French omelets! First, Danny's son was served, then Danny. The omelets were a work of art. Eggs bacon, cheese, vegetables, all cooked to a crispy-around-the-edges perfection, and piled high with fruit. It looked mouthwatering, and I was starving. Danny's wife told me mine was special, and would be done in a few minutes. All eyes were on me when she brought my plate from the kitchen and placed it on the table.

It looked like a bowl of ketchup—I mean the whole plate was drowning in it! I tried inconspicuously to brush off some of the ketchup and hunt for the omelet. I did my best to eat all the real food, leaving a mound of ketchup behind. Danny told me later that his wife had to go to many stores to find ketchup. They had heard that Americans loved ketchup and couldn't eat any meal without it.

To coincide with the U.K. release on EMI and Link's release in France, Danny took out full-page ads in all the music magazines to announce Gypsy Queen's debut album. Because of the band's success at Midem, combined with Jack's popularity, not to mention the stunning redheaded twin sisters, the European press took a strong interest in the band. Jack returned to perform radio interviews in Paris, then live TV interviews. It was hilarious watching Jack on TV with his voice dubbed in French.

With Danny, it was meetings all day and dinner all night. Our dinners usually were held at a very exclusive and sedate restaurant, which was located just off the Champs Élysées. Dinner began at eight and lasted past midnight. Danny was host and he loved a full house, having invited whomever he came in contact with that day. Jack and I were always treated like celebrity guests. It was one thing to be late for a meeting, but being late for dinner was inexcusable.

Come midnight, after a multitude of courses and endless bottles of wine, a dessert tray heaped high with pastries, fruit, whipped cream and chocolate would be placed on the table. Danny would announce, "Tonight, I *trash* this whole restaurant!" The first night he said this, I paid scant attention because trash was one of Danny's favorite words, but then he picked up a croissant topped with whipped cream and threw it across the table and into my face. I was caught off guard, and while I tried to wipe whipped cream from my eyes, Danny threw a piece of chocolate pie at the disc jockey seated next to me. The DJ grabbed a handful of strawberries and threw them right back, but his aim was lousy and the berries rained down on the fashion designer seated next to Danny. She scooped strawberries off her lap and mashed them into Danny's hair.

The food fight was on! We threw desserts, remnants of dinner, and anything else not nailed down until food dripped from our faces, hair and clothes, and we were breathless from laughing. On some nights, Danny smashed wine glasses and ashtrays, and the other guests in the restaurant would either become disgusted or join in. Regardless, the restaurant owner never seemed to mind our nightly ritual; Danny paid well for his pleasures, and trashing restaurants was one of his passions.

As soon as Danny was satisfied that the album was selling well in France and he had German distribution in place with an affiliate of Polygram Records, he scheduled rounds of meetings and interviews in Germany. After Frankfurt and Munich, our last stop was in Hamburg. After Jack's radio interview, he and Danny and I went to a small club for a drink and to watch the stage show, which resembled a Follies show but had sexual overtones. During the intermission the lights came on and the audience went back to their drinks and conversations. As we were discussing the following day's plans, we couldn't help but notice the young couple to our right. Not only were they stunning in appearance, they had started kissing playfully, and were getting more intimate. Even uninhibited Danny could not take his eyes off them. The other patrons in the club were mostly ignoring them, so we tried not to leer at them like idiots. Just as we succeeded in not staring, the man started tearing at the woman's clothing, ripping her dress open and tearing it away from her body.

Although most of the people around us were still paying little attention, the three of us once again turned our attention their way. When the woman was completely naked, she began to tear the man's clothes off. He threw her on top of the cocktail table, and as he pounced on top of her, the lights went out, a spotlight hit them and the table started to rise. They were having passionate sex on an elevated table, and it was all part of the stage show. We later learned that this particular club was considered mild. We never did have the opportunity to visit one of the wilder clubs, but I now understood why the Beatles spent so much time in Hamburg.

The album was selling in France, Germany and the U.K., the European press was covering the band, and Jurgen Meyer had a tour scheduled. It was time to bring Gypsy Queen overseas, but before we flew them over, Danny decided he wanted to come to the United States for a short visit.

In America, Danny was a walking disaster. As soon as he met the band, he immediately saw that a problem existed between the twins and the guys. Pam and Paula wanted to be the headliners, but Pedro, Bryan, Mars and Keith were an important part of the act and didn't want to be treated like back-up players. When Danny was with the guys, he assured them that they were as important as the girls, that every member of the band was a front man, and that the European audience would be just as interested in them as they were in the twins. That was great, but when he was with the girls he assured them that they were the main attraction and that no one in Europe would be interested in the other band members. Besides, he told them having an old bass player like Mars was hurting their image. He said that in order to have longevity they needed a younger band. In private, Danny told everybody what he or she wanted to hear, and Jack and I were powerless to convince anyone otherwise.

In addition to trashing restaurants, Danny loved trashing people. One afternoon, after a busy morning spent throwing Rachel and her friends into our pool, Danny asked us why Coleman had told him to "stay away from Robyn"? When Alissa gave him the low-down, he became fascinated with Robyn and insisted on meeting her. Jack and I always refused to have anything to do with her and thought it a terrible idea to have her come over while Danny was there. Danny, who already harbored animosity toward Coleman and Stuart, as well as Joe Ricci, had now set his sights on Robyn, and he begged and pleaded to meet her.

Robyn was thrilled by the invitation and delighted to meet the legendary Danny Terbeche. She made it clear to him that she was an integral part of Wildcat Records, then she told him she managed a band and invited Danny to go with her to hear them play. While Danny quietly (for once!) sat on the couch next to Robyn, I sensed trouble and was relieved when she was summoned home to her children. Upon leaving, she asked Danny if he smoked pot and invited him over to her house. As soon as Robyn was out the door, Danny became hysterical. He said, "I go over to Robyn's house, smoke pot and fuck her!"

He returned an hour later and like a victorious warrior he shouted, "Today I trash Robyn, tomorrow I trash Mr. Coleman!"

The Gypsy Queen album had a full release, and the band was promoting it with a tour of Europe. The reviews ranged from satisfactory to rave. The press loved Pam and Paula, and the English tabloids followed them and covered their every exploit as they crisscrossed Europe. The tour ended with an encore performance at the famous Redding Festival. A photo was taken of Brian May, the lead guitar player from the band Queen with a twin on each arm. The photo appeared in dozens of periodicals topped with headlines that read "The Three Queens," or "Queen Meets Queen." As the band's popularity grew, so did record sales. As of yet, the numbers had not reached a profitable level, but Jack and I knew that their limited success would open doors in America. It was our intention to bring the album home to EMI by way of their international arm.

Nearly penniless again, Jack and I knew if we were to continue with Wildcat Records we would need to break away from Coleman and his oil wells. Every investor we unwittingly presented to Coleman eventually realized they had been swindled, and looked to Jack and me for answers. Naturally, we had no answers and had a hard time convincing them Coleman had broken every promise he'd made us, too.

Just as Gypsy Queen was about to turn a profit, like out of a scene from *The Godfather* where all at once several characters are killed off, Wildcat Records was to suffer devastating blows.

While Jack and I concentrated on bringing the record home, Coleman still had his hooks in Joe Ricci, Jr. and he persuaded him to buy an eight-million-dollar yacht-building facility in Ft. Lauderdale. Shortly afterwards a dispute erupted between the two and Joe decided he no longer wanted anything to do with Coleman Schwartz.

Danny decided he alone was responsible for the success of the Gypsy Queen album and decided he no longer wanted anything to do with Joe Ricci.

Pam and Paula decided they no longer wanted anything to do with their entire band. When Jack and I reminded them that the band was also under contract, the twins decided they no longer wanted anything to do with anyone, and they simply quit.

Pam and Paula immediately began rehearsing with their new band—even before telling the old band they were all fired! They found younger musicians with more hair and tighter pants. They had the looks, but lacked the talent.

The girls called a meeting, and Pedro, Bryan, Mars, Keith, Augie, Jack, Chris, Alissa and I attended. The twins broke the news to the band that they were fired. Pedro, who had been with the band since its inception, took it the hardest. With tears in his eyes he pointed to his hairline and said to Pam and Paula, "If I'm going bald, I got this way from putting up with your shit for all these years!" Jack and I tried to make the girls understand they were ruining their careers, but they insisted that Danny would love their new band and pour lots of money into it. Jack agreed to hear the new band, and when he did he knew there would not be a second Gypsy Queen album on Wildcat Records, or any other Wildcat productions for that matter. Discouraged, he and Chris packed their bags and moved back to New York.

As Gypsy Queen fizzled out in Europe, Danny ran out of funds. He had made promises to the band he couldn't keep, so he tried to reunite with Joe Ricci, Jr., but the damage had been done. Danny withdrew all support.

Joe Ricci tried to pick up the pieces of the company, and for a while he was supporting not only the twins but Rick Dufay as well.

Aside from outstanding legal issues, Wildcat Records was over.

CHAPTER 37

The 2.2

I was still mourning the demise of Wildcat Records when I got a call from our lawyer, Tom Morgan. The judge had unexpectedly settled a case and was ready to hear ours. We had two days to prepare before we were to appear in court.

After a week of testimony and only two hours of deliberation, the jury was ready to render their decision. Just moments before, we had turned down what was the largest sum of money ever offered us. We were in the stairwell when Tom told us the lawyer from Zayre's had made his final settlement offer—eighty thousand dollars! This was the last of five offers that had begun at twenty-five thousand, and in rapid succession we turned them all down. It felt like we were playing a game. We would decline their offer, and five minutes later Tom would reappear with a higher number.

So here we stood, waiting outside the historic Dade County Courthouse across from the building where Tom's office was. I watched Tom as he dodged cars and crossed the street. The last thing I expected was for him to tell us that the jury had reached its verdict. As Tom hurried us into the courtroom, in our excitement neither Alissa nor I had told him we'd changed our minds and decided to accept the eighty-thousand dollars.

The bailiff said, "Please rise!"

The judge entered and sat down, then the nine jurors silently filed in and took their seats. I reached for Alissa's hand as she stood silently next to me. My mind raced with anticipation, and in the short time before the verdict was read, I reflected on the past three years.

During the time I was managing Jack, Alissa and I were arrested and jailed on grand-theft charges as we attempted to exchange a printer at a Zayre's Department Store. Had Jones not lied and said we walked in empty-handed and walked out with an Okidata printer, we would not have been arrested, nor would the subsequent chain of events have taken place. Though we were now the plaintiffs, it wasn't long ago that we were defendants. Alissa and I had faced the possibility of spending five years in prison and losing Brian and Rachel, but it was Alissa who had suffered the most during the past three years. Though I was mostly concerned with the fight, I was not aware of the real damages I was yet to suffer.

My final thought before the courtroom quieted down was, "Regardless of whether we win an award or not, this will be the end as well as the opportunity for a new beginning. We will put this in our past and move forward with our lives."

A slip of paper was handed to the bailiff. All eyes were on the paper as it was given to the judge. The judge looked at it and gave it back to the bailiff.

The bailiff cleared his throat. "Ahem. The jury awards to Kenneth Geringer five hundred thousand dollars, plus punitive damages of fifty thousand dollars. To Alissa Geringer the amount of seven hundred thousand dollars, plus punitive damages of one million dollars."

We had just been awarded 2.2 million dollars! Inside me, emotions were flying as I envisioned a second opportunity for all of us—Alissa and myself, Brian and Rachel. Though I had not been prepared to win such a huge fortune, I was less prepared for what happened next.

As we turned toward each other, with a tear running down her cheek, Alissa said, "I want a divorce. I'm in love with someone else."

Nobody told me there'd be days like this!

Epilogue

The handcuffs pinched my wrists painfully as an officer grabbed each arm and half-dragged and half-carried me through the crowds that pushed against us like the waves of a stormy sea. Once outside the club, I was jammed into the back of an unmarked police car and when it started to roll forward I twisted my head around and watched the crowd grow small as we gained distance. Several miles down Hollywood Boulevard the car stopped at a lone trailer that had the words Mobile Command Center painted on the side and existed for the sole purpose of finding and arresting Luther Campbell and his 2 Live Crew.

I was pulled from the car, rushed up the metal steps and through a plastic door. Immediately several deputies peppered me with demands.

"Where is Luther?"

"What is he driving?"

"You know where that scumbag is! Tell us!"

Before I had the chance to tell them all to go to hell, a voice crackled over the two-way radio triumphantly announcing that the getaway car had been spotted. Then, a few moments later, it blared that the suspects were in custody. There was a sudden rush of activity in the tiny trailer, as if unexpected guests were about to arrive, and as I felt the cuffs loosen and drop off, I was issued a stern warning.

"We're gonna keep a mean eye on you, kid. We don't like you or your shitty club and this town would be better off without your kind around. We can get rid of you like this!" And he snapped his fingers.

As I rubbed life back into my wrists I pondered his words. I had my life's blood as well as the Zayre's money invested in the club, and I could lose it all in an instant if I stepped over the line that had been drawn in the sand. This I believed wholeheartedly, and even more so in the months to follow as I saw my customers harassed and physically assaulted by both Hollywood and Broward County police officers, while the town of Hollywood conspired with local agencies to make life at Club Futura a living hell.

Maybe my time had come. Was I finally defeated? Had they won? Perhaps I should stop listening to myself. Wouldn't life be a lot easier if I hid my beliefs and philosophies away in a little box and stopped challenging what I couldn't tolerate?

I tried. With my mouth shut I conducted myself in the way of the meek and never once rose to the bait. Business went on as usual through the beatings, harassment, surveillances, inspections and fines for trumped-up code violations. Until one day several months down the road when the phone in my office rang . . .

"Hello?"

"Ken? This is Irving Azoff from Giant Records. I got a group here, called 2 Much Joy. Four clean-cut, white college boys from Scarsdale, N.Y. We want to send them down to Club Futura next week to perform the exact same concert Luther and The 2 Live Crew did, illegal lyrics and all. Whaddya think?"

What did I think? What do you think I thought?

The Players

Peter Hultberg, his wife Marilyn, daughter Samantha and son Gabriel live in Brooklyn, New York. Wherever I go, I know I have a best friend.

Carl Cooperstein has disappeared. He was last seen in 1988 by my parents, working as a dishwasher in a luncheonette in Hialeah, Florida.

Neil Levine is president of one of New York's hottest rap labels. Like Ahmet Ertegun, Neil got his start promoting records out of the trunk of his car.

Ross went public, started Apple Cosmetics, and in the mid '90s, I saw Ross at the Palm Beach Federal Courthouse. He was under indictment for stock fraud.

George Mazzola and Lauren Smolkin are married and have a new drummer, son Jesse A. (Jam) Mazzola. They're still pursuing their dream of a record deal while performing nightly in local South Florida clubs.

Coleman (Houdini) Schwartz: Several years after the demise of Wildcat Records, I heard Coleman had died. And if you believe that, then I have some oil wells you may be interested in . . .

Jack made his comeback! I last saw him in NY, while he was in the studio, producing a Slash (guitar player from Guns n' Roses) album. He was also in pre-production for the next Aerosmith album.

Chris and Jack became drug free and are happily married. With Chris by his side, Jack made a big comeback. I always knew he would. What a ride the three of us went on!

(Though I bet Rick Dufay is still trying to get Jack to finish his album!)

Yoko and Ken: In 1995 I met with Yoko at her art exhibit in Palm

Beach Florida. She indicated to me that she would like to support my censorship fight. At the meeting was Sean Lennon, to whom I gave a copy of the song "Beautiful Boy" from the Bermuda tape. (I told Sean that the tape was really from Jack Douglas who once told me he wanted to give Sean a copy of that song when he turned eighteen. Sean put the tape in his pocket and his index finger to his mouth and said, "Shhh—Jack Douglas . . . we don't mention that name!")

Sean in his early twenties—looking more like a rebellious teen, barefoot, and with long cascading hair almost touching his waist—was happy to receive the tape and said he had never heard that unreleased version. I was with my daughter Rachel, a drummer who immediately identified with Sean and his girlfriend, and while they talked about Sean's band, I met with Yoko and her escort Sam Havadtoy.

While looking at Sam and Yoko, I couldn't help but imagine John standing there next to this frail and aging Yoko. Sam, who had on Lennon-type glasses, was about John's height and physique, clean-shaven, with longish hair, and from a distance it appeared to be John standing there, clutched by Yoko. I wondered if Sam felt any of John's pain. Did he become as dependent upon Yoko as John once was, and would he eventually one day be reborn and seek his independence as John had been about to do? Nah! Aside from the uncanny resemblance, this man had no relation to John Lennon, and I came to the quick conclusion that Sam Havadtoy was nothing more than a dressed-up Hungarian gigolo.

Brian is completing his degrees in Asian Studies, Geology and Education at SUNY New Paltz. Someday he plans to live and work in Japan. Our fourteen-year fight with the public school system is over. Brian now thinks of himself as quite smart.

Rachel just graduated with honors from SUNY New Paltz with a Bachelor's degree in Political Science. She is a talented jazz drummer, and after taking some time off to pursue her other passion, entering (and winning) snowboarding competitions while living in British Columbia, Canada, she plans to attend law school.

Alissa and Ken: This is not **The End**

Special Thanks and Acknowledgments

First and foremost I cannot begin to thank my wife for tirelessly reading, editing and making sure every word in the manuscript was fit to print.

Twenty-five years ago the manuscript was started as a journal. When I came across it a few years back I sent the writings to an anonymous friend. Without her initial excitement and encouragement for me to write this book, it would never have happened.

Grandma Jean Happy 90th Birthday.
My parents: for everything.
Brian and Rachel—two funny, intelligent people I love immensely.
Joseph M Quesada, for preserving the Skunk Hollow Archives as well as being the current Skunk Hollow Webmaster: www.skunkhollow.org
Robert Aulicino for cover design: www.aulicinodesign.com
Gail Kearns for her copyediting: GMKEA@aol.com

I sincerely thank all the wonderful characters who appear in this book. I hope they are as proud of the parts they've played in the development of this story as they are of their contribution to this work.

And Last
Augie Treto, a shining star, may he rest in peace

All the characters in this book are real. The names Pete Scarpachi, Uncle Sonny, Uncle Sallie, Benny Rodriguez and Mike Varanci were all changed to protect... *me*.

Front cover photo:
(left to right): Ken, age 12, mother Doris, and sister Amy, age 8, November, 1968 by Martin Geringer.
Lyrics from Reggaenomics, copyright© Ken Geringer and Ezra St. Juste.
Lyrics from Sweet Mama, copyright© Pearl Livingston-Marley.

Jack and the John Lennon Sessions: The Meeting, The Call, The Sessions, The Fall, and The Aftermath are all taken from conversations between Jack Douglas and the author.

Nobody Told Me
**CD Soundtrack Available at
www.hipway.com**

Track 1   **Rockland County**
(J. Scherman) John Scherman—guitars, slide Jonathan
Best—lead vocal, piano Gary Soloman—bass, guitar,
vocals Joe Quesada—drums Anthony Franklin—
vocals Dave Fox—saxophone Joseph Keyser—trumpet
Robby Fisch—trumpet. Copyright 1981 Skunk Hollow
Records 'Skunk Tracks'.

Track 2   **The Coop Experience**
George Mazzola—guitar Carl Cooperstein—bass
Ken Geringer—drums.

Track 3   **Oh! Darling**
(Lennon-McCartney) Lauren Smolkin-Mazzola—vocals
George Mazzola—guitar Tony Schittina—bass
Ken Geringer—drums.

Track 4   **Shaleur Pour Leve**
(Ezra St. Juste-Timmy St. Juste) BMI, Trucker Man
Records.

Track 5   **Reggaenomics**
(E. St. Juste—K. Geringer) Ezra St. Juste—vocals, bass
Pearl Livingston-Marley—vocals David Snider—
guitar Mark Davenport—backup vocals, keyboards
Ken Geringer—drums. Produced by E. St. Juste-
K. Geringer for Fantail Productions.

Track 6   **Sweet Mama**
(P. Livingston-Marley) Pearl Livingston-Marley—
vocals Ezra St. Juste—backup vocals, bass Marc
Davenport—backup vocals, keyboards David Snider—
guitar Ken Geringer—drums. Produced by
E. St. Juste and K. Geringer.

Track 7 **Love Me**
(George Mazzola—Lauren Smolkin-Mazzola) Lauren
Smolkin-Mazzola—vocals George Mazzola—guitar,
backup vocals Jimmy Finnen—bass Marc
Davenport— keyboards, backup vocals Matthew
Hill—drums, backup vocals. Executive Producer K.
Geringer. Produced by Jack Douglas for Fantail
Productions, CoCo Music Publishing.

Track 8 **My Love is Real**
(George Mazzola—Lauren Smolkin-Mazzola) Lauren
Smolkin- Mazzola—vocals George Mazzola—guitar,
backup vocals Jimmy Finnen—bass Marc Davenport—
keyboards, backup vocals Matthew Hill—drums, back-
up vocals. Executive Producer—Ken Geringer.
Produced by Jack Douglas for Fantail Productions,
CoCo Music Publishing.

Track 9 **Don't Rush Me**
(P. Mattioli—P. Riera—A. Treto)
Paula Mattioli, Pamela Mattioli—vocals Pedro Riera—
guitar, vocals Bryan Le Mar—guitar Peter (Mars)
Cowling—bass guitar Keith Daniel Cronin—drums
Augie Treto—guitar Tim Divine—keyboards.
Executive Producers, K. Geringer and J. Douglas.
Produced by Jack Douglas for Wildcat Records, 1987
Black Gold Music Inc (BMI) Gypsy Queen.

Track 10 **Basement Jam**
George Mazzola—guitar Carl Cooperstein—bass
Ken Geringer—drums.

Track 11 **Star Spangled Banner**
George Mazzola—guitar Carl Cooperstein—bass
Ken Geringer—drums.